Theology for Changing Times

Theology for Changing Times

John Atherton and the Future of Public Theology

Edited by
Christopher R. Baker
and
Elaine L. Graham

scm press

© the Editors and Contributors 2018

Published in 2018 by SCM Press
Editorial office
3rd Floor, Invicta House,
108–114 Golden Lane,
London EC1Y 0TG, UK
www.scmpress.co.uk

SCM Press is an imprint of Hymns Ancient & Modern Ltd
(a registered charity)

Hymns Ancient & Modern® is a registered trademark of
Hymns Ancient & Modern Ltd
13A Hellesdon Park Road, Norwich,
Norfolk NR6 5DR, UK

All rights reserved. No part of this publication may be reproduced,
stored in a retrieval system, or transmitted,
in any form or by any means, electronic, mechanical,
photocopying or otherwise, without the prior permission of
the publisher, SCM Press.

The Authors have asserted their right under the Copyright,
Designs and Patents Act 1988
to be identified as the Authors of this Work

British Library Cataloguing in Publication data

A catalogue record for this book is available
from the British Library

978 0 334 05695 9

Typeset by Regent Typesetting
Printed and bound by
CPI Group (UK) Ltd

Contents

List of Contributors	vii
Preface by Lesley Atherton	ix
Acknowledgements	xi

1. Introduction: Genealogies, Typologies and Reformulations 1
   Christopher Baker and Elaine Graham

2. By Their Fruits You Shall Know Them: The Economics of Material Wellbeing and a Christianity Fit for Purpose 20
   John Atherton

3. Grounded and Inclusive: Public Theology from the Grass Roots 37
   Hilary Russell

4. 'The Manchester School': University, Cathedral, William Temple Foundation 50
   Peter Sedgwick

5. Christian Social Ethics and Political Economy 65
   Carl-Henric Grenholm

6. John Atherton: Industry, the City and the Age of Incarnation 81
   Malcolm Brown

7. Economic Activity, Economic Theory and Morality 96
   Ian Steedman

8. Faith, Finance and the Digital 110
   John Reader

9. Bending it Like Atherton: Doing Public Theology in an Age of Public Anger 124
   William Storrar

10 Flourishing and Ambiguity in UK Urban Mission   143
    Anna Ruddick

11 Alternative Possible Futures: Unearthing a Catholic Public
    Theology for Northern Ireland   158
    Maria Power

12 Afterword: Genealogy and Generativity   175
    Christopher Baker and Elaine Graham

Index of Names and Subjects   187

List of Contributors

John Atherton (1939–2016) was, until his retirement in 2004, Canon Theologian of Manchester Cathedral, Honorary Lecturer in Christian Social Ethics at the University of Manchester and Secretary of the William Temple Foundation. He was awarded an honorary doctorate by the University of Uppsala in 2004 and was, latterly, Visiting Research Professor in Religion and Economics at the University of Chester.

Lesley Atherton is John's daughter and assisted her father with his administration, email, IT support, typing and editing for the last few years of his life and considers it a privilege to have done so.

Christopher Baker is William Temple Professor of Religion and Public Life at Goldsmiths, University of London and Director of the William Temple Foundation.

Malcolm Brown is Director of Mission and Public Affairs for the Archbishops' Council of the Church of England. He was formerly Principal of the Eastern Region Ministry Course within the Cambridge Theological Foundation, having previously spent ten years as Executive Secretary of the William Temple Foundation.

Elaine Graham is Grosvenor Research Professor of Practical Theology at the University of Chester and Canon Theologian of Chester Cathedral.

Carl-Henric Grenholm is Professor Emeritus of Ethics at Uppsala University, Sweden. His main areas of research are the relationship between ethics and economics, ethical theory, ethical reflection in Lutheran theology, and the contribution of ethics to political theory.

Maria Power is Lecturer in Religion and Peacebuilding at the University of Liverpool and a Visiting Research Fellow at St Mary's University. Her research focuses on the role of the Catholic Church in the public square in Northern Ireland.

John Reader is Rector of the Ironstone Benefice in the Diocese of Oxford. He is an Associate Research Fellow and Trustee of the William Temple Foundation; Honorary Senior Lecturer for the Institute of Education, University of Worcester, and a tutor for the Christian Rural Environmental Studies Course.

Anna Ruddick is a community theologian and researcher who facilitates theological reflection and learning for leaders, congregations and Christian organizations seeking to deepen and strengthen their relationships with their local community. Anna currently represents Livability as Community Engagement Associate, and Urban Life as a Core team member. She is also a Research Fellow at Bristol Baptist College, and a Trustee of the William Temple Foundation.

Hilary Russell is Emeritus Professor, John Moores University European Institute of Urban Affairs, a Lay Canon of Liverpool Cathedral and Chair of Churches Together in Merseyside. She has been closely involved in Church Action on Poverty and Together for the Common Good and is the author of *Poverty Close to Home: Political and Theological Challenge of Poverty in Britain* (1995) and *A Faithful Presence: Working Together for the Common Good* (2015).

Peter Sedgwick was Principal of St Michael's College, Llandaff, a former staff member of the Church of England Board for Social Responsibility and is a Trustee of the William Temple Foundation.

Ian Steedman was Professor of Economics at the University of Manchester between 1976 and 1995 before moving to be Research Professor of Economics at Manchester Metropolitan University until his retirement in 2006. He is now Emeritus Professor, an Honorary Research Fellow at the University of Chester and a Senior Research Fellow of the William Temple Foundation.

William Storrar is the Director of the Center of Theological Inquiry in Princeton, New Jersey, an independent institution with an international visiting scholar programme for interdisciplinary research in religion.

Preface

LESLEY ATHERTON

John Atherton was my father, my boss and my best friend. Although we saw or spoke to each other almost daily, I always looked forward to the time we spent together. I still smile remembering his countless IT support phone calls or his requests for just 'twenty minutes' of my time, which would usually turn into a good three hours in his office. These sessions would inevitably be punctuated by a cuppa (scheduled for the same times each day, and always accompanied by a small biscuit) and a lot of stimulating conversation.

Dad would begin his research with a concept, and would then read massively around that subject. He could have single-handedly kept Amazon in business, and virtually none of the publications he purchased were recreational fiction. His relaxation, apart from reading and rereading the occasional historical detective novel, was his work.

He kept two very large shelving units for the purposes of storing the books he'd used for his most recent research – and each reference book would include its own sheaf of illegible scribbled notes. Once his research was completed, he'd take time to compile, to clarify and consider his notes, transforming them to an equally illegible pile of A4 that only he (and occasionally I) could decipher.

When he was ready to compile his first drafts, we would get together in his cosy office and he'd dictate to me in person from behind his huge stack of papers. Each page would be deciphered by Dad and relayed to me with an occasional, 'What does that say, Lesley Anne?' I would check and make guesses – and we would muddle through. He'd dictate so speedily at times that I didn't always get to grips with the concepts behind his work, but later, when we proof-read and I had the luxury of reading his work section by section, I would realize just what he'd created.

I'm so proud of him: of course because of his writings, his faith and his achievements, but mainly because of the person he was. He was generous, but nobody's fool; he was a self-confessed cheerful pessimist; he was loving, respectful, protective and silly. He was not a saint and nor was he a sinner, but he certainly was one of a kind, and a great, gentle, man.

Even in his youth his personality clearly shone through. He worked with great diligence to ensure his working-class family were proud of him and he earned the position of head boy at his grammar school – a commendable achievement considering how, at just a few years old, he had sneaked out of his new nursery and walked half a mile home alone and in his wellies. His reasoning: learning wasn't for him. But his studies really *were* for him. Despite his claim that he was not a clever man, merely a hard-working one, he achieved much, and I miss him enormously.

Acknowledgements

The editors would like to thank David Shervington, our editor at SCM Press, for his encouragement and help in conceiving and completing this volume. Thanks also go to Lesley Atherton, John's daughter, who provided us with valuable resources and information.

Last, but not least, of course, we would like to thank John Atherton himself: for his body of work as well as his unswerving encouragement and support of us as colleagues and friends.

Christopher Baker
Elaine Graham
Easter 2018

I

Introduction: Genealogies, Typologies and Reformulations

CHRISTOPHER BAKER AND ELAINE GRAHAM

To read the eight major volumes of public theology that spanned John Atherton's extraordinarily rich and consistent output from the early 1980s up to his death in 2016 is to swim in an immense tide of human experience, social history, global upheaval and religious and secular change. John's public theology captures a period in history that is still shaping our collective experience. The last 40 years have been an era of turmoil and often traumatic disorientation: from the rise of Thatcherism and the big bang of financial deregulation, the collapse of the post-war global consensus and the break-up of the Soviet Union, growing social inequality and the decline of Christianity in the West, through to 9/11, the rise of grass-roots protest such as the Occupy movement, global religious revival and the current moment of dangerous and febrile nationalist populism across Europe and the USA. John's work accurately and presciently captures these historical and social movements in a way that no one else in public or political theology has done.

And yet these monographs (along with many chapters, journal articles, collaborations and edited volumes) also hold these movements and moments in a rich and optimistic canvas. They capture the ever-present outpouring of divine love and purpose into the world, and relish the constant intellectual and spiritual challenge this represents in the promise of a coherent, critical, yet also timeless theology of hope and redemption. It is the constancy of vision, experience, imagination and method that holds this both intricate and widely scoped tapestry together. As a corpus of work, it is unique in the way it creates a distinctive voice that is supremely confident in how it critically analyses and redefines intellectual and hermeneutical paradigms.

This is the rich legacy of John's work, in its constant modulations and frequencies that interweave through the past, the present and the future, that this festschrift attempts to capture. Of the many direct quotes that will adorn this volume, two sum up particularly well the fearless and compassionate, yet also grounded, ontology of John's work. They both come from the introduction to his most critically acclaimed volume, *Public Theology for Changing Times*, written on the cusp of the new millennium. The first quote articulates the method, the second defines the rationale. In the context of the exponential reach of globalization and the market, representing the new empire that has replaced the stasis generated by Cold War ideologies and mutually assured destruction, John writes:

> The task is to develop large theologies which connect in critical dialogue with the narratives demanded by global contexts and questions. There can be no retreat from the Christian task of developing public theologies of global proportions. (Atherton, 2000, p. viii)

The second quote unambiguously frames the rationale for such a public theology; namely that the work of divine healing, redemption, judgement and imagination takes place in the daily processes of labour and change in the world. 'And God created Man(chester)' was the ironic marketing sobriquet invented at the height of the rebranding of Manchester as a post-industrial centre of music, culture and the arts in 1990s. It is one that we should also apply to John's work, since time and time again the twin cities of Manchester and Salford, and his proudly held working-class Lancashire upbringing, are the crucibles from which his public theology is forged. Manchester, writes John,

> drives us deep into histories of urbanization and industrialization and their transformation as global processes. It confronts us with great global challenges, from environment to marginalization ... and therefore means developing a familiarity with a variety of disciplines from economics and politics to history and literature [and] is an unfamiliar world to many in churches and theological departments. (2000, pp. 1–2)

Alien as a northern industrial conurbation may seem to most churches and academic theological departments, for John it was a natural habitat, given his theological conviction that for any Christian, any theologian, 'absorption in the secular, in God's world and works, is one of the most exciting and creative of journeys' (2000, p. 2).

We now lay out as a 'curtain-raising' exercise what we consider to be six key dimensions or modalities of John's work which emerge out of our own memories of working closely with him, as well as those evoked by our co-workers in this volume. These modalities are: a 'Manchester School'; a genius of place (namely context and materiality from which public theology emerges); engagement with the non-theological and empirical (as an embodiment of a Christian-orientated realism and pragmatism); ecumenical social ethics; morality and the market (and how both are 'reformulated' in mutual encounter); and autoethnography ('writing oneself in' as a critical actor in the theological and intellectual landscape through which one is travelling).

1 A 'Manchester School'?

In *Christianity and the Market* (1992) John points to a chain of connection between teachers and pupils within English Christian social thought (Atherton, 1992, p. 184) stretching from the mid-nineteenth to late twentieth centuries. It begins with F. D. Maurice, B. F. Westcott and Charles Gore, who taught both William Temple and R. H. Tawney, continuing with Tawney's student Ronald Preston, who supervised John for his Manchester doctorate awarded in 1974 (on Tawney, with particular reference to *The Acquisitive Society*). John himself was aware of this legacy and once (half-jokingly, perhaps) referred to it as a form of 'apostolic succession' (Atherton, 2000, p. 79; see also Sedgwick this volume). Whether it constitutes a definable 'Manchester School', however, is another matter. Later in this volume, Peter Sedgwick rejects this notion – and he is right to do so if what is meant is some kind of rigid orthodoxy, or quaint form of ancestor worship. What it does signal, however – and where perhaps it remains a helpful reference point – is what it says about John himself: undoubtedly, shaped by the Temple-Preston tradition of Anglican social thought, but also indelibly, uniquely forged in the social and economic crucible of Manchester and Salford, as the world's first industrial cities (2000, pp. 1–2; 2005). The shock of urbanization, the birth of political economy, the crisis of faith, the challenge of economic scarcity, the call to social solidarity; all these provided John with the raw materials of his craft.

While Manchester – cathedral and university – were the twin poles within which so much of his work was conceived, John's career also reflects a remarkable openness to changing times and influences. His conviction was, above all, that Christian social ethics must begin with the empirical realities of a situation, paying close attention to the social conditions, even as they were changing around him. In that respect, he did stand in a tradition of English social scientific empiricism that remained constant to his approach and that fuelled his intellectual curiosity up to his death; in another respect, as circumstances changed around him, as his perspective became more global, his work transcended any single influence or tradition.

So there may not have been a 'Manchester School' in any doctrinaire sense, then, although possibly it was – as Sedgwick suggests – a 'story': one that was materially embodied in the unfolding narratives of history and the theoretical systems of economics, in the built and natural environments of Lancashire and urban geography of Manchester–Salford, as well as told through these intergenerational bonds of intellectual affinity. But whatever the Manchester School, story or brand may have been, it was never purely an intellectual club. John's theology was certainly honed by his many years teaching Christian social ethics to generations of undergraduates at the University of Manchester, and in conversations with colleagues – another circle that widened over the years to reflect his connections to Uppsala and Princeton in particular. But to read his work is to rediscover, powerfully, how rooted too he was in the life of the Church – not as an ecclesiological ideal, but in the regular routines and disciplines of its liturgy and the quotidian encounters of parish life and pastoral care. John looked to integrate 'theory' with 'practice' – indeed, he would deny their separation, since the challenge was how to weave together the various dimensions of 'practical involvement, worship and theological reflection into one coherent whole, into one rich Christian way of life' (Atherton, 1988, p. 128). By *Public Theology for Changing Times* John was deliberately referring to theology as 'practical divinity' in order to capture that blend of 'a disciplined reflection on the nature and destiny of life, with regard to an ultimate frame of reference' and 'the tangible, practical consequences of that theological voice ... into and through partnership and reconciliation operating in our contexts, discerning, interpreting and promoting what is going on' (2000, p. 3).

Despite its shortcomings (and John was highly critical of the institution at times), the Church is the place in which the necessary virtues of a worldly but faithful spirituality, grounded in the rhythms of prayer, word and sacrament, are cultivated. At a personal level, and as an Anglican priest, John was always firmly committed to his local Christian community, not least because he knew it to be the place in which theological concepts such as common good, the Body of Christ (1988, pp. 25f.) or the capacious God (2000) 'took flesh' in the practices of solidarity, interdependence, human dignity and 'the ways of justice and of peace' (1988, p. 31).

Yet this is a public theology too: the Church's self-understanding as the people of God was not solely a vision for itself alone, but a reminder of the essential unity and fellowship of the entire human family and 'a potential focus of great power for Christian engagement with the corporate realities of contemporary life' (1988, p. 31). In this respect, John lived creatively within the dialectic of secular and sacred, action and reflection, convinced that this constituted the true calling of the Church

INTRODUCTION

in the world: 'Worship which is divorced from reflection and action will change nothing. It never leaves the church building' (Atherton, 1988, p. 26). This commitment to context, attention to detail, narrative and embodied change is what characterized John's essential quality, that of rootedness. This came out of a profoundly incarnational and sacramental theology which understands the affairs of the world as the place in which 'God is to be found, worshipped and served' (1983, p. 124).

2 A 'genius of place': the importance of context

John liked to quote the prospect of Friedrich Engels surveying the urban landscape of Manchester and Salford from Blackstone Edge in 1842 as an expression of how the impact of the Industrial Revolution was carved into the very contours of the physical environment (1994, p. 10). Like Engels, who portrayed the divisions of the emergent capitalist social order in spatial terms, noting the physical estrangement and separation of different classes as they passed one another, seemingly indifferent to the other's existence, on the city streets, Atherton also used the industrial and economic topography of his native Lancashire as a symbol of the profound economic, social and political change of the past 250 years. This was a story of population growth and upheaval, extremes of wealth and poverty, transformation of the built and natural environments and corresponding adjustments to human expectations – and it was written into the built environment, the stories of its population, its ideas and social movements. John also commented on the way in which, only in Manchester, could a public building, the Free Trade Hall, be named not after a saint, river or landowner but an idea – indeed a political and economic philosophy at the heart of industrial capitalism.

Yet while the immediate story of the world's first industrial conurbation may have formed the backdrop to his earlier work, as years went on John expanded his view to encompass an ever more globalized vista. If initially his curiosity was how a series of local circumstances in the north west of England – climate, financial, demographic, political – combined to effect the global eruption of industrial capitalism, then increasingly his enquiry was refracted through ever more complex and global and interdisciplinary lenses. This more global shift begins with *Public Theology for Changing Times*, a book for the new millennium where the threats and opportunities generated by globalization are even more apparent. The issue of poverty (and its corollary of wellbeing) continues to be refracted through ever complex and global and interdisciplinary lenses. 'The task is to develop large theologies which connect in critical dialogue with the narratives demanded by global contexts and questions. There can be no

5

retreat from the Christian task of developing public theologies of global proportions' (2000, p. viii).

3 Theological method: engagement with the non-theological

Continuity and change also mark his interdisciplinary engagement, as well: from a disciplined articulation of the need to incorporate the insights of secular analysis as part of a truly 'public' theology that was both accountable and relevant, to a deep engagement with later sources and world views beyond political economy that, for him, offered vital insights into human behaviour: religious studies, the economics and psychology of happiness and wellbeing, Islamic economics, evolutionary biology, and so on.

Thus in the earlier volumes, written in the 1980s and early 1990s, there is a commitment to engaging theology with social and ecclesial history (especially focusing on the north west of England), and those disciplines associated with what John constantly referred to as political economy. These included the history of economic ideas, and the history of political and philosophical ideas relating to how best to combine ethics and distribution of goods such as equality, justice and the common good. Thus Smith, Tawney, Malthus, Ricardo, Keynes, Marshall, Rawls, Weber (especially his work on religion and capitalism) and Engels interact with Temple, Preston, Niebuhr and Buber.

Later work in the early 2000s focuses on globalization and its challenge to imagine and generate a new pro-poor, pro-environment political economy (Sen, Stiglitz). This, combined with a clear trajectory on institutional church decline in the West, sees him engaging more with feminist social theorists and economists (Young), and sociology of religion (Putnam, Davie). His last phase of work, written over the last ten years, sees a much greater focus on what he calls the 'hard' (namely post-Marxist) sociology of Castells, Bourdieu, Levinas, Derrida and Hardt and Negri. It also engages with wellbeing and happiness studies, including popular psychology and behavioural economics (Seligman, Haidt, Deaton, Fogel), and their ability to measure subjective wellbeing and techno-physical wellbeing, religious studies, and the work of women theologians such as Charry and Tanner.

For John, the insights of theology and sociology, psychology and economics must all be

> united in at least as much as they address the human condition in exploratory and interpretative terms. All these disciplines, and certainly including religious studies, must therefore be concerned in their

distinctive ways with life and how things are with the world of daily life ... [and] about being able to see things from another perspective as well as from one's own. (Atherton, 2014, p. 194)

However, the Church has not been good at thinking theologically about contemporary challenges, or how the resources of the tradition can be put to work in guiding its members' everyday discipleship (Atherton, 1988, p. 134). Neither extrapolation directly from the Bible or naive adoption of secular insights will do, because these neglect what John, quoting Martin Buber, terms 'the in-between' (1988, p. 135): the necessary synthesis of sacred and secular. Rather, Christian social thought is a 'dynamic interaction between the understanding of God's purposes mediated through Christian tradition, but equally through the secular realities of life' (Atherton, 1992, p. 279). The inherited wisdom of Christian tradition is brought to bear 'for the development of faith, rather than [for] the narrowly deductively logical attempts to prove God's existence' (Atherton, 1992, p. 277). Theological reflection proceeds from the practicalities of faithful living; but in turn, its authenticity is gauged by its ability to nurture the practices of discipleship.

This is above all a dialogical process. It means to attend to empirical evidence and to bring Christian tradition to bear (Atherton, 1992, pp. 16–17): 'our understanding of God's purposes is ... always a critical dialogue with secular understandings and experiences' (p. 18). Theology combines theory and practice; it is both interpretative framework and practical wisdom; it has to interact with non-theological insights; it promotes clear values based on an understanding of the nature of God and human destiny; it must be rooted in social realities and experiences. Being independent of the current situation, it can bring new perspectives and challenges to bear; it makes strong connections between moral principles and policy options (Atherton, 1988, p. 141), something which demands the skills of mediation between tradition/belief or situation/experience, which constitute 'middle-range moral imperatives' (p. 142) but stop short of specific policy options. The method of proceeding is first to investigate and analyse what is happening; and then to bring elements of Christian thought and practice to bear; and finally to evaluate prevailing trends in social and political policy. 'Addressing our context always needs to include taking economic matters seriously, yet how we interpret them must be responsive to the changing context' (Atherton, 1992, pp. 15–16).

Empirical evidence of the changing context was integral to John's theological method. These include surveys from: popular psychology around levels of self-reported happiness and wellbeing; mortality and heath indices; human development indices from the Ice Age onwards; poverty and marginalization indices on the broad impacts of globalization on poverty, inequality and the environment. At the heart of this empirical quest lies the belief that for theology and religious studies to have a credible interdisciplinary voice, and a role in the task of reconnecting and rebuilding the fabric of public and human life, it needs to prove the added value of its impact and praxis, as well as articulating an alternative vision for society.

That is why, in his later work, John gets so excited by the growth in studies aimed at defining and articulating human happiness and wellbeing, since these can be empirically measured at both individual and national levels. The empirical study of happiness and wellbeing, along with neuroscience, becomes the interstitial space where the impacts of both progressive economics and religion can be measured and understood. Thus, *Challenging Religious Studies* contains an amazing table, which like the Synoptic Gospels lays side by side the sources of insight into human wellbeing derived from secular research on the efficacy of religion, the Christian tradition itself, and national accounts of wellbeing.[1] Each tradition identifies seven criteria for *eudaimonic* as well as hedonic happiness. However, the variables that appear most consistently across all three columns are a strong belief-system and a sense of belonging. John is clear that these two variables represent the foundations of human flourishing. Reflecting on how his active Christian faith helped him to come to terms with the death of his wife Vannie after 47 years of marriage, he writes: 'As a classic Anglican, my experience suggests both believing and belonging in equal doses, the one supporting, and being essential for, the robust nature of the other' (2014, p. 70).

4 Ecumenical social ethics

In line with his intellectual commitment to interdisciplinarity as a way of developing 'practical divinity' was his commitment to cooperation with and between religions. Traditionally, this has always included dialogue between Abrahamic faiths, but must now extend to Eastern religions including Buddhism, Hinduism and Confucianism, as well as 'the collaboration between established religions and growing secular spiritualities' (Atherton, 2014, p. 20). For John, the articulation and development of an ecumenical social ethics that moves from intrafaith to interfaith (2007, p. 8), is integral to the role and impact that religion can play in addressing the wealth, wellbeing and inequalities of nations.

First, an ecumenical social ethics, based on John's reading of key theological categories. *Oikonomia* describes the activity of human stewardship of God's economy (in other words, the whole created order), which is 'the partnership between God and ourselves for our sustenance and the transformation of the world' (2000, p. 16). For John, the shared task of *oikonomia* is grounded in the churches' distinctive identity, which is expressed through its everyday worship, nurture and mission:

> Being church is about an identity which includes dialogue and outreach through worship and service as its distinctive heart. Making connections with other 'convictions and aspirations' to address common problematics becomes an intimate part of its mission and ministry. (2003, p. 132)

This performative *oikonomia* is more fully developed in *Public Theology for Changing Times* as part of the great 'partnership and reconciliation' typology that depicts the current era of religious, political, social and economic change that has occurred since 1750. The age of partnership and reconciliation follows on from the age of voluntarism and atonement, through the age of incarnation and the state. It appears towards the end of the 1960s, becoming clearer during the accelerated processes of globalization in the 1980s and 90s. It develops from many strands, first as a new pragmatism engendered by the dominance of the market economy, which becomes enshrined in the policy turn towards the so-called 'Third Way', which lay at the heart of the Clinton administration of 1992–2000 in the USA and Blair's New Labour project in the UK from 1997. Partnership and reconciliation develops in the light of the collapse of the Soviet Union and a growing assertiveness of religion that seriously questions the underlying binaries of old twentieth-century modernism. It also occurs within the complexity and embedded interconnectedness generated by globalization, and the scale of the problems it generates in terms of marginalization, population and the environment. All these major shifts mean that we have no choice but to develop an ethic of partnership and reconciliation as both a moral and a policy imperative. John quotes the anthropologist and ethicist Nigel Boyle to summarizing effect: 'There is one world and it is not endless, and we have to work out among ourselves how we are to live in it together or we shall die in it separately', before adding, 'And that is about partnership and reconciliation' (2003, p. 84).

So an ecumenical social ethics emerges from the age of partnership and reconciliation as an ethical and humanitarian response to the problematic of globalization, and is characterized by intrafaith, interfaith and interdisciplinary research, reflection and praxis (Atherton, 2014, pp. 19–21). This often mundane and embedded praxis is explored in several localized case studies in his books. It includes: relational agency (that is, personal agency that is held and perfected by the relational agency of others and that in turn leads to the formation of character and virtues); the provision of a telos or goal in life which 'connects human purposes to God's purposes'; the consistency found within religion between theory and output that helps to 'generate a *logic of practice*, as the embodiment of ethical norms ... known as praxis'; and finally an 'ecumenical social ethics' that is 'rooted most powerfully, [as] the contemporary engagement with the Other as Other'.

5 Morality of the market

This key intellectual, theological and moral theme runs through the whole of John's work. Despite ranging over many varied topics, and including both poles of poverty and wealth creation, John's concerns are linked by a common thread: a concern for human flourishing and how that might best be achieved. It is also reflected in his consistent interest in the conundrum of scarcity as the fundamental problem of political economy. The capacity of the market to effect basic social goods – and thus fulfilling the fundamental problem of scarcity – and the market as the least worst means of achieving that, began to emerge in *Faith in the Nation* (1988) and comprised a key theme in *Christianity and the Market* (1992). The secret, as John gradually came to recognize, lay in processes of material advancement: a liberation from the impediments of subsistence and want, as exemplified in his consideration in *Challenging Religious Studies* of how the advent of industrial capitalism (reprising, thus, his enduring fascination with the 'Great Transition' of the late eighteenth century as symbolized by the rise of Manchester-Salford) truly represented an unprecedented and definitive breakthrough in human history, resulting in exponential gains in terms of mortality, health, wellbeing and social stability.

Furthermore, as Malcolm Brown has noted, John acknowledged if not the legitimacy of the market then its existence, in the eyes of its advocates, as a *moral* undertaking (Brown, 2014, p. 8). Embracing the market 'as an efficient and preferred mechanism for the production and allocation of resources' (Atherton, 1988, p. 110) is a necessary consideration, albeit constrained by principles of participation and democracy. Markets are the most effective means of ensuring economic growth, even though at this stage John still envisages this as occurring within a model of social market or market socialism (Atherton, 1988, pp. 111–13).

At the heart of this all-pervasive theme of the market is the driving idea of interconnection or integration. Strongly influenced by Bourdieu's work on religious capital, John argues that while religion and economics are separate fields of human experience and activity, they can nevertheless be in dialogue with one another. This is because the significance of wealth creation and distribution, so integral to both human and national development and wellbeing, cannot be divorced from deep insights into the true nature of human happiness and ethics that is located in transcendent as well as material goods. The task is to link the insights and practice of both disciplines in order to address the greatest problematic of the current age, namely globalization and the attendant marginalization and inequality it brings, while lifting at the same time billions out of abject poverty and giving a purpose for living and development.

John sums up both the challenge and supreme importance of engaging morality with the market. Morality, he argues, should never be deployed to 'underwrite' one particular economic system, whether market economics or state-sponsored socialism (2000, p. 64). The stories we tell ourselves about human development and wellbeing, claims John, are 'rather about a continuing interaction, of market and challenges, of politics and economics, of morality and "realities"' (2000, p. 64). In John's view, religion interacts with the market in three critical ways: to critique, to reformulate and to transfigure.

Critique of the market

The *critical* function of religion is uppermost in John's earlier writing (for example, *Faith in the Nation* and *Christianity and the Market*), especially after his controversial shift towards a recognition of the market as an ineluctable dimension of public life with which Christian social ethics will have to engage. A desire for a return to neo-Christendom, or the creation of a series of alternative and counter-cultural Christian enclaves, is not an adequate response to the mainstreaming of the market. For him, inherently Christian values and ethics are already contained in the market, including the values of self-interest, freedom, individualism and efficiency. However, they need to be harnessed and balanced with other values such as altruism, interdependence and redistribution.

In *Faith in the Nation*, for example, he refracts these values through the concepts of the Body of Christ and the common good. The Body of Christ speaks of interdependence and complementarity in the following ways: it is a sign and instrument of the Kingdom; it generates solidarity in the face of suffering and embodies and offers a corporate life rooted in common worship that is nevertheless conditioned by hope and realism regarding the shortcomings of religion; the Church as the family of God at work in the world; and a new community that anticipates the unity of humanity under God. These insights are brought together by making the connections between moral principles and policy ideas, something, as we have already highlighted, that demands the skills of mediation between the resources of tradition and belief, together with situation and experience in order to produce 'middle-range moral imperatives' (Atherton, 1988, p. 141).

Reformulation of the market

In his later work, John sees the engagement of morality in the market as more far-reaching and dynamic, moving from critique to *reformulation*. In *Marginalization* he distances himself more fully from pre-existing categories of thought (such as the common good) in favour of a more confident interdisciplinary reformulation of 'Christian political economy'. This is based on what he calls the plenitude of God, which, he argues, subverts the scarcity economics paradigm introduced by Thomas Malthus, and which had become the basis of modern economics. In defiance of this, however, figures such as Whateley, Sumner, Copleston, Tucker and Berkeley (Atherton, 2003, pp. 144–5) argued from a Christian standpoint that 'the economy that underpins God's new order is centred on "abundance and extraordinary generosity", epitomised in the gracious self-giving of God in Christ'. Christians

> are therefore called to participate in that divine economy by their way of life, including through sharing in the Eucharist where 'resources are neither scarce nor subject to competition' ... [and] Distribution is made subject only to the condition of one's baptism ... [therefore] there need be no poor among us. (2003, p. 144)

John articulates some contemporary points of connection between economics and theology that elaborate how a Christian political economy can actively contribute to a reformulation of the market for the sake of a globally sustainable economy for all. First, he stresses the connection between economics and ethics via the thought of the 'ethical' thinking of key figures such as Adam Smith and Amartya Sen. This is not at the expense of rejecting market mechanisms, but aims for their 'reformulation'. This will focus on correcting and broadening the implicitly defective anthropology inherent in neoclassical economics – most notably in ideas about 'economic man' in terms of human nature and behaviour; efficiency in relation to debates about production and distribution; and the role of governance. Second, John argues that it is possible to have both efficiency and justice. Learning from the experience of South East Asian economies, he quotes Sen: 'Justice is good for the economy.' The market economy flourishes on the foundation of pro-poor and pro-environment policies and technologies. Third, as part of the evidence base for this assertion, Sweden and Japan are offered as good examples of thriving and innovative economies, supported by and through good governance structures.

Finally, the Jubilee 2000 campaign to relieve global debt is a good case study of the 'the interaction between Christian tradition and the global economic problematic of marginalization through tackling international debt'. John augments this example with further case studies from religious traditions, including Muslim interest-free banking. He then lists examples throughout the last two centuries of experiments of alternative and prophetic religious thought and practice, ranging from liberation theology, the Christendom Group, the Guild of St Matthew, Christian Socialism and Radical Orthodoxy. John refers to this as a 'heteroclitical' tradition, which went on to create 'fissures and cracks' within secular and positivist discourses on economics and the market by, in Zygmunt Bauman's phrase, 'Questioning the ostensibly unquestionable premises of our way of life' (Atherton, 2003, p. 176).

The whole interaction of these points of connection based on religious experience and imagination, intellectual rigour and empirical research is likened to the 'perichoretic dance of the Trinity'; 'it is that dialogic or perichoretic logic, linking divine and ecological realities, which takes us into contemporary change, into the great marginalization problematic and therefore into the reconnecting of Christianity with that total context' (Atherton, 2003, p. 179).

Transfiguration of the market

The final function of religion in relation to the market is to *transfigure* it, as explored in his 2008 volume, *Transfiguring Capitalism*. This is possibly the most ambitious book John wrote, in terms of size and scope. There are three interconnecting parts to the book. The first part overviews the shifting global context by including sections on Empires, Capitalism, Globalization and Religion as the coming together of politics, economics, global capitalism, religious studies and the sociology of social capital. The second part details the religious field, focusing primarily on the idea that a resurgent religion might so interact with and shape economics that it moves it towards the wellbeing of humans and the planet, and in doing so helps economics to rediscover its original ethos as contributing to life in all its fullness and abundance. This approach reveals overlapping themes between religion and economics based on ideas of happiness, sympathy, cooperation, trust and ideas of gift economics; overlaps which not only generate an excess of wellbeing but in the process help to promote economic sustainability and an economics based on the values of reciprocity, partnership and team working. John defines this interchange as 'faithful economics', namely 'the space where faith, ethics, and economy overlap' (2008, p. 145). He concludes: 'It is that ability to promote a more relational form of economy which addresses the lessons of the happiness hypothesis and so creates a more ethically adequate economy' (2008, p. 145).

If faithful economics presents the general interaction of the religious field with the economics field, then Part 3 of *Transfiguring Capitalism* moves to the specific ways in which faithful economics work. These include: faith-based contributions to a post-scarcity anthropology; collaborative working in the form of interfaith ethics; and a refurbished Christian social ethics. At its heart is a *theological* economics based on Kathryn Tanner's *Economy of Grace*. Religion, taking Tanner's lead, represents for John an alternative field of organized economy in the production and distribution of distinct goods. These goods include physical, psychological and spiritual contributions to the public sphere based on God's grace, and reflect an uncompetitive distribution that depletes neither our responses nor our resources, but impels us to build up others as we have been built up. Unconditional giving is universal giving and develops practices of mutual benefit, and John unpacks policy examples based on these ideas over a nine-page section in the book (2008, pp. 273–82) with ideas ranging from taxation to welfare.

The final chapter of the book, however, is where he deconstructs the biblical account of the transfiguration of Christ on the mountain 'at the midpoint of his ministry' in the Gospels and in 2 Peter. He highlights the multilevelled ways that religion interpenetrates and suffuses capitalism and transfigures it. These include: the transfiguration of the material world; the imaginary power of the law and the prophets; the offer of ethics and the formation of character; a recognition of the transcendent – 'the hidden presence in all events'; and the validation of interim ethics, 'as we live in between the appearance of Christ on the holy mountain and his appearance at the end'. In a typical piece of Athertonian rhetoric, all these elements are magisterially brought into a coherent and passionate whole, moving seamlessly from the material to the sacred while keeping one's sights firmly set on the challenge of living with integrity in a complex and contradictory world. He writes:

> The features of transfiguration as materiality, tradition and transcendence therefore generate a more comprehensive model or framework, which is both survey of the constitution of wellbeing and the process for engaging it. It is a connection beautifully captured by the concept of wholeness, an intimate part of the pursuit of wellbeing, which includes economic life but increasingly its interaction with wider experiences or understandings of what it means to be human in a post-scarcity age. For wholeness is associated in the English language with the word holiness. (2008, p. 285)

6 Public theology and autoethnography

The final defining feature of John's theology is the extent to which he consistently wrote himself into the complex historical social, economic and theological drama he so expertly defined and mapped. We have already alluded to the fact that the cities of Manchester and Salford, together with the economic history of the north-west region of England, are central characters in the telling of this narrative; commenting, debunking and illuminating these grand sweeps of history and ideas, dressed in colourful and local garb. Surely the third central character in John's work is John himself. It is both his innate confidence in his own abilities, but also the detached way he sees his life as part of a wider social pattern, that creates this unique ability. However, this view is always earthed, never hubristic. In fact, it is often disarmingly confessional and personal. John understands that it is the ordinariness of his life and upbringing that is precisely the source of its transcendent and salvific qualities. He speaks as one who knows his value as a human being, both in this life and in the life to come.

Autoethnography, a technique in which the researcher's imaginative reconstructions of their own life-experience are a key site of reflection and knowledge-making, may be a relatively recent arrival into the practical theological methodological canon (Ellis, 2004; Walton, 2014), but John had already been quietly employing his own life as source and resource for many years. It returns us, in a sense, to where we began this appreciation: in the deep rootedness and commitment to the texture of everyday life that gave his work such richness and integrity.

Attention to lived experience and personal narrative begins, perhaps, with his use of case studies in *The Scandal of Poverty*. He constructs four typical experiences of poverty in order to dispel the sterility and formality of statistical and quantitative measures and to correct misunderstandings and prejudices (1983, pp. 5–18). The causes of poverty may be structural but its impact is always personal (1983, pp. 51f.).

Three further examples show John's particular use of this kind of life-writing as research in relation to himself. In *Challenging Religious Studies*, written under considerable duress due to illness, John traces how his personal life history and those of his forebears illuminates his work. He reflects, for example, on the huge strides in techno-physical evolution that have released millions from acute poverty and the sorrow of premature child deaths. Only just over a century ago, he reflects, 75% of all deaths recorded in the parish of Chopwell, in the diocese of Durham, were infants of less than a year old. He then recalls his own family history. 'My grandmother (on my father's side), gave birth in 1900 to a son, John Robert Atherton, who died well before the age of one. There is every chance I was named after him' (2014, p. 41). He also poignantly recalls the precious gift he presented as an only child to his own parents:

> For recent generations, parents have fought and hoped ... that their children would make a better life for themselves than their parents. This has certainly been the case in my own family, classic English working class (my father was a plumber) and putting their hopes on their one child, born at the end of the Great Depression in 1939, and his ability to escape from their relative poverty into modest prosperity, higher education and more robust health. I was that precious (to them!) child, on which their hopes for a better life were placed. (2014, p. 2)

This undoubtedly colours his approach to 'the Great Transition' of the industrial period and to continuing currents of globalization and economic development to this day.

Another example illustrates the wider point he is making about the contribution of lived religious faith to happiness and wellbeing as defined by popular psychology, and particularly the work of Martin Seligman. Seligman developed his PERMA framework for happiness and wellbeing: the acronym stands for Positive emotions, Engagement, Relationships, Meaning and Achievement. During the preparation of the text for his final volume, John's wife Vannie died. Still raw with grief, John decided to take the online PERMA survey himself. He defines with moving candour the insights that the survey gives, and that he knows will help him move on in the months and years ahead.

> The proof of the pudding is in the eating. So in February, 2011, I completed the surveys for each of these five constituent parts ... I decided at first it wasn't worth doing the initial one, positive emotions, because my wife of nearly 47 years had died suddenly several weeks before. Ours had been a lifelong, rich and happy partnership. So I was pretty devastated ... I knew what my emotions were, and they were the opposite of positive! Fortunately I read further and realized Seligman himself judged he was not very good at positive emotions, yet clearly recognized that his life was flourishing. And that was because he scored highly on engagement, meaning, accomplishment and positive relationships. And I did. And that research, confirmed by my completing the personal surveys on the five features of wellbeing, greatly helped me to survive my wife's death gracefully. (2014, pp. 56–7)

A final example will resonate with anyone who visited John and Vannie's home in Adlington in Lancashire. Adorned on all the walls were pictures of local landscapes, several of which make appearances in John's works. One of his favourites was a series of views of Pendle Hill across different

INTRODUCTION

seasons. The hill dominates the whole of north-east Lancashire. In *Transfiguring Capitalism* he reflects:

> It's a place of important histories and stories, from the Pendle Witches, cruelly done to death in the name of religion ... the seminal memory for the Quakers of their founder George Fox climbing the Hill's summit and having a greater vision of the heavenly host, to the growth of the industrial revolution and urban living in the city and towns of North East Lancashire, now home to large immigrant populations, sign of the impact on British society of world faiths like Islam, and the symbol of global flows par excellence. It is that multidimensional history, it is that profound plurality, which is so tangibly confirmed and exhibited by ... [these] pictures. (2008, p. 15)

These three examples represent John's finely honed intuition that the macro only makes sense if it is refracted in the micro; that the vast global, cultural and religious shifts he defines as the laboratory of public theology only connect and have credibility if they can demonstrate how they impact on the lives of local communities and individuals.

With John's challenges thus ringing in our ears, we undertake this act of critical *homage* and investigation with the help of fellow travellers who have contributed to this volume. Many of them knew John as a lifelong friend and interlocutor. Hilary Russell offers a more detailed account of the various contexts and issues that informed John's work, affirming the view in this Introduction of his commitment to theologizing on behalf of grass-roots causes and the life of the Church. In common with a number of contributions, Peter Sedgwick's chapter identifies certain features as quintessentially 'Athertonian': a serious engagement with non-theological sources, and particularly political economy; a stubborn refusal to dodge the hard questions; and a prioritization of human wellbeing and flourishing. Querying the existence of a 'Manchester School' of Christian social ethics, Sedgwick nevertheless concedes that the city served both as empirical source of much of John's work, as well as occupying a major symbolic place as a benchmark against which to measure and ground the broader, increasingly global, sweep of his concerns.

Carl-Henric Grenholm represents John's valued links with the University of Uppsala, which honoured him with an honorary doctorate in 2004. Grenholm carefully outlines John's changing perspective on the market and the evolution of his thought from a concern with the problem of poverty to the historical dynamics of wealth creation and thence to the problematic of wellbeing. Throughout this, argues Grenholm, there was a characteristic concern to articulate a theological voice that was capable of responding convincingly to its economic and political context.

Finally, Malcolm Brown considers the legacy of industrial mission, arguing that its history after 1945 reflects the tension within Christian social thought between the theologies of atonement and incarnation, something to which John frequently drew attention (Atherton, 1994, p. 15). While industrial mission's insistence on a theology of Incarnation has fallen from favour, new ways of combining the two traditions are beginning to resemble John's call (which we touch on above) for a greater synthesis that embodies the tasks of partnership, reconciliation and mission.

Other contributors to this collection have found a critical inspiration from engaging with John's work as they traverse other intellectual disciplines. Ian Steedman, a leading welfare economist, long-standing friend and conversation partner of John, provides a nuanced critique of the morality of the market and endorses John's characterization of the market as 'ambiguously positive' (Atherton, 1992, p. 212). It is important, argues Steedman, to be circumspect about the moral nature of the market – remembering we are talking about economic actors rather than impersonal forces – and how the goods of equity and justice have to be balanced with those of material prosperity and efficiency.

John Reader chooses to consider the phenomenon of the information economy, and the impact of one particular new technology, that of 'blockchain'. In contrast to the traditional emphasis on economic actors, Reader raises the prospect that increasingly the global economy will be driven by mechanisms such as algorithms and rapid transactions of data, largely independent of human decision-making. Reader considers how religious practices, and especially alternative ways of inhabiting time and space, might offer critical vantage points; and he ends with a typically Athertonian question: 'Who benefits?'

Since John died in June 2016, the world has seen the rise of populist political movements such as Brexit and the election of Donald Trump. In his essay, Will Storrar offers some timely reflections on the political implications of these new trends. Can such disaffection and anger with the democratic process, and what that says about the health of our very democratic processes, he asks, be 'bent' or redirected to constructive and equitable ends? Storrar picks up John's concerns for the psychological and emotional dimensions of economic change, reminding us once again of the ambivalence of economic prosperity, not least in its impact on mental health and wellbeing, which in turn may have ramifications for the future of democracy itself.

Finally, other writers have used John's work as the platform for their own reflections on the future directions that theologically informed enquiry needs to take. Drawing on her doctoral research into the work of the Eden Network in inner-city Manchester, Anna Ruddick demonstrates how the twin strands of incarnation and atonement, as highlighted in John's work, are undergoing a new synthesis in the form of what she terms 'missional pastoral care'. Traditional approaches to mission as personal evangelism have evolved into an alternative strategy of long-term, incarnational presence within and alongside local communities and the valuing of material, physical and subjective wellbeing as sustainable outcomes.

Mindful of John's rootedness in a particular tradition of Anglican social thought, Maria Power considers the prospects for a related tradition, that of Roman Catholic Social Teaching (CST). While CST is proving increasingly popular within mainstream political thinking, Power argues that it is not as developed or focused a body of teaching as is often assumed. Rather, it needs its own processes of contextualization, and by way of illustration Power uses her own work on peacebuilding and reconciliation in Ireland to demonstrate the purpose and potential of a Catholic public theology.

As editors, we have been delighted to see the diversity of our contributors' dialogue with John and his work, since it creates many different ways into an understanding of the many modalities of John's writing. We hope these essays connect together to create a whole new body of work that will enable us to take John's legacy forward, since so much of it remains to be properly explored and teased out further.

Note

1 Some of this material is contained within John's essay for this volume; see Chapter 2.

References

Atherton, J. R., 1983, *The Scandal of Poverty: Priorities for the Emerging Church*, London: Mowbray.
Atherton, J. R., 1988, *Faith in the Nation: A Christian Vision for Britain*, London: SPCK.
Atherton, J. R., 1992, *Christianity and the Market: Christian Social Thought for Our Times*, London: SPCK.
Atherton, J. R., 2000, *Public Theology for Changing Times*, London: SPCK.
Atherton, J. R., 2003, *Marginalization*, London: SCM Press.
Atherton, J. R., 2008, *Transfiguring Capitalism: An Enquiry into Religion and Social Change*, London: SCM Press.
Atherton, J. R., 2014, *Challenging Religious Studies: The Wealth, Wellbeing and Inequalities of Nations*, London: SCM Press.
Ellis, C. 2004, *The Ethnographic I: A Methodological Novel about Autoethnography*, Walnut Creek, CA: AltaMira Press.
Walton, H., 2014, *Writing Methods in Theological Reflection*, London: SCM Press.

2

By Their Fruits You Shall Know Them: The Economics of Material Wellbeing and a Christianity Fit for Purpose[1]

JOHN ATHERTON

The most progressive changes in economic history occurred after 1800, namely the increases in living standards, the decline in poverty, and improvements in life expectancy. We are no longer poor, and we die in old age, not as children. Economists refer to these changes as people being freed from slavery, a trend beginning with Nobel economics laureate Robert Fogel's *The Escape from Hunger and Premature Death* (2004) and continued by another economics laureate Angus Deaton's *The Great Escape: Health, Wealth and the Origins of Inequality* (2013).

Standards of living and health lie at the centre of our understanding of human wellbeing. Their story is the account of 'the world of daily life' (Bellah, 2011, p. 2); of the struggle to survive and improve life, the history of how people have managed 'to make their lives better' (Deaton, 2013, p. xiv).

This is everybody's agenda. It certainly should be at the heart of Christianity with the gospel's aspiration, 'that they might have life, and have it more abundantly' (John 10.10, KJV). Historically, its record of promoting greater wellbeing has been mixed in practice and even more in theory, particularly since 1800 when the Industrial and then Mortality Revolutions began spreading their beneficial consequences across the world. So much of Christianity's theory and practice was framed before 1800 that it lacked tools to engage such progressive change, especially economic change and economics.

This chapter is part of an exercise to engage these changes and so build bridges between Christianity and economics. The first stage was concluded in 2014 by my *Challenging Religious Studies: The Wealth, Wellbeing and Inequalities of Nations*. Its entry point was Deaton's *Great Escape: Health, Wealth and the Origins of Inequality*. Out of this emerged my working model for a rebuilt Christianity's engagement with economics and economic change. For Deaton's book explores from the perspective of economics the essential features of contemporary wellbeing, income, health and subjective wellbeing. My own book, *Challenging Religious Studies*, developed this model for Christianity's engagement with economics, initially through that third feature, subjective wellbeing, and to a lesser extent with the second, health. This chapter will address that first perspective on wellbeing, income as material wellbeing, at the heart of modern economics and economic life.

This further testing of the model begins, first, with an account of modern material wellbeing, focused on income (or money), with all that it offers access to, from historic basics of material wellbeing such as food, clothing and housing, to more recently education, good participatory governance, healthcare and leisure. The chapter then, secondly, moves on to rebuilding a Christianity fit for the purpose of engaging with the economics of material wellbeing and income. This will use the economists' tool of revealed preferences (studying what people actually do about their material wellbeing, including their standards of living). This confirms the published first part of this research project, that Christianity requires a reordering or reprioritizing process by focusing on its practices before its ethics and beliefs. In other words, 'by their fruits ye shall know them' (Matthew 7.16, 20, KJV). Having completed work on the economics of material wellbeing, Christianity's side of the collaboration between disciplines clearly needs further research.

The latter statement on interdisciplinary work is a reminder that engaging Industrial and Mortality Revolutions requires such a research character. For the economist Easterlin, the world's most formidable problems are not of any one discipline. Rather, their solutions must 'recognise multidisciplinary training and research' (Easterlin, 2004, p. 249). It's what I describe as learning to live in more than one place at once (Atherton, 2014, pp. 193f.; Clements, 2013). It's about living in different disciplines, in this case economics and Christianity, in the incarnational sense of the Word becoming flesh and dwelling among us (John 1.15; Atherton, 2014, p. 197).

The economics of material wellbeing and income

The account of the sudden growth of income and therefore of living standards from 1800 for Deaton represents 'perhaps the greatest escape in all of human history, and certainly the most rapid one'. The economics of such material wellbeing is measured by incomes, with money as reasonable indicator of 'people's ability to buy the things on which material wellbeing depends' (Deaton, 2013, p. 16). Income is therefore central to greater wellbeing as key component of food, clothing and housing, but also as facilitator of other aspects of wellbeing, including education, healthcare, participatory governance, welfare and society. Economists measure such progress across nations by increases in per capita income (the Gross National Product – GNP – divided by population). Such a consideration of increasing incomes is related to decreasing poverty but also increasing inequality.

First, the historic increase of income resulted from the Industrial Revolution's 'long-term and continuing economic growth' (Deaton, 2013, p. 34). From 1820 to 1992 the world's inhabitants' average income grew between seven and eight times, constituting a 'historically unprecedented increase in living standards' (Deaton, 2013, pp. 4–5, 167). In the USA, leader of this revolution, per capita income rose from $8,000 in 1929 to $43,238 in 2012, an amazing fourfold increase in only 80 years and the result of economic growth of 1.9% per annum, astonishing to our ancestors, but not to us (Deaton, 2013, p. 170).

Second, decreasing poverty was one of the greatest consequences of increasing incomes. So between 1820 and 1992 the fraction of the world's population in extreme poverty dropped from 84% to 24% (Deaton, 2013, p. 167). This achievement was nothing to do with liberation theology!

Third, increasing inequality, the classic indicator of great divergences, of paradoxes of development, accompanied these progressive changes in incomes and poverty. Such income inequality since the Industrial Revolution has occurred particularly between nations. The wealthiest countries are 256 times richer than the poorest (Deaton, 2013, p. 20). Inequalities within nations, like the USA, have returned to rapidly accelerating processes since the 1970s. In the USA, the bottom 90% is 'barely holding onto the living standards of its parents' (Deaton, 2013, pp. 189, 205). The real gains have been made particularly by the top 1%. Nobel economist Stiglitz has summarized these developments in *Vanity Fair*: 'Of the 1%, for the 1%, by the 1%' (Stiglitz, 2012, p. xxxix).

To grasp the nature and extent of these transformations it is best to locate them in historical contexts. In 1798, Thomas Malthus published the *Essay on the Principle of Population* with its thesis that expanding populations increasingly outstrip the growth in food, shelter and clothing necessary to resource them. That gap could only be closed by education or morality (meaning marrying later, so having fewer children), or by starvation, war, disease. This Malthusian Trap operated throughout history from 14000 BC to AD 1800. So the world of daily life was shaped by one factor, 'in the long run births had to equal deaths' (Clark, 2007, p. 19). Before 1800, rates of technological advance were so low that incomes could not escape the Malthusian equilibrium. The only way to improve living standards was to lower population levels by reducing fertility or increasing mortality. Average living standards meant living 'a pinched and straightened existence' (Clark, 2007, p. 38), working every hour God sent you, with a poor diet so low in calories as to produce short people, often unable to work, with poor clothing, and living in crowded insanitary housing. That was the world before 1800, throughout secular and Christian history. That was what was changed by the Industrial Revolution breaking the Malthusian Trap, changing 'forever the possibilities for material consumption' with all that brings for wellbeing (Clark, 2007, p. 2). So income per person began its inexorable rise, delivering billions out of poverty.

Importantly, this growth in income was not an isolated achievement in wellbeing. It related to Deaton's other two features of wellbeing, health and subjective wellbeing, in that, generally speaking, higher incomes were associated with better health and subjective wellbeing. So better incomes and health over generations are reflected in increasing population heights. Before 1800, people were smaller, indicating calorific nutritional deficiencies, especially in childhood. The European male's average height in the mid-nineteenth century was 166.7cm; by 1980, it was 178.6cm (Deaton, 2013, pp. 158, 160). For Fogel, in eighteenth-century Britain, low calorific intakes meant meagre energy for work, low stature and high mortality rates. The Industrial Revolution brought higher incomes, and so higher calorific food intakes, greater wellbeing and stronger economic growth – what is referred to as the thermodynamic factor, constituting 30% of British economic growth since 1790 (Fogel, 2004, p. 33). It is these links between income, food, health and economic growth that illustrate the interaction between these central features of progressive human wellbeing.

Because of this centrality of material wellbeing to wellbeing in general, it is worth exploring debates in economics questioning this significance of increasing income for increasing wellbeing. These arguments are particularly relevant to conversations between Christianity and economics, with the former's long history of critical suspicion of material wellbeing, money and consumption. Whatever wellbeing is about, it's not about that at all for much of Christianity! There are two arguments over these matters in contemporary economics, relating to post-materialism and whether greater incomes make us happier.

First, arguments by economists over the emerging significance of a post-materialist age began in the mid-nineteenth century with J. S. Mill, founder of mainstream classical economics, and were repeated by reformer of the following neoclassical economics, J. M. Keynes, looking forward, in 1931, to the day when the 'economic problem will take the back seat where it belongs' (Keynes, 1932, p. vi). Fogel argued more recently that 'The touchstone of wellbeing ... will be measured ... in terms of the quality of health and the opportunity for self-realisation', what he terms 'spiritual rather than material resources' (Fogel, 1997, p. 1905). But it was American political scientist Inglehart who argued that empirical evidence demonstrated the emergence of increasingly post-materialist societies in the USA and Europe. For him, post-materialist values have 'tended to neutralise the emphasis on economic accumulation' (Inglehart, 1988, p. 1203). This is obviously an appealing argument to the religious, being pro-spiritual and anti-economics/materialist. Yet on examining surveys from 1975–94 Easterlin found quite different trends reflecting the significance of the materialist in relation to social concerns: 'the percentage of people naming the materialist response as part of the good life exceeded that of people giving the non-materialist response' (the difference rose from 7 to 21% – suggesting clear shifts towards materialist values, not away from them) (Easterlin, 2004, p. 51). Deaton and Easterlin conclude, therefore, that the material remains of decisive importance for human wellbeing, as it always has been. Christianity needs to come to terms with that, but is not very good at it.

Second, economists like Easterlin and Layard have argued that subjective wellbeing as happiness does not increase with higher incomes, using surveys of nations with higher economic growth and income per capita. Again, this reinforces Christian opinion that happiness is not about higher incomes primarily. Yet research now points the other way in this highly contested relationship between income and subjective wellbeing. Within nations, richer people experience greater subjective wellbeing than poorer people. This is particularly the case with life satisfaction, indicating the relationship between higher incomes and life satisfaction as 'remarkably similar', 'both at higher levels of incomes as at lower levels' (Sacks, Stevenson and Wolfers, 2012, p. 67). This overturns the orthodoxy of Layard that increasing happiness only benefits *lower* incomes, say about $10,000, so above that increasing incomes does not produce increasing happiness (Easterlin, 2004, pp. 23–31; Layard, 2005, p. 33). This new evidence also contradicts mainstream economic assumptions that the marginal wellbeing impact of 'a dollar of income diminishes as income increases' (Sacks, Stevenson and Wolfers, 2012, p. 61).

Similarly, emotional wellbeing measures of happiness also indicate rises with nations' average incomes, but the relationship is much weaker and less uniform than with life satisfaction. So Pakistanis and Kenyans experience greater such happiness than Danes and Italians. This limited relationship between income and experienced happiness also holds within rich economies like the USA. So beyond an income of $70,000 per annum, 'additional money does nothing to improve happiness', even though those with more money report they have better lives (life evaluation) (Deaton,

2013, pp. 52–3). So money matters only up to a point for improving such happiness, leading Graham to talk of the 'paradox of happy peasants and miserable millionaires' (Graham, 2009). Higher incomes improve evaluations of life but not emotional wellbeing.

Given this new evidence that higher incomes are very significant for wellbeing, it is worth finally summarizing the nature and role of incomes in material wellbeing both in contemporary and historical contexts.

Material wellbeing is 'typically measured by income, the amount of money people have to spend or save' (Deaton, 2013, p. 16). What Americans spend their money on can be divided between goods and services, income spent on goods constituting a third of the total in 2012, divided between durable goods, a third, say on cars, furniture, clothes, and non-durable goods, say on food (7.5% rising to 13% when you include food consumed away from home). In terms of services, the two largest items were housing and utilities, representing 18% of consumer expenditure, and healthcare at 16%. These income-resourced expenditures represent 'the stuff of material wellbeing' (Deaton, 2013, pp. 171–2). Yet many often criticize such bedrocks of life. 'Spending more, we are often told, does not bring us better lives, and religious authorities regularly warn against materialism' (Deaton, 2013, p. 172). Yet such opinions neglect the enormous benefit for human wellbeing of the escape from the Malthusian Trap which dominated and scarred most lives for most of human history.

The French historian Braudel's three-volumed *Civilization and Capitalism, 15th–18th Century*, traces the evolution of such material wellbeing up to the Industrial Revolution. The first volume engages *The Structures of Everyday Life*, classically centred on the historically continuing bases of material wellbeing, food, clothing and housing, from the fifteenth to the eighteenth century (and for most of history) (Braudel, 1981, 1982, 1984). It was these material essentials for wellbeing that were transformed by the Industrial Revolution, even though they still form the basis of current income expenditure. It is this story of dramatic contemporary change in material wellbeing, say from 1870 to the present, that has been charted in US history by Robert Gordon's *The Rise and Fall of American Growth: The US Standard of Living Since the Civil War*. Life in 1870 was closer to the Malthusian Trap. What happened after turned the whole world of material wellbeing upside down profoundly for the better. In 1870, Boston had 250,000 citizens sharing the streets with 50,000 horses (Gordon, 2016, p. 48)! Women carried water and fuel into the house and took sewage and ashes out. The labour extended to cooking on fires, hand washing clothes, making clothes, and was immense. Then came two revolutions in 1879, Edison's electric light and Benz's internal combustion engine, transforming life for ever, along with the production of nutritious safe food and drink and good cheap clothing (the rise of mail catalogues and department stores) and the connectivity of housing in terms of piped clean water, sanitation systems, electricity and electrical appliances, central heating and then air conditioning, and telephones representing continuing advances in communications. And from the house, the car and then the aeroplane opened the world to all with incomes. It is an astonishing story of the development of material wellbeing.

Material wellbeing is intimately linked to incomes or money. It is the former that dominates economic understandings, but the undue focus on the latter has led Christians, especially theologians and church leaders, to at best profound misunderstandings of material wellbeing and income. Money, as Braudel so carefully traces its history, needs to be located in a schema of three levels, first the local, where most life has been and is lived. This constitutes the ordinary world of daily life, or material wellbeing and income. Second, impinging on, yet transcending, the local, trade developed through the spread of local and regional markets in the Middle Ages. Third, the development of trade evolved, increasingly internationally, generating financial systems based on the deployment of money and its substitutes in and through increasingly complex financial systems and banking (Braudel, 1982, pp. 21–3). The necessary growing sophistication of such systems involves a history of both the essential constructive undergirding of material wellbeing and income, and yet also inevitable volatilities, the latest dramatic upheaval occurring in 2007–08. The latter relates particularly to the emerging trend in this dimension, of developing a life of its own. It is this dimension that church leaders and theologians have often concentrated on in terms of their Pauline-type denunciations of money. These are again regularly mistaken in their understandings of such systems, but even more so in their diversion from focusing on the centrality of Braudel's first and second levels for the ordinary basics of material wellbeing (though supported by the third level), of food, clothing, housing, energy and communications. This typology therefore allows us to begin to engage the second part of this research more adequately, namely the development of a Christianity fit for the purpose of accurately engaging such material wellbeing.

Rebuilding Christianity to engage the economics of material wellbeing and income

A Christianity formed before 1800 is inevitably going to struggle to make sense of radical changes in material wellbeing and income inaugurated by the Industrial and Mortality Revolutions. It is not the world of the Bible or the development of Christian doctrines and beliefs. Beginning from the account of the economics of material wellbeing and income in the first section of this chapter, of what the world of daily life is actually like, it should be possible to begin a reconstruction of Christianity fit for the purpose of engaging in constructive conversations with the economics of material wellbeing. This will involve testing the model of Christianity, its transmission processes and measurement systems, as developed for engaging the economics of subjective wellbeing and health, but now with reference to Deaton's material wellbeing and income.

It is important to begin by recognizing, demonstrated in the first section of this chapter, the positive connections between income, health and subjective wellbeing. Generally speaking, higher incomes delivered by economic growth have profoundly positive effects on health and subjective wellbeing. My initial research enquiry focused on the latter, subjective wellbeing, because of the availability of relevant sources in economics, psychology and sociology. This enabled the remodelling of Christianity to participate in multidisciplinary engagements to promote greater human wellbeing. Importantly, this *also* provides significant economic tools for developing the economics of material wellbeing and of Christianity's involvement with it.

The economics of subjective wellbeing is recognition that it's not just whether experts say we are happier, empirically, but it's also about what people say about their wellbeing, knowledge acquired through surveys based on self-reporting techniques. As Easterlin observes, although the social sciences have a 'long and respected history' of deploying such surveys on subjective testimonies, the knowledge built up was 'unfortunately excluded from economic analysis' (Easterlin, 2014, p. 21). For Carol Graham, economics therefore relies on studying *'revealed preferences'* as the chosen measure of economic welfare, and not on the *'expressed preferences'* delivered by studying surveys of self-reported responses (Graham, 2011, pp. 7–8; my emphasis). But, as Deaton summarizes, both are needed to engage more comprehensively material wellbeing, the revealed preferences measuring income and the expressed preferences measuring subjective wellbeing, even though it is the former that is rightly given *priority*.

It is precisely that reordering that now informs the development of my model, 'Mapping Christianity's practices, ethics and beliefs from secular and religious sources of wellbeing as income in the twenty-first century' (see Table 1 below). For Christianity has traditionally focused on the rightness of theology, on doctrines and beliefs, as orthodoxy. In the later twentieth century, that ordering has begun to change. Within religious studies, practice-orientated traditions have emerged, including liberation theology's prioritizing of orthopraxis over orthodoxy, and the development of practical theology, pastoral theology, public theology,

Christian social ethics and sociological theology. That is to re-establish the religious ordering developed by the earliest humans. In Bellah's *Religion in Human Evolution* (2011, pp. 18–20), the practices and rituals of religion in early human evolution clearly emerge and dominate before the much later cognitive. The reordering of the main features of Christianity, so that practice displaces beliefs or doctrines, is therefore of the greatest importance in the formation of Christian engagements with the economics of material wellbeing. And it is also reflected in early Christian tradition in the priorities of Christ and his injunction for Christian living, namely, 'By their fruits ye shall know them' (Matthew 7.16, 20, KJV) (or by their revealed preferences as against their expressed preferences). Of course, this reprioritizing does not remove the essential contributions of ethics and beliefs to wellbeing. For example, ethics have always been associated with religious life. They have also reappeared in modern economics through the work of Nobel economics laureates Sen and Stiglitz.

Continuing the theme from theological realism, I will utilize other classic secular tools of economists as entry points into reshaping Christianity for effective engagement with economics. For example, economists develop three tools in their engagement with economic life: modelling to illuminate the world of daily life by 'stripped-down representations of the phenomena out there'; locating economics in contexts particularly informed by economic history and its increasing use of economic tools; and finally measuring such realities using 'a statistical approach' (Dasgupta, 2007, pp. 9–12). These tools are useful in terms of transferability into the redevelopment of Christianity fit for the purpose of engaging the economic life of material wellbeing.

Mapping and modelling Christianity's contribution to material wellbeing

This model was developed in relation to the economics of subjective wellbeing, drawing from secular and Christian sources (noting the correlative and causal relationships between Christianity and greater subjective wellbeing). That positive relationship is reinforced by the references to transmission processes of how Christianity influences material wellbeing for the better. Although the main features are drawn principally from subjective wellbeing literatures, they are very likely to also apply to material wellbeing, not least because of the proven empirical and positive links between income and subjective wellbeing. The assumption is made, too, that Christianity's contribution to subjective wellbeing initially continues to apply also to health, and then finally to income, because of their integral connections identified in the first section of this chapter.

The emerging model (Table 1), 'Mapping and modelling Christianity's contribution to wellbeing as income', is adapted from the original one for subjective wellbeing. It therefore notes secular arguments for the significance of Christianity's contribution to subjective wellbeing, initially, drawing from important sources and research methods in economics, psychology and sociology. These were elaborated from Christian sources, allowing the detection of clear resonances between the first two parts of the Table. Out of these interactions the model's seven constituent features emerged (see Table 1), sourced from across the three columns.

The first column identifies the shared seven features initially from supportive secular sources. These seven are regarded as particularly conducive to Christianity's effective contributions to greater wellbeing. The secular sources include Layard (economics), Diener and Seligman (psychology), Putnam (sociology) and Myers (surveys research sources on Christianity and greater wellbeing). The seven features include:

1 Comforting beliefs generating positive emotions, particularly appropriate to economic life. These include justice, faith leading to trust, hope for a better future, the ability of transformation, the acquisition of knowledge, and so on.
2 Connecting to reality greater than self – Layard's 'people who believe in God are happier' in terms of wellbeing (Layard, 2005, p. 72).
3 Experience of rituals as worship, including meditation and other spiritual (including secular) exercises.
4 Regulating lifestyle and behaviour (including as ethical). This includes restricting alcohol and drug intake; acquiring life skills, including participation in society (Methodist chapels in nineteenth-century Britain as schools of democracy for future trade union officials – Wearmouth, 1937, p. 103); contributing to society through volunteering and charitable giving (costed for the north west of England – NWRDA, 2005); coping skills for illness/mishaps in life, and so promoting better health (and economic activity) as wholeness.
5 Churchgoing as social support and networking.
6 Nurturing young people as growing up religiously and as educationally proficient (vital for human capital – for example, initially through Bible reading). This can be illustrated by the life of Humphrey Chetham (1580–1653), an important Manchester merchant also operating in London and the Low Countries, based on the cloth trade, forerunner of the later cotton industry, the basis of the Industrial Revolution. Importantly, Chetham was a Puritan/Calvinist in the first half of the seventeenth century, the early modern period, and an example of Weber's Protestant Ethic thesis. He was also an educationalist, leaving provision for chained libraries around Manchester, and for

Table 1: Mapping and modelling Christianity's contribution to wellbeing as income

Supportive secular sources of religion	Christian tradition (Sweden)	National accounts of wellbeing
1. Comforting beliefs (D) – embodied in values generating *positive emotions* (M) including forgiveness, hope, transformation (M), afterlife, compassion, humility, altruism (M, S, P), justice (P).	Hope in context of eternal life; forgiveness through Christ; awareness of sin, humility and responsibility; trust as faith in Christ; love for self, others and God as giving and receiving; justice and peace, especially for the marginalized.	Emotional wellbeing – as *positive feelings*. Satisfying life (*positive* evaluation of life). Feeling optimistic about your *future* (resilience and self-esteem).
2. Connecting to reality greater than self (D) (M): 'people who believe in God are happier' (L, M, S, P).	Engagement with God and the Other.	Meaning.
3. Experiences of ritual as worship (D), including meditation (L, P).	Eucharist, communion, hymns, liturgy.	
4. Regulation of lifestyle and behaviour: as restricting alcohol and drug intake (M); as acquisition of life skills (M), including participation in civic society (L, P); and contributing to society through volunteering and charitable giving (P); coping skills for illness, stress, loss (M) and for better health, especially mental health (S, P).	Lifestyle choice, courage to be vulnerable, vulnerability-trust, value of love for others.	Resilience and self-esteem (being able to deal with life's difficulties). Competence (feeling accomplishment from what you do, and being able to use your abilities) (as positive functioning).
5. Churchgoing as social support and networking (D, M, S, P).	Church as organization and fellowship; with family relationships, solidary with vulnerable, trust, love – giver and receiver.	Social wellbeing (supportive relationships – families, friends), trust and belonging.
6. Growing up religiously (D, S, P).	The nurturing of children, students, and the study and teaching of ethics.	Seligman addresses this in relation to schools and wellbeing.
7. All sustained by, and in turn generating a philosophy of life, including a common good (L, M, S, P).	Continuities and meaning, including through Christian tradition, linking involvement with contexts.	Positive functioning – as meaning and purpose – feeling that your own life is valuable, worthwhile and valued by others.
D – Diener and Biswas-Diener, 2008; L – Layard, 2005; M – Myers, 2008; S – Seligman, 2002; P – Putnam, 2010.	'The Gospel of Today', Strängnäs Diocese, Sweden (2009), with sections on Gospel, Kingdom of God, Conversion, Peace, Freedom, Forgiveness, Atonement, Love, Life, Grace and Mercy, Justification, and Truth.	New Economics Foundation (2009): *Personal Wellbeing*: Emotional wellbeing (positive feelings, absence of negative feelings), Satisfying life, Vitality, Resilience and self-esteem (self-esteem, optimism, resilience), Positive functioning (autonomy, competence, engagement, meaning and purpose). *Social Wellbeing*: supportive relationships, trust and belonging

the famous Chetham's Library, the first public library in England (the trustees avoided monochrome collections of Puritan-only books, but sought the best quality books in Europe). Economic historians like Ferguson (2011) saw this Puritan contribution to education as of high importance for the Industrial Revolution in terms of the development of human capital; and in its contribution to innovation and technologies, Deaton, Mokyr and Easterlin all regard such capital as more important for the great improvement in material wellbeing and health than economic growth.

7 All sustained by, and in turn generating, a philosophy of life, including a common good.

Note that it is the cumulative contribution of these seven that forms Christian tradition as an instrument for resourcing personal and communal wellbeing in the past, present and future.

The middle column is drawn from a contemporary Christian source, the Swedish Diocese of Strängnäs' conference in 2009. It illustrates intra-faith collaboration, namely the Porvöo Agreement. This amplifies the first column's seven features from specific sources in Christian traditions (from within traditions as illustrating correspondence between secular and Christian sources).

The third column confirms and extends secular material in the first column by drawing from the model used by Britain's New Economics Foundation's *National Accounts of Well-being* (2009). This combines sources from positive psychologists and economists as bases of measurement systems of national wellbeing covering 23 European nations and surveying 43,000 people. As an independent secular source, it covers five of the seven features in the other two columns, omitting Christian sources of worship and growing up religiously. This column has the additional benefit of providing research-based measurement systems for national wellbeing supportive of five of the seven features of Christianity's wellbeing contribution.

Two matters arise from this model: first, prioritizing the seven features into the most effective in promoting greater wellbeing. Some focus on beliefs like hope (Seligman, 2002, pp. 59–60), others emphasize belonging to Christian communities, especially their networking (Putnam and Campbell, 2010, pp. 491–2). Second, the nature of the relationship between the three columns, between Christian and secular contributions to greater wellbeing, is important. That relationship is certainly correlative, in terms of 'a relationship of meaning' rather than one implying cause and effect (Astley and Francis, 2013, p. 45). So the correlative does not prove the truth of Christian understandings, but it does indicate their relevance to greater wellbeing. For Seligman, and Putnam, a further significant step is taken because their research indicates features explaining why Christianity is so effective in promoting greater wellbeing. Again, this does not demonstrate the truth of Christianity. These distinctions are important in exploring the nature of the Christian model's effectiveness in promoting greater material wellbeing. Practices, ethics and beliefs account for greater wellbeing, certainly at least in giving critical enriching depth to corresponding secular human understandings. This coincides with Grenholm's partially based revelation ethics, which 'clarifies and lends depth to the moral insights that are based upon common human experiences' (Grenholm, 1993, p. 313). The result clearly suggests the importance for Christianity of that additional added value of providing an empirically researched means of religion generating an answer to what Jürgen Habermas identifies as 'an awareness of what is missing' in secular communicative reason (Graham 2013, p. 46; Habermas, 2010, pp. 15–23).

Developing the model through its transmission processes: how Christianity influences wellbeing

This is an integral part of my model. The identified transmission processes confirm the important relevance of the features for generating material wellbeing, which in turn thereby facilitates their effectiveness. Two processes have been selected from appropriate research literatures.

First, Gill's process of transposing beliefs and values into secular life, or socially constructed theological ideas, once generated, may have influence on society at large (Gill 2013, p. 9). As Max Weber noted, transposed Christian virtues may persist in society long after their initial institutional basis has been forgotten. Gill illustrates this process from the Nuffield Council of Bio-ethics (Gill, 2013, pp. 201–6).

The second transmission process is based on Putnam's 'moral freighting' through religiously based ties (Christians are evidenced as inhabiting 'a density of religious social networks' as church friends, and talking about religion with family and friends) (Putnam and Campbell, 2010, pp. 477, 470). This can be illustrated through studies of strong Quaker networks in the early modern period in business, manufacturing and banking, which were of critical significance for building trust and maintaining commercial confidence (Prior and Kirby, 1993).

This research therefore establishes a correlative and causal relationship between such religious networks and the religious being better citizens and neighbours and promoting material wellbeing. So British government minister Denham recognized in public life that 'Faith is a strong and powerful source of honesty, solidarity, generosity, the very key values which are essential to politics, to our economy and our society' (Baker, 2013, p. 343). Baker has developed further this transmission process as belonging, becoming and so participating, through research into British faith groups (Baker, 2013, p. 355).

In relation actually to measuring Christianity's contributions to wellbeing, however, Gill recognizes deep unease in theological circles over attempts to *quantify* religious experiences (Gill, 2012, p. 30). Many regard faith matters as unquantifiable. As we have seen with regard to measuring subjective wellbeing, this varies from surveying revealed preferences to surveying the self-reporting of expressed preferences. Both relate to quantitative surveys, but alongside this essential tool for engaging large complex modern societies should also be noted the value of qualitative surveys. Both are essential for developing the Christian model.

To do this, I have used complementary secular and religious tools to measure religious contributions to wellbeing in general and material wellbeing in particular. The three secular measurement systems relate to progressive change using Dasgupta's deployment of the political scientist Villacourt's definition in terms of the contributions of institutions, policies and civic agencies and attitudes to enable people to improve their wellbeing (Dasgupta, 2007, p. 159). My account of material wellbeing has clear correspondences with this definition.

These three more secular measurement tools move from pre-ethical (number 1) to the more ethical remainder.

1 Morris's *Social Development Index* is based on statistical and historical research using four traits: energy capture, urban organization, communications, and military capacities (Morris, 2011, p. 643). These reflect society's abilities to get things done. He measures social, and explicitly not moral, goods, from 14,000 BC to the present. Yet the theologian Browning usefully describes such traits as 'pre-moral goods' in terms of their strategic contribution to progressive change (Browning, 2006, p. 300).
2 *The Human Development Index* (HDI) tests the extent nations have achieved decent standards of living through measuring national GDP per capita, life expectancy at birth, and literacy (Atherton, 2003, pp. 162–5). The theologian Hicks has refined and developed this metric as an Inequality Adjusted Human Development Index to take account of income inequalities within nations (Hicks, 2000). This tool therefore engages the inequality paradox of development.
3 The *Index of Sustainable Economic Welfare* has been developed by the economist Daly and the theologian Cobb, and runs environmental alongside social and economic indicators (Daly and Cobb, 1990).

These three secular tools are complemented by three metrics for measuring religious contributions to greater wellbeing:

4 A *Religion and Happiness Index*, developed by Leslie Francis, deploying the secular Oxford Happiness Inventory of positive psychology alongside his scale of attitudes to religion (Francis, 2010). It indicates positive associations between attitudes to religion and happiness, linked particularly to subjective wellbeing. It therefore has potential for extension to health and then income.
5 *Putnam's Religiosity Index* measures American religiosity. This overlaps with my model's seven features, and constitutes a major source for measuring volunteering, trust (key economic virtue) and civic participation. It also measures religious commitments to religious programmes engaging income inequality and government roles in poverty alleviation (Putnam and Campbell, 2010, pp. 18–23, Appendix 1).
6 Baker's *Belonging, Becoming and Participation Index* gives depth to Putnam's moral freighting transmission process (Baker, 2013). So it measures religion's religious capital (practical outputs, so easy to link to material wellbeing) and spiritual capital (measuring motivating and energizing forces, so links to my beliefs, God, worship and ritual, regulating lifestyles, behaviour and values in my seven model's features).

These six measurement systems illustrate the possibility and the feasibility of developing measurement systems in relation to religion's contribution to improving material wellbeing. This would have the necessary added value, in terms of 'by their fruits ye shall know them', of refocusing on actual revealed practices of Christianity in relation to greater material wellbeing and away from the dominance of its expressed preferences in terms of the work of theologians and church leaders in Christian history. 'In an increasingly performance-orientated society, metrics matter. What we measure affects what we do. If we have the wrong metrics we will strive for the wrong things' (Stiglitz, Sen and Fitoussi, 2010, p. xvii). Measuring the fruits begins to allow the radical correction of the perceptions of Christian history.

Note

1 This chapter has been revised for inclusion in this volume. An earlier version was published as J. R. Atherton, 'Det materiella välståndets ekonomi och en effektiv krisendum', in Normunds Kamergrauzis (ed.), *En gråtande gud och den förvirrade människan*, Stockholm: Verbum, 2017, pp. 189–216.

References

Astley, J. and Francis, L., 2013, *Exploring Ordinary Theology: Everyday Christian Believing and the Church*, Farnham: Ashgate.
Atherton, J. R., 2003, *Marginalization*, London: SCM Press.
Atherton, J. R., 2014, *Challenging Religious Studies: The Wealth, Wellbeing and Inequalities of Nations*, London: SCM Press.
Atherton, J. R., Graham, E. and Steedman, I. (eds), 2010, *The Practices of Happiness: Political Economy, Religion and Wellbeing*, Abingdon: Routledge.
Baker, C., 2013, 'Moral Freighting and Civic Engagement: A UK Perspective on Putnam and Campbell's Theory of Religious-Based Social Action', *Sociology of Religion: A Quarterly Review* 74:3, pp. 343–69.
Beales, C., 2014, *Humanising Work: Co-operatives, Credit Unions and the Challenge of Mass Unemployment*, Milton Keynes: Rainmaker Books.
Bellah, R., 2011, *Religion in Human Evolution from the Paleolithic to the Axial Age*, Cambridge, MA: Harvard University Press.
Braudel, F., 1981, *Civilization and Capitalism, 15th–18th Century, Vol. 1, The Structures of Everyday Life: The Limits of the Possible*, London: William Collins.
Braudel, F., 1982, *Vol. 2, The Wheels of Commerce*, London: William Collins.
Braudel, F., 1984, *Vol. 3, The Perspective of the World*, London: William Collins.
Browning, D., 'Human Dignity, Human Complexity, and Human Good', in Soulen, R. and Woodhead, L. (eds), 2006, *God and Human Dignity*, Grand Rapids, MI: Eerdmans.
Clark, G., 2007, *A Farewell to Alms: A Brief Economic History of the World*, Princeton, NJ: Princeton University Press.
Clements, K., 2013, *Ecumenical Dynamics: Living in More than One Place at Once*, Geneva, World Council of Churches.
Daly, H. and Cobb, J., 1990, *For the Common Good: Redirecting the Economy Towards Community, the Environment and a Sustainable Future*, London: Merlin Press.
Dasgupta, P., 2007, *Economics: A Very Short Introduction*, Oxford: Oxford University Press.
Deaton, A., 2013, *The Great Escape: Health, Wealth and the Origins of Inequality*, Princeton, NJ: Princeton University Press.
Diener, E. and Biswas-Diener, R., 2008, *Happiness: Unlocking the Mysteries of Psychological Wealth*, Oxford: Blackwell.
Easterlin, R., 1974, 'Does Economic Growth Improve the Human Lot?', in David, P. and Reder, M. (eds), *Nations and Households in Economic Growth: Essays in Honor of Moses Abramovitz*, New York: Academic Press Inc.
Easterlin, R., 2004, *The Reluctant Economist: Perspectives on Economics, Economic History and Demography*, Cambridge: Cambridge University Press.
Ferguson, N., 2011, *Civilization: The West and the Rest*, London: Allen Lane.
Fogel, R., 1997, 'Economic and Social Structure for an Aging Population', *Philosophical Transactions of the Royal Society of London* 352, pp. 1905–17.
Fogel, R., 2004, *The Escape from Hunger and Premature Death, 1700–2100: Europe, America, and the Third World*, Cambridge: Cambridge University Press.
Francis, L., 2010, 'Religion and Happiness: Perspectives from the Psychology of Religion, Positive Psychology and Empirical Theology', in Atherton, Graham, and Steedman, *The Practices of Happiness*.
Gill, R., 2012, *Theology in a Social Context: Sociological Theology Volume 1*, Farnham: Ashgate.

Gill, R., 2013, *Society Shaped by Theology: Sociological Theology Volume 3*, Farnham: Ashgate.
Gordon, R., 2016, *The Rise and Fall of American Growth: The U.S. Standard of Living Since the Civil War*, Princeton, NJ: Princeton University Press.
Graham, C., 2009, *Happiness around the World: The Paradox of Happy Peasants and Miserable Millionaires*, Oxford: Oxford University Press.
Graham, C., 2011, *The Pursuit of Happiness: An Economy of Wellbeing*, Washington, DC: Brookings Institution.
Graham, E., 2013, *Between a Rock and a Hard Place: Public Theology in a Post-Secular Age*, London: SCM Press.
Grenholm, Carl-Henric, 1993, *Protestant Work Ethics: A Study of Work Ethical Theories in Contemporary Protestant Theology*, Uppsala: Uppsala University Press.
Habermas, J., 2010, 'An Awareness of What is Missing', in Habermas, J. et al., *An Awareness of What is Missing: Faith and Reason in a Post-Secular Age*, Cambridge: Polity Press.
Hicks, D., 2000, *Inequality and Christian Ethics*, Cambridge: Cambridge University Press.
Inglehart, R., 1988, 'The Renaissance of Political Culture', *American Political Science Review* 82:4 (December), pp. 1203–30.
Kamergrauzis, N., 2001, *The Persistence of Christian Realism: A Study of the Social Ethics of Ronald H. Preston*, Uppsala: Uppsala University Press.
Keynes, J., 1932, *Essays in Persuasion*, New York: Harcourt-Brace.
Layard, R., 2005, *Happiness: Lessons from a New Science*, London: Allen Lane.
Malthus, T., 1798, *An Essay on the Principle of Population*, ed. A. Flew, Harmondsworth: Penguin Books.
Morris, I., 2011, *Why the West Rules – For Now: The Patterns of History, and What They Reveal about the Future*, London: Profile Books.
Myers, D., 2008, 'Religion and Human Flourishing', in Eid, M. and Larsen, R. (eds), *The Science of Subjective Wellbeing*, New York: The Guildford Press.
New Economics Foundation, 2009, *National Accounts of Well-being: Bringing Real Wealth onto the Balance Sheet*, London: New Economics Foundation.
NWRDA, 2005, *Faith in England's Northwest: Economic Impact Assessment*, Warrington: Northwest Regional Development Agency.
Prior, A. and Kirby, M., 1993, 'The Society of Friends and the Family Firm, 1700–1830', *Business History* 35:4, pp. 66–85.
Putnam, R. and Campbell, D., 2010, *American Grace: How Religion Divides and Unites Us*, New York: Simon & Schuster.
Sacks, D., Stevenson, B. and Wolfers, J., 2012, 'Subjective Wellbeing, Income, Economic Development and Growth', in Booth, P. (ed.), *... and the Pursuit of Happiness: Wellbeing and the Role of Government*, London: The Institute of Economic Affairs.
Seligman, M., 2002, *Authentic Happiness: Using the New Positive Psychology to Realize Your Potential for Deep Fulfilment*, London: Nicholas Brealey Publishing.
Seligman, M., 2011, *Flourish: A New Understanding of Happiness and Wellbeing and How to Achieve Them*, London: Nicholas Brealey Publishing.
Stiglitz, J., Sen, A., Fitoussi, J.-P. (eds), 2010, *Mis-Measuring Our Lives: Why GDP Doesn't Add Up*, London: New Press.
Stiglitz, J., 2012, *The Price of Inequality*, London: Penguin Books.
Wearmouth, R., 1937, *Methodism and the Working-Class Movements of England 1800–1950*, London: Epworth Press.

3

Grounded and Inclusive: Public Theology from the Grass Roots

HILARY RUSSELL

if our words are to speak with authenticity (and authority) they must be rooted, incarnated in our familiar world ... (Mayne, 2006, loc. 3126)

For my pond is the centre of Manchester, its past, present and future, a story which is now the world's. My vocation is to show how natural it is for an understanding of God and his purposes for the world to be fully part of that context. (Atherton, 2000, p. 1)

John Atherton's theological method can be seen as a journey, always grounded but perhaps becoming ever more rooted in a variety of ways that, by Michael Mayne's criterion, give it both authenticity and authority. It is a journey I witnessed, at least from the mid-1980s onwards, when I knew him first as my tutor on the William Temple Foundation Certificate in Religious Studies course, then as a fellow trustee of both Church Action on Poverty and the William Temple Foundation. This chapter tries to trace some aspects of this journey, illustrate the dimensions that make it 'public theology from the grass roots' and indicate some of the emerging messages.

In my bones

John took a huge pride in Manchester. He saw it as the locus of modernization processes that shaped the world. (He used to conduct tours of Manchester and surrounding areas, tracing industrial and economic growth and change since the Industrial Revolution.) Manchester was not just his academic base or a source of subject matter. He described it as being 'in my bones' (2003, p. xiii). Three institutions in the city were indispensable to his immersion in urban realities: the William Temple Foundation, the diocese and the cathedral. The Foundation had been founded to build on Archbishop Temple's deep interest in poverty, which was intensified and informed by his long-standing friendship with Richard Tawney and William Beveridge, two architects of the welfare state. John's PhD thesis was on R. H. Tawney as a Christian social moralist. His supervisor and colleague in Manchester University was Ronald Preston, who had been influenced by Tawney while a student at the LSE.

John was indebted to Preston not just for his friendship and support but also for giving him an 'awareness of standing in a great tradition of Christian social thought and practice' (Atherton, 2003, p. xii). His involvement in the Diocesan Board for Social Responsibility gave him access to statistical data about the diocese and insights into the role and capacity of churches in deprived areas. In the late 1990s/early 2000s, the diocese worked on its strategic involvement in urban churches. As well as having a Partnership Officer to promote church involvement in regeneration initiatives, there were two influential reports. The first, *Changing Church and Society: Developing a Strategy for Mission in the Urban Priority Areas of the Diocese of Manchester* (1998), led to further activity based on a second report, *Becoming One Body: Beyond Changing Church and Society* (2001). Research for these fed into a case study in John's book on *Marginalization* (2003). Manchester Cathedral gave John a spiritual and practical home from 1984 to 2004. 'It roots me in the daily worship and service of a community at the heart of Manchester' (2003, p. xiii). He was grateful to his chapter colleagues for their support in his theological tasks and, as Canon Theologian, he stimulated a wider network of theological reflection which in turn fed into and kindled his own research.

As well as being acutely aware of his immediate context, John deployed stories from his own family history as a way of exemplifying wider and longer-term changes (2014, p. 23). For instance, he compared his own life and opportunities with those of his forebears. His working-class parents could hope for their son to escape their relative poverty and enjoy higher education, better health and greater financial security, a trend he was much less confident would continue for his own children and grandchildren (2014, p. 2).

A dark shadow over British society

Concern about poverty and how to address it in theory and in practice was a theme running throughout his life and ministry. It was shaped first when he served in inner-city parishes in Aberdeen, Glasgow and Manchester, and developed further when he moved in 1974 to work for the William Temple Foundation. The paradox of poverty and its co-existence with wealth in an affluent society was the 'problematic', an entry point that always characterized John's theological method. It was not merely a theoretical concern, but arose because of what he had seen for himself. Intertwining personal experience and intellectual grappling was an abiding feature of his work. In the early 1980s, when he wrote *The Scandal of Poverty*, he was Joint Director of the William Temple Foundation, an honorary lecturer in the University of Manchester Department of Social and Pastoral Theology and chair of the Diocese of Manchester Board for Social Responsibility. He found rich meaning in his research in Salford in the 1970s working with unemployed young people, 'for we uncovered the statistical reality of that unemployment and always saw these facts on the face of the young unemployed' (2014, p. 19). He was also one of the founders of the newly formed Church Action on Poverty. He was, therefore, well positioned to address the topic backed by the Foundation's research, the stories emerging from parishes and the direct witness of people experiencing poverty. His aim was to examine 'what poverty really is and what it drives us to do, in the firm belief that this is a way in which God is to be found, worshipped and served' (Atherton, 1983, p. 124).

The book revolves around two main questions: what it means to be poor and why the churches must be involved in the question of poverty. He saw poverty as one of the signs of the times, communicating a reality that it was imperative to take seriously. It was 'precisely through this reality that the truths of the Christian understanding of the human have to be proclaimed'. In other words, what was happening to the poor was a sign offered to the Church. This focus continued to be the axis around which his work revolved. As a perspective that informed all his thinking, it is a lens through which both to review his subsequent writings and to recognize their potential to inform grass-roots action to address poverty and inequality. He brought together material from a range of secular as well as religious sources, but always emphasized the significance of 'ordinary theology' (Astley and Francis, 2013); that is, what most church members believe and do rather than what church leaders tell them to believe and do.

Seminal and significant but ...

In the early to mid-1980s, representing the Foundation, John acted as a consultant to the Archbishop's Commission on Urban Priority Areas and was involved in drafting its report, *Faith in the City* (1985). While acknowledging it as a seminal report and applauding its significance in maintaining the Church of England's faltering engagement with urban society (Atherton, 2003, p. 45), he was nevertheless critical. On the one hand, he felt it was insufficiently sharp in its analysis and prescriptions. It washed over some forms of capitalist injustice; a compromise that avoided the need for real change. The report mainly stayed in the 'soft centre of consensus politics, of Butskellism or neo-Keynesianism' (Atherton, 1988, p. 67). Other commentators at the time were similarly critical: 'There is an indictment of the effects of capitalism – or rather the "modern consumer society" – but the assumption is only that it needs to be given a kinder face, not that its very basis should be questioned' (Russell, 1987, p. 32). The Commission was overoptimistic about the nature of the political scene and those engaged in it, seeming to assume that people across the political spectrum still upheld the aim of a fair society, whereas it had been jettisoned by the New Right and was no longer a guiding principle for political policy (Raymond Plant, cited in Russell, 1995, p. 53).

On the other hand, John pointed out the report's theological weaknesses:

> *Faith in the City* stands as a monument to a series of legitimately concerned Christian reports on grave social problems which in the end founder on the rock of inadequate theological reflection ... In a society more complex and changing than ever before, the Church has to learn to think harder, and in more detail and more comprehensively than ever before. (1988, p. 143)

The nub of his criticism was the report's failure to distinguish middle-range moral imperatives from the policy options required to implement them. John argued that these policy options related to political programmes that ranged from democratic capitalist to democratic socialist ones, whereas *Faith in the City* conflated imperatives and options into detailed recommendations, giving 'the strong impression that they were therefore achievable only by [SDP/Liberal] Alliance or Labour Party means. It therefore disenfranchised Conservatives of the social market kind.' He regarded promoting overrestrictive political allegiances that would not achieve major change in an increasingly affluent democracy as defective theological method (1988, pp. 142–3). This kind of statement gave ammunition to those who suspected that he had moved from socialism to conservatism; a suspicion he acknowledged, but strongly refuted (1992, p. 284). As he said later, he was more concerned about commentary that was morally and empirically inadequate. 'Connecting poverty and economic systems invariably leads church leaders and theologians to condemn the latter on behalf of the former, and therefore to fail both' (2014, p. 9).

Getting a measure of change

John's critique of *Faith in the City* gives insights into the contrasting way that he worked. His involvement in the report increased his anxiety to explore the central economic nature of the problem of poverty. This stage of his journey was represented both in *Faith in the Nation* (1988) and *Christianity and the Market* (1992). As with all his books, the choice of topic went hand in hand with his perceptions of, and concern about, what was happening in wider society. At the same time as gratitude for the blessings of this life, 'unease always returns and in very direct ways as the reports of conflicts and divisions, unemployment and deprivation, and cuts in public services sooner or later break into our own private lives in however small a way', such as the effect of bus deregulation on his elderly mother's life (1988, p. 1). But John also perceived that these were only outward expressions of more deep-seated stresses and behind them was a society and economy in major transition. He was increasingly aware that traditional politics and economics seemed not to have a measure of these changes and, further, that the Church was part of this mismatch, rarely transcending well-worn analyses and tired solutions. Thus, *Faith in the Nation* was not just an attempt to analyse contemporary change and examine political and economic options. He set out to scrutinize existing political and economic categories in the light of Christian belief. He sketched out tentative outlines for a Christian vision for our society – a participating and reciprocal society. The book is about the vocation of Christians in political and economic affairs at all levels of society, which, John said, is why it necessarily had to include a chapter on spirituality and theological reflection. Again, he underlined his view that 'our understanding and use of theology limits the quality and consequently the impact' of our contributions on social affairs' (1988, p. 2).

Similarly, in *Christianity and the Market*, he quotes F. D. Maurice: 'No man I think will ever be of much use to his generation who does not apply himself mainly to the questions which are occupying those who belong to it.' It had become more and more evident to John that making sense of the world increasingly entailed understanding economics. The market economy, therefore, was an appropriate entry point for engaging with the contemporary context. Such a study has to reflect 'its interconnections and dynamism. It has to range across systems, nations, disciplines and histories' (1992, p. 2). His panorama was becoming wider and more ambitious, but it was still depicted with the same determination to make connections between Christian thought and practice and context. The market economy 'offers one of the greatest challenges to Christianity, just as Christianity in its turn challenges that context by its refusal to be fully integrated into it' (1992, p. 2).

My concern is more with his processes of thought so this is not the place to go into the content of John's discussion, but his argument here demonstrates his divergence from the approach he criticized in *Faith in the City*. His survey of three responses to the market economy – conservative, radical and liberal – convinced him that though each had strengths and weaknesses to contribute to Christian social thought, no single response stood out as an adequate principal vehicle for the job of reformulation. What is required is rather a position of detached concern, 'a listening to, while distancing from, all three responses'. Whereas theologians he admired, such as Ronald Preston and J. P. Wogaman, would have worked from the mainstream liberal tradition, John concluded that the end of the dominance of the mainstream liberal tradition forces

> us to engage in an open interaction between market and challenges, between economics and theology. It frees the liberal response to play a more constructive role in relationship to, and on a par with, the conservative and radical responses. For that is all it is and should be. (1992, pp. 200–1)

There is a way in which John was preoccupied with change. He recognized that we are living in a period of immense change: accelerating technological and scientific development, globalization and the accompanying multiplication of interconnections and interdependencies. He saw his life as increasingly a journey of openness to change. Responding to a changing context became a catalyst for personal change and development (Atherton, 1992, p. 284). It was also a challenge to locate Christian social thought and practice in this evolving context. In *Public Theology for Changing Times*, he explored aspects of globalization 'for and through an understanding of public theology, God, Christ and the Church'. In stating that there can be 'no retreat from the Christian task of developing public theologies of global proportions', he stressed that theology must be integral. It cannot just be an afterthought tacked on to secular commentaries (2000, p. viii).

One of John's frustrations, therefore, was that 'religions in general, and in my case, Christianity in particular, have at best persistently refused to take these matters and these changes seriously. They have rarely prioritized them, as the world of daily life does and has to.' It was ever thus. John quotes an MP talking about the Church and the coalfield community in the nineteenth and twentieth centuries: 'The working man is not interested in the Prayer Book, but in the rent book'. It was this gulf he sought to bridge in *Challenging Religious Studies: The Wealth, Wellbeing and Inequalities of Nations*: 'This book is about what matters most to most people most of the time, whether as individuals, families, communities or societies' (2014, p. 1). This was his most full-frontal challenge to the failure of the Church to engage the world of people's daily lives (2014, p. 4). The book represents a continuation in so far as its 'evolution began with the poverty imperative, at the heart of the Christian concern for the vulnerable and marginalized and of modern economics' (2014, p. 8). It again demonstrates and addresses the gulf between policy and lived experience. It is again concerned with making connections. But it is also a new stage in his journey as he spans a wider canvas, delves more deeply and even more determinedly works with a two-way process of interaction:

> the one challenging the other, for their mutual benefit, that is, the wealth, wellbeing and inequality of nations, the stuff of the world of daily life of peoples, communities and societies and its interactive overlapping with the world of religious life. (2014, p. 7)

Living in more than one place at once

What characterized his approach in this his last book? Much was prefigured in earlier ones, but it is articulated more clearly here, perhaps precisely because it is what he called 'an exploratory essay' (Atherton, 2014, p. 21). Seeing things from other perspectives was a vital part, hence 'living in more than one place at once' (Clements, 2013). First, he once again excavated behind the presenting problem. Just as earlier, he had pushed beyond poverty to marginalization, he now delved down to another stratum to questions of human flourishing. Contact and collaboration with international colleagues at Princeton and Uppsala spurred him to develop themes of income, health and subjective wellbeing. Second, always interdisciplinary, he extended here into more subject areas. He looked at historical material, for example relating to hunger, nutrition and life expectancy (Atherton, 2014, p. 30), but also drew on the social sciences more generally. The study of subjective wellbeing in particular took him into psychology research. It was the economist, Angus Deaton's work that gave him 'a most useful and viable framework' (Atherton, 2014, p. 30) from which to branch out and engage with new research in what was a rapidly evolving area.

A third element of his methodology was that he not only connected with Christian social thought, but also treated belief and the Church as part of his field of inquiry. Other secular writers had attested to the significance of faith in relation to happiness. Richard Layard reports that 'one of the most robust findings of happiness research is that people who believe in God are happier' (Layard, 2005, p. 72). Recognition of transcendent values is one contributory factor. Others are the social support of churchgoing; the experience of ritual and spiritual exercises; associated styles of living, such as moderation in consumption and contributing to society through voluntary activity and charitable giving; beliefs that generate positive emotions and virtues and enable better coping skills in adversity (Atherton, 2014, p. 65). Robert Putnam in the United States similarly found empirical evidence for the religiously observant being better neighbours, better citizens and more active in community life. Putnam's research arose from his wider work on social capital. He talks about 'moral freighting', the capacity to carry their practices, virtues and beliefs into wider society and promote wellbeing. Chris Baker's qualitative research with different faith groups has elaborated how such moral freighting works (Baker, 2013).

John's promotion of the idea of 'ordinary theology' (though not necessarily much using this terminology) led him to the linked concept of 'ordinary church': not the Church that church leaders say it is or tell it to be but 'the Church as it is, full of ordinary folk doing ordinary things, yet which are also extraordinary, not least because, for example, they produce people who generate higher wellbeing' (2014, pp. 75–6). He endorsed Keith Clements' view that community is the essence of Christianity and that churchgoing involves 'real community with others in all their awkwardness, bearing and forbearing, giving and forgiving' (Clements, 2013, p. 131). The value of these insights became more apparent to John during his years in retirement as an 'ordinary' member of his local church, seeing church life from the grass roots and, when widowed, being sustained by ordinary churchgoing and surrounded by the normality of ordinary human love (Atherton, 2014, p. 80). The significance of these material practices as the religious equivalent of the world of daily life explains why he called the book *Challenging Religious Studies* instead of 'challenging theology'. He located theology 'rightfully and respectfully' in the wider field of religious studies (2014, p. 89).

John's rationale for rooting his religious studies in the findings of other disciplines is illustrated by his quote from Bonhoeffer:

> In Christ we are offered the possibility of partaking in the reality of God and in the reality of the world, but not in one without the other. The reality of God discloses itself only by setting me entirely in the reality of the world. (Bonhoeffer, 1963, p. 195)

He provides some tools for this purposeful integration and for engaging with this wide agenda. They reflect that this is necessarily a two-way process. First, he used tools developed by economists, including modelling and statistical approaches. For instance, he developed a Christian model in relation to the three perspectives of wealth, wellbeing and inequalities of nations, drawing on economic history and statistical resources. Second, he brought together pure and applied research. Although there has been growing interest in practical theology seen in pastoral studies, the sociology of religion, public theology and Christian social ethics, this was a necessary corrective to 'the assumed dominance in religious studies of "pure" (often systematic) theology in relation to the reflections on the practice of Christians and their institutions' (Atherton, 2014, p. 18). A third tool he deployed is Ellen Charry's optometric one of monovision, because it helps to meet the difficulty in religious studies of reconciling the breadth of the agenda with engagement with the personal, with each human being. In monovision, one eye is used for close-up work and the other for distance viewing. This wholly meets John's aim to analyse the world of daily life on a large scale in the context of the nations of the world without neglecting the experience of individuals and their particular families and communities. Fourth is 'inter-ization'. (John did apologize for the term!) Here religious studies can bring added value to other interdisciplinary approaches. Christian experience suggests a three-dimensional paradigm: intra-faith between Christian denominations; interfaith relations across religions; interdisciplinary collaboration between secular and religious disciplines. For John, this last type of collaboration was most important for developing greater wellbeing, with the other two 'feeding into it, though retaining their particular identities' (2014, pp. 19–21), and with 'Christian beliefs and stories giving greater depth and meaning to the ordinary, necessary and hopefully increasing collaboration between disciplines, traditions and practical partners for the pursuit of greater human wellbeing' (2014, p. 197).

A formidable agenda but also useful pointers for us all

Probing and multifaceted, crossing geographies and histories and secular and religious disciplines, John's methodology was never going to be easy or tidy. Its intellectual breadth and rigour makes it quite difficult for many of us to grapple with and certainly to emulate. Nevertheless, widely relevant and practical messages emerge, not just for academics but for individuals and organizations seeking to develop their discipleship and forms of Christian ministry. I want to suggest some ways in which his approach can provide food for thought for parishes, for social activists and for Christians speaking in the public square.

John's definition of the Christian vocation as being to 'participate with God in transforming the world' emphasizes the importance of theological reflection. Developing a Christian social vision that can help to promote a participating and reciprocal society requires an adequate theology. Love and worship, though essential, are not sufficient. This is pertinent at all levels in the Church. For parish churches, engaging in the reality of local life must be the starting point for their mission and ministry and, as an entry point to contemporary developments, this will also be the basis for formulating an adequate theology. It means taking public issues seriously as well as private troubles. In turn, it entails not only drawing on the research of other disciplines, but also hearing insights gleaned from a range of perspectives. Parishioners can be well placed to see how wider economic forces and political policies play out in their neighbourhoods and communities. They may themselves span numerous vantage points as parents or grandparents, teachers or social workers, doctors or nurses, managers or trade unionists, retail workers or builders, people on benefits or stockbrokers, job centre staff or local councillors. Many Christians, too, are involved in social action, as volunteers in foodbanks, debt counselling or homelessness projects or running community outreach initiatives in their church. People sitting in our pews Sunday by Sunday have a wealth of expertise, yet the Church often does not look beyond their potential to play a part in the management and maintenance of the church fabric and institution. There is often little knowledge of, or value placed on, their Monday to Saturday lives and they are seldom made aware that they have a theological contribution to make.

Often what activists witness will provoke indignation at manifest injustices and structural inequalities and lead them into campaigning. Here John had some cautionary words. He talked about 'the soft option of prophecy' (2014, p. 4). What he meant was that it can be all too easy to say what we are against, more difficult also to take responsibility for the harder work of constructing alternatives: 'It is easy to preach good news to the poor and condemn their rich oppressors, whether people or systems. It is immensely more difficult to deliver' (2003, p. 105). He also warned against too narrow a focus. For him, that meant shifting from a preferential option for the poor to 'a bias for inclusivity', which questions both the naive assumption that economic growth will trickle down to benefit all and oversimple reliance on a bias to the poor. 'To ignore the possibilities and likelihood of economic growth is as imbalanced as ignoring structural inequalities. A bias for inclusivity seeks to encompass both' (2003, p. 117).

How does listening to different perspectives, seeing situations from the points of view of all the players fit with taking the side of the poor and powerless? Are there times when we should take sides, even at risk of oversimplifying? Are there occasions when different people within the Church rightly play different roles? An example from Liverpool, though dating from nearly 30 years ago, illustrates this broader view. In March

1989, it was announced that the Birds Eye factory in Kirkby, Merseyside, was to close with the loss of 1,000 jobs. Members of the local churches, Anglican, Roman Catholic and Methodist, all felt they had a duty to their community and acted in concert. They held a vigil at the factory gates and met with management and unions. Subsequently they published a joint statement calling on management to reconsider their decision. The Church leaders also acted. Archbishop Derek Worlock, Bishop David Sheppard and Dr John Newton, the Free Church Moderator, shared in the Good Friday procession for the Stations of the Cross in Kirkby, to be present with local people at a time of hurt. But, having concluded that the management decision would not be reversed, they put energy into board-room talks to try to ensure the firm would leave some sort of useful legacy.

Although the resulting programme for community benefit scarcely made up for the loss of jobs, it was some small compensation. There was a major debate at the diocesan synod taking place a week after the factory closure. A motion had been put to synod recommending that the Church Commissioners withdraw their investment in Unilever, the Birds Eye parent company. Papers by one of the local clergy, a personnel officer from the factory and the divisional trade union organizer were presented and the Bishop of Liverpool also made a statement. At the heart of the debate was the question: what should be the response of the Church to such a situation? Whose story should take precedence? That of the managers who felt decisions were forced on them by the reality of competition or that of local residents who felt hurt and helpless? Pastoral care for all parties, community involvement and solidarity, negotiation, protest and prophetic witness were all valid responses to a problem of such complexity, even though they represented different reactions. Arguably the challenge for the Church was to acknowledge this diversity and embrace it in a loving and open way.

John himself recognized the need for lobbying, for engaging 'the powers', for being active in the political arena. Seeing different points of view does not equate to enfeebled even-handedness, nor does it mean failing to challenge systemic injustices. The distinctiveness of Church Action on Poverty (CAP) as a campaigning organization owed much to his huge influence. CAP was unusual at the time in bringing together three strands of work: raising awareness about poverty inside and outside the churches; making explicit connections with Christian thinking to find ways in which to face the contradictions between our beliefs and practices if our theology is to be meaningful to people who are marginalized; political – but not party political – involvement because public policies determine so much about the nature of society and the life chances of individuals. In his later advocacy of a bias for inclusivity or 'differentiated solidarity', John was looking for a formula combining concerns for the whole and for the marginalized. The associated task was to bring back the marginalized into full participation in church and society (Atherton, 2003, p. 119), which has been a key role of CAP over the 30 or more years since its inception.

John believed Christians potentially have something useful to offer to public discourse, provided they have a theology relevant to the broader context and commensurate with the complexity of public concerns. The question is not whether religious arguments qualify for a public role, but what kind of arguments. John adopted the three criteria of the American theologian, R. F. Thiemann, for evaluating religious contributions in the public sphere. First, they must be broadly accessible, using language and concepts that are recognizable to the wider public. The challenge is greater 'given the impact of plural post-industrial and postmodern contexts of competing narratives, including other faiths'. Churches can no longer claim a public voice by right. Further, the increasing significance of difference and plurality calls for them to rethink their traditional commitment to the common good to make room for diversity (Atherton, 2003, pp. 123–4). Second, because there will be inevitable disagreements, mutual respect must remain central. Such respect must go beyond mere toleration to accepting the moral agency of those who disagree. This has implications for democratic living. It underlines the importance of creating spaces of encounter where people can safely explore their common ground and their differences. Third, to have moral integrity, statements must be underpinned by consistency of speech and action. If Christians are to criticize aspects of society, they must ensure their own (church) house is in order (2003, p. 125).

I said earlier that John's journey was one of responding to social and economic change. As it progressed, the more he was also preoccupied with making connections. Linkages became increasingly important: the intellectual and the personal, religious studies and other disciplines, praxis and theological reflection, ecumenism and interfaith, political economy and the human, the environment and the nature of God. He summed it up himself: 'it is as though the Christian task becomes participation in the making of a great patchwork quilt, weaving these different insights and experiences into a whole, a rich tapestry of immense variety' (2003, p. 178).

References

Astley, J. and Francis, L., 2013, *Exploring Ordinary Theology: Everyday Christian Believing and the Church*, Farnham: Ashgate.
Atherton, J. R., 1983, *The Scandal of Poverty: Priorities for the Emerging Church*, London: Mowbray.
Atherton, J. R., 1988, *Faith in the Nation: A Christian Vision for Britain*, London: SPCK.
Atherton, J. R., 1992, *Christianity and the Market: Christian Social Thought for Our Times*, London: SPCK.
Atherton, J. R., 2000, *Public Theology for Changing Times*, London: SPCK.
Atherton, J. R., 2003, *Marginalization*, London: SCM Press.
Atherton, J. R., 2014, *Challenging Religious Studies: The Wealth, Wellbeing and Inequalities of Nations*, London: SCM Press.
Baker, C. R., 2013, 'Moral Freighting and Civic Engagement: A UK Perspective on Putnam and Campbell's Theory of Religious-Based Social Action', *Sociology of Religion: A Quarterly Review* 74:3, pp. 343–69.
Bonhoeffer, D., 1964, *Ethics*, ed. E. Bethge, trans. N. Horton Smith, London: Collins, Fontana Library.
Charry, E., 2010, *God and the Art of Happiness*, Grand Rapids, MI: Eerdmans.
Clements, K., 2013, *Ecumenical Dynamics: Living in More than One Place at Once*, Geneva: WCC Publications.
Deaton, A., 2013, *The Great Escape: Health, Wealth and the Origins of Inequality*, Princeton, NJ: Princeton University Press.
Faith in the City: A Call for Action by Church and Nation, 1985, Report of the Archbishop of Canterbury's Commission on Urban Priority Areas, London: Church House Publishing.
Forrester, D. B., 1997, *Christian Justice and Public Policy*, Cambridge: Cambridge University Press.
Layard, R., 2005, *Happiness: Lessons from a New Science*, London: Allen Lane.
Mayne, M., 2006, *The Enduring Melody*, London: Darton, Longman & Todd (digital edn, 2013, Andrews UK Ltd).
Preston, R. H., 1979, *Religion and the Persistence of Capitalism*, London: SCM Press.
Putnam, R. and Campbell, D., 2010, *American Grace: How Religion Divides and Unites Us*, New York: Simon & Schuster.
Russell, H. (ed.), 1987, *Faith in Our City: The Message of the Archbishop of Canterbury's Commission on Urban Priority Areas for Faith and Public Policy in Merseyside and Region*, Liverpool: Liverpool Diocesan Publishing Co. Ltd.
Russell, H., 1995, *Poverty Close to Home: A Christian Understanding*, London: Mowbray.
Ward, G., 2000, *Cities of God*, London and New York: Routledge.
Wogaman, J. P., 1988, *Christian Perspectives on Politics*, London: SCM Press.

4

'The Manchester School': University, Cathedral, William Temple Foundation[1]

PETER SEDGWICK

Preston and Atherton

The idea of 'the Manchester School' in public theology refers to the influence of Ronald Preston and John Atherton as they worked and taught in Manchester from 1947, when Preston moved to work at Manchester University, until Atherton's death in 2016. Atherton was then living in Lancashire, and assisting at St Katharine's Church, Black Rod, near to where he was born. The Manchester School of public theology covers a period of nearly 70 years, and involves Manchester Cathedral, the University of Manchester, and the creation of the William Temple Foundation in Manchester. John Atherton was deeply indebted to his doctoral supervisor Ronald Preston. Preston, who lived from 1913 to 2001, had been taught in turn by the great economic historian and social activist R. H Tawney at the London School of Economics, and this influence was to shape Preston throughout his life. However, the historian Lawrence Goldman in his magisterial biography of Tawney noted that Preston also questioned Tawney's rejection of self-advancement and profit as a valuable social force (Atherton, 2005; Goldman, 2013; Preston, 1966).

Preston had also met William Temple, when Preston was a young man in his twenties. Temple had been Bishop of Manchester from 1921 to 1929, although there is no evidence that his writings reflected a particular Mancunian perspective. Stephen Spencer said that Manchester did not take him to heart: 'he could not in the end be described as a great pastoral bishop' (Spencer, 2001, p. 46; Iremonger, 1946, pp. 282–344). What Manchester did give Temple was two things. First, it showed him that his great friend Tawney was correct in his analysis of industrial poverty and class division. Temple believed that anyway, but his experience of constant visiting of parishes showed him how deep poverty was in the lives of working people, never mind those without work. This encounter with daily hardship deeply ingrained in Temple a belief that poverty and class division strongly prevented people flourishing, and was a major obstacle to religious faith. Second, Temple was briefly involved in attempting to mediate nationally the 1926 coal stoppage after the end of the General Strike. This was not successful but it did show organized labour where Temple's commitment was. Temple became in 1929 the enormously influential Archbishop of York, and then in 1942 Archbishop of Canterbury. His writings did more than anything to shape Christian social thought in the twentieth century. Temple died in 1944, at the height of his powers, aged 63 (Hastings, 2005; Dackson, 2006). Temple was very close to Tawney, although again in reviewing *The Acquisitive Society* Temple doubted Tawney's rejection of self-interest. Preston and Atherton's work can be seen as an extended coda to Temple's thought in both British theology and social policy. A coda in music is the concluding passage of a piece or movement, typically forming an addition to the basic structure.

Preston wrote extensively about Temple all his life, and Temple's theology lies constantly in the background of Atherton's thought (Preston, 1969; 1981a; 1981b; 1987; Atherton, 1992; 1994). Atherton once described Preston as being in a tradition from Temple 'almost as an apostolic succession' (Atherton, 2000, p. 79). Temple and Atherton united in their understanding of the Christian faith. This faith is an incarnational, sacramental appreciation of how human life reflects God's nature and action, but equally how the sinfulness of humanity through injustice results in profound economic and social misery for many people. Atherton wrote of Temple's thought that it was 'his embodying of the Anglo-Saxon tradition of incarnational theology in debates for a modern welfare state and Keynesian economics' (Atherton, Baker and Graham, 2003). The reference is to Temple's *Christianity and Social Order*, which expounded his commitment to the Christian principles of freedom, fellowship and service as being at the heart of social order (Temple, 1942). Preston in particular developed the idea of 'middle axioms', standing between Christian principles and detailed social and economic policies (Preston, 1981, pp. 37–44).

Ronald Preston was appointed a lecturer in Christian ethics in 1947, and warden of a Manchester University hall of residence, through a joint initiative of the Bishop of Manchester and the Vice-Chancellor of Manchester University. It was the first ever appointment of a lecturer in Christian ethics in England apart from the Regius Professorship at Oxford. Preston moved to Manchester Cathedral in 1957 as residentiary canon theologian. In 1970, he became Professor of Social and Pastoral Theology at Manchester University, while continuing to hold a canonry at the cathedral, until he retired in 1980. He remained very active until his death in 2001. Preston worked closely with John Atherton. They first met in 1970, and interacted very closely for the next 30 years (Atherton, 2004, p. 21).

I remember meeting them both for the first time, when I was in my thirties, in 1986. Atherton and I had become members of the Church of England's Industrial and Economic Affairs Committee. Preston had previously been a member. The effect of meeting them together was overwhelming. Both men took it for granted that you would be fully versed in the details of the economic debates between Keynesians and monetarists of the Chicago School, such as Hayek or Friedman. The Chicago school also influenced Brian Griffiths, who was Margaret Thatcher's economic advisor, and who briefly was a member of the same committee, and Patrick Minford, who was a leading academic economist who strongly supported the Conservative government and has been a profound Eurosceptic all his life. Both Preston and Atherton also knew that economic debate had to be grounded in day-to-day industrial reality, and as a result Preston and Atherton knew industrial life very deeply, especially in north-west England. Both men had also given a huge amount of time to reflecting on the relationship of theology to economics and industrial life, in what was called 'public theology'. Finally, both men were deeply rooted in the Church's response to industry and economic life, through the organization called Industrial Mission. This was embodied in the relationship of Manchester Cathedral to the social and economic outreach of the churches ecumenically in the region, but above all in the work of the Manchester Diocesan Board for Social Responsibility (BSR). Atherton chaired the Board for many years, while being canon theologian at the Cathedral. It was two sides of one coin. Chris Beales, who had been an industrial chaplain and was Secretary of the Church of England Industrial and Economic Affairs Committee in the mid-1980s, of which Atherton and myself were members, remembers the period well, in a personal email to the author:

> John's pragmatism was an important aspect of his life and work – though more through the Boards for Social Responsibility at diocesan and national levels. He chaired Linking Up Inter-Faith, which worked nationally from a base in the Manchester BSR, on urban regeneration.

The 1980s were a turbulent time in British social theology for two reasons. First, there was mass unemployment, the collapse of Britain's industrial base, especially in the Midlands and the North, and social unrest in British cities. Second, there was the influence of liberation theology, originating in South America, which impacted on the Temple–Preston tradition. John Atherton advised, but was not a member of, the working party that wrote the famous Church of England report, *Faith in the City*, in 1985 (Atherton, 2014, p. 179). His views were consonant with the report (Morris, 2018). It was the high-water mark of the influence of the Temple–Preston–Atherton approach. Beales remembers the tensions well: 'I remember lots of talk about the inadequacy of "middle axioms" in the face of Thatcherism and mass unemployment (especially with the challenges posed by Liberation Theology to our work as industrial chaplains).'

Atherton did not stand alone in his work. Those influenced by him included Malcolm Brown and Chris Baker. Atherton supervised the doctoral thesis of Malcolm Brown, which was on Temple, Preston and other theologians, in their dialogue with economic life. Like Preston, Atherton was a residentiary canon at Manchester Cathedral, while teaching at Manchester University. Atherton taught through the William Temple Foundation. The William Temple Foundation was, and is, a remarkable institution. It was founded in memory of Archbishop William Temple, who died in 1944. The William Temple College trained both lay men and women to relate Christian faith to the realities of the secular world (Elwyn, 1996, pp. 229–30). In 1971, the College moved to the Manchester Business School and was renamed the William Temple Foundation, conceiving itself as a 'college without walls' in the field of Christian social ethics. The Foundation was an ecumenical research institute concerned with theology, economics and urban life, engaged in training programmes, research, publishing and teaching. The Foundation's first Director was David Jenkins, who later became Bishop of Durham. Jenkins was soon joined by Atherton, who succeeded Jenkins as Director. In turn, the Directors (or Executive Secretaries) after Atherton were Malcolm Brown, from 1991 to 2000, and Chris Baker, from 2001 until the present day. Atherton, however, remained deeply involved with the Foundation until his death in 2016.

During the 1980s the Foundation took a leading role in developing community work among British churches. It also developed European church networks, bringing together theologians, economists and activists to develop common agendas. Since 2001, under the leadership of the Foundation's current Director of Research, Chris Baker, the emphasis has been on urban change, or what Baker describes as the post-secular city. This involves use of the concepts of religious and spiritual capital, in relation to wellbeing. The Foundation also continued to work on economic affairs, especially in the final works of John Atherton.

It was this extraordinary combination of place, individuals and style of theology that led to the description of the work of Preston, Atherton, Brown, Baker and others as being the 'Manchester School'. A few examples may be given. Baker himself writes about:

the Manchester school of public theology, arising back from Temple's time as Bishop of Manchester through the work of Ronald Preston and Tony Dyson, and carried on for a while by Elaine Graham and myself. What is the Manchester school? I would define it as an empirical form of public theology, rooted in an interdisciplinary, critical but progressive enquiry into political, social, cultural and economic change, and the role of religion, theology and the church in those changes, all deeply embedded in the spirit and study of Manchester as a global city and how its ebb and flow illuminates our understanding of the world. In a book chapter co-written by Elaine Graham and myself for a volume entitled *Pathways to the Public Square*, John (Atherton) wrote: 'In taking Manchester as a case study of what it means to do theology in public, we identify three ways in which it provides a striking archetypal example of the key factors to which public theology must attend: (1) The realities of economic growth and political economy. (2) Human dimensions in terms of marginalization. (3) Church as implicated in changing forms of urban life.' Those three tenets stayed with him throughout his life. (Baker, 2016a; 2016b)

Two more examples may be given of the recognition of this group as the 'Manchester School'. Malcolm Brown, in a tribute after Atherton's death, wrote:

> John's PhD thesis was on Tawney whose work remained close to his heart all his life. Preston, his supervisor, had known both Tawney and Temple ... These continuities, within an evolving theological understanding, growing as new challenges and perspectives came into play, typified John's keen sense of how a tradition develops. His own researches, continuing until his death, took him well beyond Tawney, Temple or Preston and engaged with some of the most recent international interdisciplinary studies. (Brown, 2016)

A final description of the school by the veteran social ethicist Duncan Forrester describes the Manchester School as part of Ecumenical Social Ethics. This flourished from the 1940s to the 1980s. It drew on a Western consensus that was explicitly or implicitly Christian, or at least regarded the Christian faith as worthy of respect. It was interdisciplinary, and used what were called 'middle axioms'. These were propositions derived from the Christian tradition but which were acceptable in social and economic policy, such as the value of human flourishing, or the importance of personality. Ecumenical Social Ethics tended to Keynesianism in economics. Forrester saw Preston as 'its last great prophet' but the project collapsed in the 1980s. It was too cautious, middle class and conservative to deal with liberation theology. However, Forrester also saw Atherton as believing that 'the tradition of Ecumenical Social Ethics as still capable of speaking perceptively and prophetically to church and society today' (Forrester, 2008).

Against the idea of a tradition

Many other illustrations of the influence of the 'Manchester School' could be given, as well as attacks on it by John Hughes, and the followers of Stanley Hauerwas (Hughes, 2016, pp. 157, 175). However, at this point I want to make an abrupt U-turn, and ask whether the tradition existed at all. There is no doubt that Preston and Atherton were deeply influenced by Tawney and Temple, that they interacted closely despite their difference in ages (Preston was born in 1901, Atherton in 1939), that both taught in Manchester, and that Atherton was regarded with enormous respect by Brown and Baker. There was also, as noted above, the institutional influence of the William Temple Foundation. But is there more than this? This might seem surprising: do the last three pages not demonstrate this quite clearly?

Most discussion of tradition in political philosophy and theology in the last 40 years has drawn on MacIntyre's *After Virtue* (1985) and his reformulation of tradition. A classic way of doing this is Brown's *After the Market* (Brown, 2004, pp. 57–8). Atherton was not entirely convinced by this approach: his references to MacIntyre are always coded, but on the whole critical. He saw value in the practice of the virtues as MacIntyre described, and recognized both the need for the exercise of those virtues to change the established order and the need to interact with the wider society, including challenging the existing order (Atherton, 2008, pp. 7, 220). The practice of those virtues could be described as 'an historically extended, socially embodied argument'. He accepted this definition of a tradition in MacIntyre's writing, and found this 'particularly creative' (Atherton, 2003, p. 108). Where MacIntyre was also useful was in explaining how a tradition, religious or otherwise, became 'inadequate for engagement with a changing context'. That led to 'epistemological crisis', and Atherton used MacIntyre to support his engagement with 'an enlarged narrative' (Atherton, 2008, pp. 157, 233). The reference to story, or narrative, is important.

As Atherton engaged with faiths other than Christianity in Manchester, other disciplines and experiences, he rejected any model that sought to say that the Church was a closed community with a distinctive economic viewpoint. All it had was distinctive sources as it engaged with ever-changing cultures and communities. That was the Manchester story in the early twentieth century for Atherton (Atherton, 2003, pp. 177–8). But references in *Marginalization, Transfiguring Capitalism* and *Challenging Religious Studies* to MacIntyre do not support any theory of largely incompatible traditions as found in MacIntyre – a different approach from Brown (Brown, 2004, p. 68). Atherton sought to avoid 'the universalism and foundationalism of a common human essence' alongside 'the MacIntyre post-modernism of rival and incommensurable moral premises' (Atherton, 2003, pp. 67, 127). Nor are there references in Atherton's work to the Manchester School. The only reference in all his writings to the 'Manchester School' is not to public theology at all but instead to the free-trade group of economists in the nineteenth century, including Cobden (Atherton, 2014, p. 165). Atherton knew that he stood within a tradition of thinkers indebted to Charles Gore, William Temple and R. H. Tawney, but he never saw this group as being in any sense a 'school'. Indeed, as he aged and his thought ranged wider, the references to the tradition he stood in became less. You can find such a reference in *Public Theology for Changing Times*, but his last book simply cites the growing number of 'public theologians' engaging 'with varying degrees of adequacy' with economics. The reference to degrees of adequacy is a typical, wry Athertonian comment (Atherton, 2000, p. 79; 2014, p. 15)!

The Manchester Story, not the Manchester School

Atherton's alternative to talking of the 'Manchester School' was subtle. He followed Tawney, the subject of his own doctoral work. 'By teaching history, [Tawney] could help working-class students understand how their industries and communities had emerged and developed, and provide them with the intellectual means to change them for the better' (Goldman, 2013–14). This could be said of Atherton above all. Atherton saw the narrative of Manchester's industrialization as standing in the Tawney mould in three ways. First, there was intellectual analysis. To take but one of Atherton's many books, *Transfiguring Capitalism*, there was an analysis of contemporary financial capitalism, with the globalization and dematerializing of money, and the very different operation of social capital. Second, there was the display of this analysis in a historical narrative, using the emergence of global capitalism during the British Empire in 1900 and Temple's understanding of intermediate social groups as part of social capital in 1942. Atherton especially used the historical narrative of nineteenth-century Manchester, which he knew so well. Third, for those who heard and understood aright there was the moral transformation of its subject.

Atherton appealed to a concept he had found in the US Anglican theologian Kathryn Tanner, which was 'the economy of grace' (Atherton, 2008, pp. 258–9, 272–82, 286–8). This appeal to moral exhortation at the end of a tightly argued study is deeply Pauline. The technical biblical term is 'paraenesis' (Gk: *parainesis*). Paraenesis refers to moral exhortation aimed at a particular social group, precisely because of their social context, and as the conclusion of a tightly knit argument. Romans 12 is the classic example of paraenesis, where after Paul's lengthy exposition of justification and righteousness, a small, persecuted social group in Rome is told to 'bless those who persecute you' (Rom. 12.14; Dunn, 1998, p. 672). Goldman refers to the impact Tawney had in his lectures to working people before the First World War. One of his colleagues said that if there were more lecturers like Tawney, England would be turned upside down in a few years' time. The moral passion arising from close intellectual analysis and historical narrative is twentieth-century paraenesis. The challenge was there to transfigure those who heard Tawney. The appeal was to join trade unions or political parties, and change the deeply unjust British political and economic system. Atherton concludes *Transfiguring Capitalism* in a similar way. He makes reference to Kathryn Tanner's *Economy of Grace* (Tanner, 2005), and the way economics can be transfigured. It is again an example of paraenesis, following his beloved Tawney. But it is neither sentimental nor merely exhortatory. It is an appeal to the reader to become involved in fighting global capitalism (Atherton, 2008, pp. 283–9).

These views are summed up in the chapter already mentioned above by Baker.

> How are those who observe the phenomenon of the urban condition to communicate and assimilate its significance? Is it an occasion for exhilaration and wonder; or something which calls forth dismay at the diminution of the quality of life it produces? (Atherton, Baker and Graham, 2003)

We should note that this is quite deliberately an emotional reaction, and this point will be taken up in a moment here. Very simply, Atherton knew people felt passionate about the need for change. He wrote about Manchester because he was from Lancashire, and he retired there as well. The story was *his story*, and so was *his-tory*. Manchester's *story*, rather than being part of a *school*, was the story of the life and death of British industrial development.

And though he was read by the world, he always taught local students, took part in local industrial mission and social responsibility work, and was renowned for this. The cathedral, the diocese and the university were not part of a school, but a story and a place. In so teaching students, preaching and working with industrial mission and social responsibility, Atherton enabled (to quote once more Goldman on Tawney) 'the intellectual means to change them for the better'. Atherton knew this, and said so to me, on several occasions. By contrast, listen to Atherton on Preston: 'You will find little sense of my excitement inhabiting such a historic and contemporary fulcrum of change. He is much more part of the mid-twentieth-century rational tradition of universalising particular experiences' (Atherton, 2004, p. 21). Atherton and I were great friends with Preston. We both spoke at his funeral in Manchester Cathedral, which was the same building as Atherton's memorial service was to be held in 15 years later. But Atherton knew that Preston was different from him in a profound way. Atherton's alternative was to be contextual and earthed, listening to those who suffer injustice. Atherton knew the importance of never being 'disconnected from particular narratives and experiences' (Atherton, 2004, pp. 20, 27–8).

Atherton also held different views from Kenneth Leech. He distrusted his commitment to socialism as failing to engage with the reality of economics as a discipline, especially the classical tradition since Adam Smith. Yet both Atherton and Leech sought social justice, and both came from the north west of England. Leech was born in the same year as Atherton in a Manchester suburb, and retired to the North West. Both were committed to local, contextual theology, and the centrality of praxis, or action in tandem with theory (Leech, 2006). Both celebrated the importance of narrative and local experience in all their books, even if Leech spent most of his time in East London, where his local examples are set, before retiring back to where he had grown up. The difference between them was, however, important.

Even before his death in 2016, Atherton was sharply critical of the Corbyn–McDonnell ascendancy in the British Labour Party, as embodying Leech's views in a major political party. Atherton felt Leech's economic thought was highly inadequate and a form of wish-fulfilment. While despairing of the failure of the Conservative Party in Britain to overcome its nationalist prejudices and its lack of economic and social regulation, Atherton was deeply committed to market economics. He felt Corbyn represented a retreat before the forces of globalization. Atherton's commitment to the benefits of the market after 1992 looked like a change of mind. Yet it was not. The collapse of Communism in Eastern Europe, the potential of the market economy to deliver benefits and the changing context meant that his ideals remained the same but the challenge was 'to stand up for the poor and marginalized, and at the same time make the best use of the opportunities for the common good the market economy presented' (Morris 2018).

The theological and political significance of emotions

Atherton's work changed in the decade after 2000. Before that he wrote on poverty, social policy, the market and political change. Increasingly after 2000, in his sixties, he was fascinated by the relationship of religion to human flourishing, wellbeing and happiness. In two working parties, you can see the ideas begin to develop. In the first working party, of which I was a member, which was published as *Through the Eye of a Needle: Theological Conversations over Political Economy*, there are a few references to happiness. In Atherton's own book, *Transfiguring Capitalism*, there is a whole chapter on happiness. Atherton then arranged a second extended symposium, which resulted in *The Practices of Happiness: Political Economy, Religion and Wellbeing*. Finally, there is the last of Atherton's own books, *Challenging Religious Studies: The Wealth, Wellbeing and Inequalities of Nations*, where the study of emotions and happiness is to the fore (Atherton and Skinner, 2007; 2014).

But how do we interpret what we hear as we experience it and listen to it? Atherton was very intrigued before his death at my introducing him to Joshua Hordern's work on 'political affections' (Hordern, 2013). Hordern engages with Habermas and Scruton at length. Cognitive theorists of emotions argue that emotions are object-directed, at external objective realities, and express our rational assessment of this reality emotionally. (Hordern uses the traditional term for this in philosophy, which is affections, but I will keep the term emotions, for the sake of using the common-sense term.) Emotions are ways of knowing and living in the reality that we encounter. We are never just angry, but angry at x. This describes Tawney and Atherton's approach to working-class pride, anger, sense of place and above all hope for a better society very well. There can be local, political and religious expressions of emotions. All enable civic participation and social change. The key is to use this emotion to see what it is emotion *about*. Atherton would have explored this new epistemology with me had he lived. Sadly, he did not.

What was missing from Atherton's work on positive emotions was a way of interpreting the work of psychologists in terms of political theory, and of looping back positive emotions to a sense of place, history, religion, and so on (Atherton, 2014, pp. 54–82). What his last book needed was Hordern's argument. Emotions are 'participative beginnings of understanding'. We do not grow up without emotions and then acquire them along the way. The emotional analogue of the reality that we are born into communities is that these communities have common objects of love. We engage in emotions before we engage in discursive reasoning and, as Hordern says, for he is no anti-rationalist, values that appear to emotions are 'the *first* ethical facts, the *half-light* of ethics' (Hordern,

2013, p. 77, emphasis original). Tawney and Atherton took this half-light of ethical understanding, provided an intellectual justification or critique of it, embedded it in a historical narrative, and then returned it to the hearer (or reader) as moral exhortation or paraenesis. This is not the Manchester School, but the story of Manchester people.

It is, above all, a story of memory and historical narrative. Israelite festivals are about memory and serving the needy (Hordern, 2013, pp. 147–51). The analogue in Atherton is of course wellbeing, with which his final book ends (Atherton, 2014, p. 197). Atherton valued Manchester Cathedral because this was a place of communal festive celebration of God's presence in Manchester, where his preaching explored the call for social justice and the reality of God in the world of work and unemployment. There is a moving tribute to the Cathedral in *Marginalization* (Atherton, 2003, p. xiii). Yet he also charted the relentless decline of the number attending Anglican churches in Manchester. He was never sentimental (Atherton, 2003, pp. 100–1). Eve Poole said to me in a personal email that Atherton's relationship to the cathedral was one of embodiment: 'In many ways, he was trying to be a personification of the cathedral he loved so much – to be a physical manifestation of public Christian hospitality in the heart of the marketplace, with all the tension, mess, boldness and glory that involves.' That is a perceptive observation.

The 'evaluative intentionality' of emotions for Hordern is a form of moral insight whereby human beings participate and shape the 'created order of value'. Our emotions are not simply individual. There is 'intersubjective verification', or social solidarity. The epistemological ability of socially stabilized emotions provides ways of evaluation, participation, recognition of the moral authority of political leaders and processes, and the initiation of action (Hordern, 2013, pp. 40, 77, 81). Hordern evidences resentment, alienation and disillusionment of transnational political bodies that devalue the affection people feel for locality and place, where they were rooted. Although Atherton would have strongly disagreed with Hordern's scepticism with the European Union, he would have resonated with the argument that political emotion is generated by the local community, 'which has cared for the individual who has come into the world, received nurture, and learnt to live ... [It] takes particular form towards past and present political representatives and other public servants' (Hordern, 2013, p. 224). Local identity and community life provide socially stabilized emotions. This can of course legitimate pathological emotions as well, such as racism or ethnic violence, but Hordern is concerned to deepen Atherton's riposte to Preston's emphasis on the rational and universal. The local, and affective, matters, and has a political dimension. What Atherton needed to do was to take the transposition of theological virtues into political society and see how this worked emotionally as well. Hordern knows that ethnocentric nationalism can oppress vulnerable groups, but it is precisely the transposition of theological virtues into society that will prevent and challenge this. Above all, a political leader must elicit proper emotion to overcome the great deficit of trust that can so easily paralyse the most oppressed and marginalized groups with a weary cynicism that no one cares and it is all hopeless (Hordern, 2013, pp. 270–1).

The continuing legacy

What was Atherton's legacy? It is threefold, and all aspects of this legacy must be held together. Chris Beales puts it well in an email to me:

> His most important legacy was to take economics very seriously and be willing to face up to the awkward questions. Relating the harsh word of economics to happiness and human flourishing – and to see that as the proper concern of the Church – is what influenced me. I think that's why he was a doer and not only a thinker.

This has to be correct. Very few theologians of the present day get the relationship of economics, theology and social justice correct. Atherton's painstaking analysis of economic theory, social reality and the possibility of political and economic reform remains an enormous legacy that is hardly found in contemporary theology. Albino Barrera or Eve Poole are some of the very few, and very different, theologians who get this correct (Barrera, 2005; 2011; Poole 2010; 2015). The challenge to British social theology, and especially the Church of England, is to retrieve this legacy and not simply be indebted to Catholic Social Teaching, highly valuable and important though that is.

The second aspect of this legacy, which can only follow after this first step, is the emphasis on listening to the local experience of the marginalized (Atherton, 2004, p. 27). This has of course then to go through the process Atherton leant from Tawney. It must be analysed, embedded in historical narrative and then given back. Atherton puts it beautifully in *Marginalization*: 'You can't generalize from stories. They must never be substituted for reasoned argument. They must complement it.' The social sciences must be joined by ways of communicating the voices of the marginalized (Atherton, 2003, p. 114). In terms of emotions, Hordern is very sharp on Hauerwas. Hauerwas says feelings are important because they inform us about our own character. Hordern is correct when he says feelings matter not because they show us how we are Christian but because they help us 'understand the world outside ourselves' (Hordern,

2013 p. 290). Atherton would have said Amen to that. And especially understand Manchester.

Third, and last of all, Atherton's enormous legacy is the way he takes emotional solidarity and agreement into community organizing and so extends social trust on community organizing and social capital (Hordern, 2013, p. 256; Atherton, 2014, p. 191). Social capital is another way of expressing emotional political embodiment. What aspects of the 'Atherton' approach might be offered for the future of public and practical theology? The answer is surely that all social theology must be both performative and praxis-orientated (Atherton, 2004, p. 31).

This chapter does not deny that people have often read the involvement of Preston, Atherton, cathedral, university and Foundation as a 'school'. But I don't think that Atherton saw it like that. For him, it was a story, the story of the people of Manchester and Lancashire, where he was born, worked and died. This is not anti-intellectual: far from it. What I think is needed in the next generation is two things. First, Atherton's deep appreciation of economic analysis and the contemporary global market must be regained. That is a huge weakness at the moment in public theology. Second, we need to take Hordern's work and place it alongside Tawney and Atherton, and see how emotions, intellectual analysis, historical narrative and praxis can contribute to a public theology that overcomes distrust and cynicism. This will find the joy of the Christian faith transposed into the wellbeing of local people. That would take further the telling of the Manchester story, to which Atherton was so committed.

Note

1 I would like to thank Chris Beales, Jeremy Morris and Eve Poole for very helpful comments on this chapter.

References

Atherton, J. R., 1992, *Christianity and the Market*, London: SPCK.
Atherton, J. R. (ed.), 1994, *Social Christianity: A Reader*, London: SPCK.
Atherton, J. R., 2000, *Public Theology for Changing Times*, London: SPCK.
Atherton, J. R., Baker, C. R. and Graham, E. L., 2003, 'A "Genius of Place"? Manchester as a Case Study in Public Theology', in E. Graham and A. Rowlands (eds), *Pathways to the Public Square: Practical Theology in an Age of Pluralism* (International Academy of Practical Theology, Manchester), Münster: LIT Verlag.
Atherton, J. R., 2003, *Marginalization*, London: SCM Press.
Atherton, J. R., 2004, 'Marginalisation, Manchester and the Scope of Public Theology', in E. Graham and E. Reed (eds), *The Future of Christian Social Ethics: Essays on the Work of Ronald Preston, Studies in Christian Ethics* 17(2), London: T&T Clark.

Atherton, J. R., 2005, 'Ronald Preston', in *Oxford Dictionary of National Biography*, Oxford: Oxford University Press.
Atherton, J. R., 2008, *Transfiguring Capitalism: An Enquiry into Religion and Social Change*, London: SCM Press.
Atherton, J. R., 2014, *Challenging Religious Studies: The Wealth, Wellbeing and Inequalities of Nations*, London: SCM Press.
Atherton, J. R. and Skinner, H. (eds), 2007, *Through the Eye of a Needle: Theological Conversations over Political Economy*, Peterborough: Epworth.
Atherton, J. R., Graham, E. L. and Steedman, I. (eds), 2011, *The Practices of Happiness: Political Economy, Religion and Wellbeing*, Abingdon: Routledge.
Baker, C. R., 2016a, 'John Atherton: An Academic Appreciation', http://williamtemplefoundation.org.uk/wp-content/uploads/2016/06/John-Atherton-Academic-Appreciation.pdf.
Baker, C. R., 2016b, 'John Atherton', *Church Times*, 1 July.
Barrera, A., 2005, *Economic Compulsion and Christian Ethics*, Cambridge: Cambridge University Press.
Barrera, A., 2011, *Market Complicity and Christian Ethics*, Cambridge: Cambridge University Press.
Brown, M., 2004, *After the Market: Economics, Moral Agreement and the Churches' Mission*, Religions and Discourse Vol. 23, Oxford: Peter Lang.
Brown, M., 2016, 'John Atherton', www.workchaplaincyuk.org.uk/wp-content/uploads/2016/07/John-Atherton-obituary.pdf.
Dackson, W., 2006, 'Archbishop William Temple and Public Theology in a Post-Christian Context', *Journal of Anglican Studies* 4(2), pp. 239–52.
Dunn, J. D. G., 1998, *The Theology of Paul the Apostle*, Edinburgh: T&T Clark.
Elwyn, T., 1996, 'Industrial Mission', *Baptist Quarterly* 36(5), pp. 228–40.
Forrester, D. B., 2008, review of John Atherton and Hannah Skinner (eds), *Through the Eye of a Needle: Theological Conversations over Political Economy* (2007), *Studies in Christian Ethics* 21(3), pp. 425–6.
Goldman, L., 2013, *The Life of R. H. Tawney: Socialism and History*, London: Bloomsbury.
Goldman, L., 2014, 'Tawney's Century', *The Oxford Historian* 11, p. 48.
Hastings, A., 2005, 'William Temple', *Oxford Dictionary of National Biography*: Oxford: Oxford University Press.
Hordern, J., 2013, *Political Affections*, Oxford: Oxford University Press.
Hughes, J., 2016, *Graced Life*, ed. Matthew Bullimore, London: SCM Press.
Iremonger, F. A., 1946, *William Temple*, London: Oxford University Press.
Leech, K., 2006, 'The Soul and the City: Urban Ministry and Theology 1956–2006', The Samuel Ferguson Lecture 2006, University of Manchester, http://urblog.typepad.com/urblog/2006/10/soul_and_the_ci.html
MacIntyre, A., 1985, *After Virtue*, London: SCM Press.
Morris, J., 2018, 'Manchester Cathedral 1983 to the Present', in J. Gregory and M. Powell (eds), *A History of Manchester's Collegiate Church and Cathedral, 1421 to the Present*, Manchester: Manchester University Press.
Poole, E., 2010, *The Church and Capitalism: Theology and the Market*, Basingstoke: Palgrave Macmillan.
Poole, E., 2015, *Capitalism's Toxic Assumptions*, London: Bloomsbury.
Preston, R. H., 1966, 'R. H. Tawney as a Christian Moralist', *Theology* 64, pp. 157–64, reprinted in *Religion and the Persistence of Capitalism*, London: SCM Press, 1977.

Preston, R. H., 1969, 'William Temple after Twenty-Five Years', *Church Quarterly* 2(2).
Preston, R. H., 1981a, 'William Temple as a Social Theologian', *Theology* 84(701).
Preston, R. H., 1981b, 'Thirty-five Years Later, 1941–1976: William Temple's *Christianity and Social Order*', *Explorations in Theology* 9, London: SCM Press.
Preston, R. H., 1987, 'Church and Society: Do We Need Another William Temple?' in *The Future of Christian Ethics*, London: SCM Press.
Spencer, S., 2001, *William Temple: A Calling to Prophecy*, London: SPCK.
Tanner, K., 2005, *Economies of Grace*, Minneapolis, MN: Fortress Press.
Temple, W., 1942, *Christianity and Social Order*, London: Penguin.

5

Christian Social Ethics and Political Economy

CARL-HENRIC GRENHOLM

Political economy is the study of the interaction between politics and economics. The main problem of political economy has always been how to regard the role of the state and the government in relation to production and mechanisms for resource allocation. Researchers within this field have often been involved in a critical examination of capitalism, socialism and various types of market economy. Is a capitalist market economy the best way to increase human wealth, or should we prefer a society with a socialist planned economy?

An important task for political economy today is to give a critical analysis of global capitalism and the market economy. We are living in a world characterized by economic globalization. It involves the growth of transnational companies, free world trade and a global financial market. The importance of the global market economy has increased and worldwide economic relations have intensified. In an integrated capitalist economy, national governments are gradually losing influence in economic affairs, and the financial markets operate independently of national borders. How should we evaluate this global capitalist economy?

Research within political economy has often been involved in an interdisciplinary dialogue with moral philosophy and political philosophy. One reason for this is that a critical examination of various economic systems implies serious ethical issues concerning our conceptions of justice, freedom and political participation. This means that political economy is also of great interest in Christian social ethics. But what is the outcome of this interest? What perspectives can ethical reflection within the Christian tradition offer for an examination of market economics and alternative economic systems? The purpose of this chapter is to investigate one important contribution of Christian social ethics to political economy as a critical discourse on global capitalism. My analysis will focus upon John Atherton's efforts to reformulate the tradition of Christian political economy.

Within British Christian social ethics there is a long tradition of dialogue with political economy and critical engagement with capitalism. In *Religion and the Rise of Capitalism* (1926), R. H. Tawney demonstrated the link between the rise of capitalism and the emergence of Protestantism. V. A. Demant published later *Religion and the Decline of Capitalism* (1952), which almost announced the emerging end of capitalism due to its intrinsic contradictions. A different perspective was elaborated by Ronald Preston, in his two volumes, *Religion and the Persistence of Capitalism* (1979) and *Religion and the Ambiguities of Capitalism* (1991). Preston acknowledged the continuing significance of market economy, even if he agreed that capitalism has some weaknesses and needs to be reformed (Atherton, 2007, pp. 233f.).

In his research, John Atherton has made most important contributions to this tradition of dialogue between Christian social ethics and political economy. In *Christianity and the Market* (1992) he gave a critical analysis of different Christian responses to market economy and argued that the market is the least harmful alternative, even if it has some serious limitations. In his later *Marginalization* (2003) he argued that a reformulation of Christian political economy is necessary in order to deal with marginalization processes. Finally, in *Transfiguring Capitalism* (2008) he developed a broader and more critical perspective on global capitalism, and he also proposed a distinctively Christian contribution to political economy. His main objective was to demonstrate that religion has an important role in promoting global change and transcending capitalism.

In this chapter I will analyse these three publications by John Atherton in order to clarify his understanding of Christian social ethics and its contribution to political economy. My thesis is that Atherton in these publications takes at least two different perspectives in his critical examination of global capitalism and the market economy. They are related to various approaches to methodological issues in Christian social ethics. In his later research he argues that there is a distinctively Christian contribution to social ethics, and this position is related to a sharp critique of transnational capitalism.

My intention in this chapter is also to evaluate Atherton's efforts to reformulate the tradition of Christian political economy. I agree with him that in order to give a theological contribution to critical economic reflection it is necessary to consider what kind of Christian social ethics we prefer. Different methodological positions are related to various views concerning the theological foundations of ethical reflection. My argument is in favour of Atherton's later opinion that there are at least some distinctively Christian contributions to ethical reflection.

In order to reformulate Christian political economy it is necessary to consider the relationship between ethics and economics. From Atherton's research we can learn that a major Christian contribution to economics is that justice is a primary moral ideal. In my view a strong argument in favour of this ideal is the principle of human dignity. This means that justice is not only an equal distribution of social goods but also liberation from oppression and marginalization, which implies a revision of existing power structures. From this perspective a radical critique of the global market economy is urgent.

A Christian response to market economy

John Atherton published his *Christianity and the Market* in 1992, three years after communism was rejected in Eastern Europe. In this particular context the purpose of his study was to construct an adequate Christian response to market economies. Atherton gave a clarifying analysis of market economies in a changing world, and he argued that the market economy manifests itself in a number of forms. One of his main interests in this study was to examine the socializing of the market economy as a rejection of raw laissez-faire capitalism. From this perspective he gave a critical analysis of three different Christian responses (Atherton, 1992, pp. 64f.).

The first one is the *conservative* response to the market economy. This is a Christian neo-conservatism with a fundamental commitment to the market system as an economic system. According to this position, the role of the state should be limited in the economic sphere, and the extension of the power of the state is regarded as detrimental to liberty and the efficient functioning of the market. Communism and socialism are rejected as forms of idolatry, and religious values are regarded to be important in resourcing democracy and the market. One proponent for this position is the British economist Brian Griffiths, who was a member of the Conservative Party and an adviser to Margaret Thatcher. As a lay theologian he argued that there is a clear Christian moral case for the market economy (Atherton, 1992, pp. 87f., 90f.).

The second position is the *radical* response to the market economy. It rejects capitalism and market economy, primarily due to their social consequences. In order to promote social justice and liberation from oppression, the state should take a strong role in the economic sphere, and we should strive for both political and economic democracy. Theologians taking this position argue in favour of a Christian socialism, which sometimes is influenced by a Marxist analysis of capitalism. One proponent for this position is the German theologian Ulrich Duchrow, who argues that the rejection of the global market economy is a matter of faith itself, a *status confessionis*. Christian support of market economy is a heresy, since it is a support of oppression in the Third World (Atherton, 1992, pp. 120f., 124f.)

The third perspective on market economy is the *liberal* response. It accepts the market economy, but it is also aware of its limitations and social consequences. This position values social and political goals, and it gives priority to democracy. The market is subordinated to political life, which means that the response is committed to mixed economies, with a major role for the state as an overall planner and limited producer, undergirded by a strong welfare state. This mainstream liberalism is related to Christian realism in the tradition of Reinhold Niebuhr. Proponents of the response are Ronald Preston and J. Philip Wogaman, who have developed their social ethical approach in a close dialogue with contemporary economics (Atherton, 1992, pp. 159f., 162f., 164f., 172f.).

What, then, is Atherton's position? When he started this project he was part of the mainstream liberal tradition, and his approach to social ethics was similar to that of Reinhold Niebuhr and Ronald Preston. His intention was to reformulate Christian realism with its implications for economics and the market. However, he came to the conclusion that this position was not feasible. Instead, he became convinced that we should listen and learn from all three responses. This means that we should engage in an open interaction between market economy and its challenges (Atherton, 1992, pp. 200f.).

From the conservative response we should learn that the market is the best available economy and the most effective means for allocating resources. Atherton argues that we should build a more realistic appraisal of the market and acknowledge the autonomous nature of economic mechanisms (1992, pp. 208f., 215f.). At the same time we should also learn from the radical response that there are great challenges to the market economy in the contemporary context. One major challenge is poverty, in advanced economies as well as in the Third World, but there are also severe environmental issues and the pressure for participation in decision-making. Underlying these challenges is a deep concern for human dignity and the whole created order (1992, pp. 235–41).

Atherton still agrees with the liberal response that the market economy can be reformed into democratic social market capitalism with a mixed economy and a welfare state in which politics have priority over economics. However, his thesis is that the dynamic for Christian social ethics should be the interaction between the market economy and its challenges. Understanding this relationship presupposes recognition of the relative autonomy of market economy as the least harmful economic system. At the same time it presupposes that we take the challenges seriously, and admit that adequate living cannot be developed from the basis of the market economy alone (1992, pp. 198f., 264f.).

One conclusion in Atherton's study of *Christianity and the Market* is that we have to accept the strange death of economic socialism. As a radical protest against the evils of capitalism, socialism has been important, and it displays adequate characteristics of all the great challenges to market economy. However, neither centrally planned economies nor democratic socialism are feasible options as economic systems today. What we need are continuing reforms of the social market economy, but socialism as a human project no longer exists as a realistic radical way for operating modern economies (1992, p. 235). Atherton writes:

> Affirming the market as the best available economy in the contemporary context is now an essential part of Christian social witness. To do so is to reject the economic determinism of both libertarian and Marxist ideologies. It is to face up to economic necessities, and to work for purposeful change in relation to these constraints. (Atherton, 1992, p. 213)

On marginalization and global capitalism

In his later publications, John Atherton developed his research on Christian contributions to political economy, adopting a more critical approach to the contemporary economic order. His main focus was now on the new capitalism, with a global market economy, transnational corporations and a growing financial market. In his study *Marginalization*, he examined the marginalization processes that are results of this global capitalism. These processes are related to poverty and the grave inequalities in the world between poor and rich. Marginalization has a relational character, like deprivation, and it means that the poor are separated from the ability to participate in society (Atherton, 2003, pp. 60f.).

In order to give a critical examination of marginalization, we need a theory of global justice. Atherton was, to a large extent, influenced by Amartya Sen and his capability approach, according to which justice means more than a fair distribution of resources. Justice means that every human should have the freedom and capability to be oneself and to pursue one's own self-chosen purposes. Another theory of justice that Atherton referred to is the theory of Iris Marion Young, according to which justice means freedom from oppression and domination. From this perspective marginalization is a major form of structural injustice (Atherton, 2003, pp. 65–72).

What, then, would be the contribution of Christian social ethics to a critique of marginalization processes in global capitalism? In this study, Atherton argues that theology should be a performative discipline. This means that Christian social ethics should be developed in a process of interaction between praxis and theological reflection. It should be related to a praxis of solidarity with the marginalized, and it should take preference for the poor and oppressed. From this perspective it would be possible to develop a public theology that is broadly accessible even in a secularized society (2003, pp. 108–25).

Above all, Atherton argues that theology should contribute to normative social theory as Christian political economy. There are severe shortcomings of radical orthodoxy and liberation theology, he argues, since they reject any dialogue with contemporary economics. Instead we should reformulate the tradition of Christian political economy, where there is a clear linkage between economics, politics and Christianity (2003, p. 146).

According to Atherton, a reformulation of Christian political economy means, first of all, identifying the connection between ethics and economics. From Amartya Sen we learn that a dialogue between ethics and economics is necessary. Second, an important task for Christian political economy would be to find ways of measuring marginalization and strategies to reduce it. Third, performative theology should identify ways in which Christianity and other faith traditions can express religious insights for enlarging the economic project. There are distinctive Christian contributions to economic reflection, and at the same time we should learn from mainstream Christian social thought that a constructive relationship and a mutual dialogue is necessary between Christian social ethics and economics (2003, pp. 148f.).

This programme for Christian political economy is further developed by Atherton in his impressive study *Transfiguring Capitalism*. The intention of this study was to contribute to the debate within British social ethics over the relationship between religion and capitalism. However, it expanded to be an examination of the contributions of religion to global change and the necessary maintenance of our world. As such, it still has a focus on political economy and its relationship to Christian social ethics (Atherton, 2008, pp. 1, 5).

In his critical examination of capitalism, Atherton argues that this system today should be understood in a global context. Economic globalization means increased trade and export, the growth of transnational corporations and a global financial market. It is also related to political globalization, which means that nation states are intersecting internationally to manage trade and finance. At the same time we have seen the rise of the American empire. This is a new global empire of capitalism, which represents dominance in the economic realm, but which is also reinforced by power in the military and political fields (2008, pp. 25f., 56f.).

In order to give a theological contribution to political economy and a critical perspective on global capitalism, Atherton maintains that it is necessary to elaborate a clear position within Christian social ethics. This position includes a theological anthropology and a vision of human flourishing. According to a Christian view of humans, personal agency is understood as foundationally relational, which means that agency is formed as character through participation in communities. It also includes personalist ethics and an image of the common good. Since we always are living in relationship to others, we should give priority to our common good and not to individual preferences. This implies a critique of the atomistic individualism that is presupposed in a neo-liberal understanding of the market economy (Atherton, 2008, pp. 217–22).

According to Atherton, Christian social ethics should be a performative discipline that is involved in both theory and practice. It should be the result of collaborative work, which is evident from the ecumenical contributions to social ethical reflection. Today it is also necessary to develop interfaith collaboration in this field, taking into account various religious perspectives on the environment, the global economy and global ethics (2008, pp. 8f., 229f.).

Christian social ethics has developed a variety of traditions and different methodological approaches. In *Transfiguring Capitalism*, Atherton proposes a typology for Christian social ethics with two clusters, representing two ends of a continuum. The first one is the idea of an overlapping consensus, according to which there is a common morality that is shared by various faiths and secular world views. The second one is the idea that Christian ethics has a content that is distinctively different from mainstream convictions. There is also a third, hybrid type, representing the continuing interaction of the two ends of the spectrum (2008, pp. 247f.).

What, then, is the contribution of Christian social ethics to political economy? First of all, Atherton argues that it is necessary to understand the importance of ethics within economic theory. There are ethical dimensions of economics, which should be acknowledged by the neo-classical paradigm as well. Second, he argues that there is a distinctively religious contribution to the ethical reflection on global economy. This contribution is the idea of faithful economics (Atherton, 2003, pp. 262f.).

In order to clarify this distinctively Christian pursuit, Atherton argues that we should strive for what Kathryn Tanner has called 'an economy of grace'. God's grace is offered free to all, not biased to the rich and powerful; it is characterized by unconditional and universal giving, and it is related to a principle of non-competition in a community of mutual benefit. In a similar way, the global economy should be characterized by economic independence, unconditional giving and a principle of non-competitiveness and mutually beneficial spirals. We should strive for an egalitarian society with a welfare policy and an inclination to co-operation (Atherton, 2008, pp. 269f., 275f., 279f.).

Faithful economics is thus 'an economy of grace', and its role, according to Atherton, is to develop ways to achieve the objective of transcending capitalism. He argues that the story of the transfiguration, when Jesus on the mountain was declared to be the Son of God, illustrates what this distinctive religious contribution can mean for the transformation of the global economy. An economy of grace should be our perspective in a critical engagement with global capitalism, when we acknowledge its achievements and, at the same time, move beyond it because of its fundamental contradictions. The objective should be to transcend capitalism and to develop an alternative faith-based understanding of ethics and economics (Atherton, 2008, pp. 283f.).

Reason and revelation in Christian social ethics

What are the contributions of Christian social ethics to political economy as a critical discourse on global capitalism? We have seen that there are different responses to market economy among contemporary theologians. As Atherton has shown, they are related to quite different interpretations of Christian social ethics. Within theological social thought there are a variety of methodological approaches and various understandings of the relationship between the content of Christian ethics and ethical models in other traditions. They are also related to different views concerning the theological foundations of ethical reflection.

Interestingly enough, John Atherton seems to revise his approach to these methodological issues in his later research. His social ethical theory is to a large extent influenced by the tradition of Christian realism as developed by Reinhold Niebuhr, Ronald Preston and J. Philip Wogaman. Atherton agrees with these theologians that the content of Christian social ethics coincides with ethical models in other world views, and that it is based on ordinary rational considerations and human experiences. This means that there is an overlapping consensus concerning moral conceptions in a pluralistic society (Wogaman, 1988, pp. 89f.).

This is the theological position that Atherton defends in *Christianity and the Market*. He also argues that we should take a contextual approach to economic ethics. When making an evaluation of the market economy, we should not refer to universal moral principles. Instead, we should make a rational judgement about what is the most adequate and least harmful economic system in our present context. We should accept the relative autonomy of economics and resist the temptation to subordinate economic realities to Christian values. In contrast, we should recognize the legitimate contribution of economics to the formation of Christian social thought (Atherton, 1992, pp. 278f.).

In this study, Atherton's conclusion is that there is no distinctively Christian contribution to social ethics. Instead, we should accept that Christian social thought is formed in the contemporary context and needs to learn from the secular realities of life. Atherton writes:

> The result is that we can be liberated from the impulsive desire to produce the distinctively Christian, when addressing such matters as the contemporary economy. We can reject with confidence those pre-modern attempts to impose, however decisively or subtly, religious understandings on secular life. (Atherton, 1992, p. 279)

As we have seen, Atherton's approach to Christian social ethics seems to be quite the opposite in *Transfiguring Capitalism*. In this study he argues that there is a distinctively Christian contribution to political economy, which he calls faithful economics. He also defends an economy of grace as a unique Christian perspective on global capitalism. From this perspective we should strive for unconditional and universal giving and non-competition in a community of mutual benefit. Here it is quite obvious that there is a unique content in Christian social ethics (Atherton, 2003, pp. 258f., 266f.).

How should we understand this contradiction in Atherton's methodological approach? It would be helpful to reflect upon his proposal for a typology of Christian social ethics. This proposal is mentioned already in *Through the Eye of a Needle* (2007), where he makes a distinction between three methodological approaches. The first one is the mainstream liberal tradition, which emphasizes the role of reason in social ethics and argues that there is an overlapping consensus with some common moral convictions in a pluralistic society. The second one is a post-liberal or radical Christian position which takes Scripture and tradition much more seriously and emphasizes that there are convictions in Christian ethics that are distinctively different from the mainstream. The third position is a hybrid type, which takes Christian tradition and its particular contributions seriously and at the same time strives for collaboration with other traditions and is prepared to learn from a wide variety of models (Atherton, 2007, pp. 230f., 259).

It is important to note that these three approaches are related to different positions on the theological justification of moral convictions. The first position can be called an *identity theory*, which maintains that the content of Christian social ethics is in no way different from ethical models in other traditions. This theory presupposes that human reason is sufficient for understanding what is good and right. The divine revelation in Christ is not a prerequisite for moral insight. According to this position, ethics is primarily based upon the doctrine of creation. This is the natural law theory in Catholic theology, and it is also the position of Lutheran social thought with its theory of the two kingdoms (Grenholm, 2003, pp. 257f., 261f.).

The second position can be called a *contrast theory*, which maintains that Christian social ethics has a content that is unique and distinctively different from ethical models within liberalism and alternative traditions. This theory presupposes that moral conceptions are developed within various traditions and social contexts. It also presupposes that all arguments that can be given to justify moral judgements are ultimately based upon the revelation in Christ. Our character as moral agents and our moral convictions are formed by our membership in a Christian church where we listen to stories about Jesus. According to this position, Christology and eschatology are important as theological foundations for ethical reflection. This is the new traditionalism as developed by Stanley Hauerwas and John Milbank (Hauerwas, 1986, pp. 36f., 51f., 89f.; see also Grenholm, 2003, pp. 113f.).

There are, in my opinion, convincing arguments against both of these approaches. One objection to the first is that it presupposes a view of human beings which is too optimistic. Human sin, not least as it appears in structural injustices, means that we sometimes have limited moral insight, and therefore we need the guidance of divine revelation in ethics. Another objection is that the identity theory does not contain resources for a critical perspective on existing political and economic structures. It is a position that tends to be legitimizing, in the sense that it supports the prevailing society and the authorities in power.

A strong argument against the contrast theory is that it presupposes a view of human beings that is too pessimistic. As created in the image of God, humans are rational beings with a capacity to develop at least partial moral insight through rational consideration. Another objection is that this position is difficult to combine with a mutual critique of and a rational dialogue on social ethical issues in a pluralistic society. With this approach, Christian social ethics develops a rather exclusive character with limited relevance. It is a rather sectarian position, which means that the Church withdraws from society and develops its own moral standards (Grenholm, 2003, pp. 261f.).

I prefer a third position, then, according to which there are some moral convictions that Christian ethics shares with other traditions, while there also is a distinctively Christian contribution to ethics. This is what I call a *combination theory*. It is related to the idea that ethics is based upon both reason and revelation, which means that some arguments that justify moral conceptions are based upon human experiences and rational considerations, while others are based upon the revelation in Christ. From this perspective Christian social ethics is based not only upon the doctrine of creation but also on Christology and eschatology.

In his critique of mainstream liberalism and new traditionalism, Jeffrey Stout has argued that there are two criteria that should be fulfilled by a reasonable interpretation of Christian social ethics. First, it should have its own identity and thereby contain recourses to take a critical position in its relationship to the prevailing society. Second, it should be open for a rational and critical dialogue on moral issues with other traditions. In my opinion, a combination theory would fulfil both of these criteria (Stout, 2004, pp. 294f.).

It is possible to interpret John Atherton's position in *Christianity and the Market* as an identity theory, according to which there is no distinctively Christian contribution to ethics. In his later research, particularly in *Transfiguring Capitalism*, he seems to be defending what I have called a combination theory. He still believes that there are some moral principles and values that are common in a pluralistic society, but he also argues that there is a unique content in Christian social ethics.

It is interesting to note that this is also the position that Atherton defended in his early publications. In *Faith in the Nation* (1988), he argued that there are some fundamental values, such as community, freedom and equality, which are accepted both in Christian social ethics and by other ethical models. This also means that social ethics is at least partly based upon common human experiences and considerations. At the same time, Atherton holds that there are specifically Christian reasons for some moral convictions, such as the principle of equal human dignity. Christology and eschatology give a distinctively Christian contribution to ethical reflection (Atherton, 1988, pp. 32f., 34f., 39f.; for an analysis of this position, see Grenholm, 1993, pp. 140f., 215f.).

Ethical impact on economic theory and practice

In his impressive research programme on religion and global change, John Atherton regarded it to be the main task to reformulate the tradition of Christian political economy. In order to do that it was necessary to reflect upon various methodological approaches to Christian social ethics. However, according to Atherton, an equally important task was that of identifying and enlarging the connection between economics and ethics. Even if the neo-classical tradition often regards economics to be a value-free science, it is urgent to recognize that there are ethical dimensions both in economic theory and practice. Therefore, we need to bring economics closer to ethics (Atherton, 2003, pp. 146f.; 2008, pp. 261f.).

As Amartya Sen has shown, there are two traditions within economics. One is 'the engineering approach', in which technical issues are focused upon. Human behaviour is modelled in very crude and simple terms, and ethical considerations are typically neglected. Rationality in economic life is often identified with the maximization of self-interest. The other tradition is 'the ethics-related tradition', which is represented by, among others, Adam Smith and John Maynard Keynes. It is often utilitarian and conceives the goal of economic life as synonymous with the good for others. As economic actors, human persons are considered not only self-interested but also concerned for others (Sen, 1992, pp. 2f., 15f., 22f.).

Sen's ambition is to contribute to a revival of the 'ethics-related tradition'. This ambition is shared by Atherton, who argues that an important task of Christian social ethics is to reconnect ethics and economics. As a researcher closely affiliated to the theological faculty at Uppsala University, he gave important contributions to a research project called 'Ethical Reflections in Economic Theory and Practice'. The purpose of this project was to study the intersections between economic and ethical discourses, with a focus on the role of ethical considerations in both economic theory and practice.

A main result of this project was the conclusion that economic analysis is not free from ethical considerations, and that the ethical approach that is presupposed in economic theory most often is a kind of utilitarianism. Welfare economics has been related to a classical utilitarianism, according to which welfare or pleasure is the intrinsic value. More important in neo-classical economics today seems to be a kind of preference utilitarianism. A decision on a market is regarded to be better than another decision if the consequences are more preference satisfaction for the individual. This seems to be the idea behind Pareto optimality as the criterion of economic efficiency (Granqvist, 2000, p. 12).

This means that there are ethical assumptions in mainstream economic theory. From the perspective of Christian social ethics these assumptions should be critically evaluated. The kind of utilitarianism that is presupposed in economic theory can be criticized in many ways. A major objection is that it does not pay attention to the problem of distribution of social values. Preference utilitarianism is typically not combined with any theory of justice, and reflection on justice is missing in mainstream economics. From an economic point of view, efficiency can be obtained even if some persons live in extreme misery and others are rolling in luxury (Sen, 1992, pp. 32f.).

According to Atherton, a primary objective for the Christian engagement with economics is poverty reduction. The persistence of absolute poverty is a scandal, and therefore government has a major role in reducing those increasing inequalities that obstruct poverty-reduction strategies. From this perspective a major Christian contribution to ethical economics would be to argue that justice is a primary moral ideal. In his later work, Atherton often referred to Richard Layard's research on happiness in order to argue that we should strive for a reduction of the inequalities between rich and poor. This is basically a utilitarian argument in favour of justice – a fair distribution of wealth would promote the happiness of both those who are poor and the well-off. I would argue that an even stronger argument in favour of justice is the principle of human dignity, according to which we should treat all human beings with equal concern and respect (Atherton, 2007, pp. 249f.).

An obvious theological argument in favour of this principle of human dignity is the conviction that all human beings are created in the image of God. However, this principle can also be supported from a christological perspective. The message about God's love in Christ is related to an idea of equality, according to which all humans have an equal worth before God independent of their merits. Justification by grace alone means that all humans are loved by God independent of their race, gender, social position and moral value. This trust in God's love implies a principle of human dignity that includes an ideal of equal concern and respect.

From this perspective it would be reasonable to defend an egalitarian conception of justice, according to which justice means an equal distribution of social goods. As Amartya Sen has shown, there are different opinions among political philosophers concerning what object should be equally distributed. His own proposal is that justice should be understood as an equal distribution of capabilities, which means that humans should have freedom to choose the lives they have reason to value. This capabilities approach means a departure from concentrating on the means of living to the actual opportunities of living (Sen, 2010, pp. 231ff.).

This egalitarian theory of justice seems to be reasonable from the perspective of a Christian conception of human dignity. However, I would argue that justice means more than an equal distribution of social goods and capabilities. As we can learn from liberation theology and Christian feminist ethics, justice can be understood as liberation from oppression. It is part of God's liberation of those humans who are oppressed, marginalized and poor. This means that an adequate conception of justice should be based upon the narratives of those who have experiences of oppression: women, people of colour and persons suffering from poverty and exploitation. From the perspective of the oppressed we can learn what justice means (Lebacqz, 1987, pp. 35, 107, 148f.).

The idea that justice is liberation from oppression is developed in a most fruitful way by Iris Marion Young. She argues that justice refers not only to a distribution of social goods but also to the institutional conditions necessary for the realization of a good life. From this perspective justice means liberation from oppression and domination. There are five forms of oppression that describe what injustice means: exploitation, marginalization, powerlessness, cultural imperialism and violence. According to Young, oppression has a structural and systematic character, which implies that justice presupposes a fundamental change of prevailing institutions. Justice cannot be reduced to a distribution of capabilities, since this would mean ignoring the social structures that determine distributive patterns (Young, 1990, pp. 15f., 38f., 48f.).

From the perspective of a Christian conception of human dignity it would be plausible to argue that justice means both an equal distribution of social goods and liberation from oppression. A main contribution of Christian social ethics to political economy would be to argue that this understanding of justice should be regarded as a primary moral principle both in economic theory and in economic practice. This means that justice as liberation from oppression is a challenge not only to neo-classical economics but also to global capitalism. It is interesting to note that this is a position that is also defended by Atherton in his later research. Both in *Marginalization* and in *Transfiguring Capitalism* he often refers not only to the capabilities approach of Sen but also to the theory of justice developed by Young. These understandings of justice gave him a critical perspective on economic globalization and contemporary transnational capitalism.

Conclusion

In this chapter I have given a critical analysis of John Atherton's contribution to the dialogue between Christian social ethics and political economy. I have also given my own perspective on the problem concerning the contributions of Christian ethical reflection to a critical examination of the contemporary economic order. My thesis is that different responses to market economy and global capitalism are related to quite different approaches to methodological issues within Christian social ethics. These various responses are also related to different interpretations of justice as an ethical impact on economic theory and practice.

It has been demonstrated that Atherton himself takes at least two different approaches in his effort to reformulate the tradition of Christian political economy. In *Christianity and the Market* he argues that the market economy is the least harmful system in the contemporary context. This position is related to an approach to social ethics according to which economic realities should not be subordinated to any Christian values, and there is no distinctively Christian contribution to social ethics.

Poverty is regarded as a challenge to market economy, but in this study Atherton does not refer to any philosophical theory of justice.

In his later research, Atherton takes a different approach in his critical examination of global capitalism. In *Transfiguring Capitalism* he argues that the idea of faithful economics is a distinctively religious contribution to the ethical reflection on political economy. We should strive for 'an economy of grace' as a way to achieve the objective of transcending capitalism. This position is related to what I call a 'combination theory', according to which ethics is based upon both reason and revelation, and there are some distinctively Christian contributions to ethics. In his later research, Atherton also refers to theories according to which justice means not only an equal distribution of capabilities but also liberation from oppression. These theories gave him a critical perspective on contemporary transnational capitalism.

How should we evaluate this development in Atherton's research on Christian political economy? What can we learn from his reflections on economics and Christian social ethics? My conclusion is that it would be fruitful to endorse and further develop the position that Atherton takes in his later research. In *Transfiguring Capitalism* it is obvious that religion can give a unique perspective on global capitalism and still be involved in a rational dialogue with various philosophical positions. Such a combination theory makes possible a radical critique of the global market economy. This is a position that I find more reasonable than what I have called an identity theory and a contrast theory.

If we accept a combination theory, Christian social ethics can promote a dialogue with other traditions and, at the same time, from a christological perspective, deliver a sharp critique of prevailing economic structures. Such a theory should also be related to an interpretation of justice that takes human dignity and the experiences of the oppressed seriously. If we accept that justice is liberation from oppression, we can see that justice presupposes a fundamental revision of existing power structures in the global political and economic order. From this perspective, Christian social ethics can challenge contemporary global capitalism, which is characterized by an expanding transnational financial market and rather weak political institutions. The task of Christian social ethics is not to prescribe what would be the best economic system, but to deliver a sharp critique of the present political and economic order.

References

Atherton, J. R., 1992, *Christianity and the Market: Christian Social Thought for Our Times*, London: SPCK.
Atherton, J. R., 1988, *Faith in the Nation: A Christian Vision for Britain*, London: SPCK.
Atherton, J. R., 2003, *Marginalization*, London: SCM Press.
Atherton, J. R., 2007, 'Emerging Directions for Christian Social Ethics and Political Economy', in J. R. Atherton and Hannah Skinner (eds), *Through the Eye of a Needle*, Peterborough: Epworth Press.
Atherton, J. R., 2008, *Transfiguring Capitalism: An Enquiry into Religion and Global Change*, London: SCM Press.
Demant, V. A., 1952, *Religion and the Decline of Capitalism*, vol. 9, London: Faber & Faber.
Granqvist, R., 2000, 'Efficiency for Rational Fools?', in Carl-Henric Grenholm and Gert Helgesson (eds), *Efficiency, Justice, and Stability: Ethical Perspectives in Economic Analysis and Practice*, Uppsala: Uppsala University Press.
Grenholm, Carl-Henric, 1993, *Protestant Work Ethics: A Study of Work Ethical Theories in Contemporary Protestant Theology*, Uppsala: Acta Universitatis Upsaliensis.
Grenholm, Carl-Henric, 2003, *Bortom humanismen: En studie i kristen etik*, Stockholm: Verbum.
Hauerwas, Stanley, 1986, *A Community of Character: Toward a Constructive Christian Social Ethic*, Notre Dame: University of Notre Dame Press.
Lebacqz, Karen, 1987, *Justice in an Unjust World*, Minneapolis, MN: Augsburg.
Preston, Ronald H., 1979, *Religion and the Persistence of Capitalism*, London: SCM Press.
Preston, Ronald H., 1991, *Religion and the Ambiguities of Capitalism*, London: SCM Press.
Sen, Amartya, 1992, *On Ethics and Economics*, Oxford: Blackwell.
Sen, Amartya, 2010, *The Idea of Justice*, London: Penguin.
Stout, Jeffrey, 2004, *Democracy and Tradition*, Princeton, NJ: Princeton University Press.
Tawney, R. H., 1926, *Religion and the Rise of Capitalism*, vol. 23, Piscataway, NJ: Transaction Publishers.
Wogaman, J. P., 1988, *Christian Perspectives on Politics*, London: SCM Press.
Young, I. M., 1990, *Justice and the Politics of Difference*, Princeton, NJ: Princeton University Press.

6

John Atherton: Industry, the City and the Age of Incarnation

MALCOLM BROWN

In 1968, having served in parishes in Aberdeen, Bury and Glasgow, John Atherton returned to north-west England as rector of St George's Church, Hulme, and as a member of the Greater Manchester Industrial Mission team (GMIM), then led by Brian Cordingley. It was a time of expansion for the team, and John was one of two new recruits. After a regional industrial mission gathering, Mike Atkinson, a veteran of Sheffield IM, observed to Cordingley that 'So-and-so is very clever, isn't he?' 'Aye,' replied Cordingley, 'and John Atherton's *bloody* clever!'[1]

John remained Manchester-based for the rest of his life and, although the Manchester Industrial Mission team predeceased him by some years, he not only supported it through good and bad times but continued to champion the practical engagement of the Church with people's working lives and with the economic forces shaping city and nation long after the IM model had run out of steam. More than this, as one of the few heavyweight theologians with practical experience of IM, and as one who accompanied the movement through a decade of 'consensus politics', on through the radical upheavals of Thatcherism into the new market monoculture of the 1990s and beyond, John's own intellectual journey represented a theological pathway through changing times that, in the end, neither the IM movement nor the wider Church chose to follow. John was clever enough to identify the trajectory of the churches' concerns well before the main trends were obvious, and clever enough to see that IM's attempt to hold together differing theological narratives and ecclesiologies would prove untenable in increasingly divided times. And, while he contributed, in *Public Theology for Changing Times* (2000), a developed theological typology that not only encapsulated his earlier writings but pointed a clear way forward, it came too late to serve an already declining movement that had given up on deep theological reflection in favour of keeping a low profile in an increasingly introspective Church.

John was fascinated by industry, not least with the role that the Manchester region played in the Industrial Revolution itself.[2] But, as that historical perspective indicates, his interest was less with the methods of, and relationships within, industry itself than with the way economics drove radical change across whole societies. It was this that drove his intellectual development and made him such a powerful contributor to church initiatives, notably *Faith in the City* (ACUPA, 1985). In this acute sense of history and change, he shared something of the perspective of the churches' early work with industry in Sheffield in the 1940s. This Sheffield experiment was the genesis of a movement that, at least from the 1950s to the 1980s, provided perhaps the deepest encounter the churches have ever had with industrial and economic life (Bagshaw, 1994; Clark, 1993). John's writings for the industrial mission movement, and his later thinking, give a framework for considering the contribution that IM made to the churches, especially the Church of England, and for understanding why it failed to make a lasting impact.

First, however, it may be helpful to sketch the origins and early thinking behind IM. Although several models of industrial mission developed more or less simultaneously, and continued to coexist, the movement's dominant narrative placed its origins in Sheffield and the powerful vision of its then Bishop, Leslie Hunter (see Hewitt, 1985). Hunter observed patterns of church life in his diocese and noted that, in common with most of the industrial conurbations of England, the Church touched the working-class majority of the population barely at all. He recruited Ted Wickham who, in the early war years had begun pastoral visiting on a chaplaincy model to an armaments factory, and sent him into the steelworks of Sheffield with carte blanche to see what happened. But Hunter's theological motivation demonstrated a considerable shift from the work Wickham had been doing to that which he was now charged to develop. The chaplaincy to the arms factory began because of the wartime introduction of seven-day shift patterns, and this encroachment on Sunday rest (and, of course, churchgoing) caused consternation among churchmen sufficient to prompt a plan to take the Church to the workers. But now, in Sheffield, Wickham was doing something rather different. The God of the middle-class churchgoer and the settled congregation was seen to be too small, too narrow and too feminized to speak to the condition of the workforces in the city's steelworks. The 'mission' element in Sheffield IM was mission to the Church, seeking to allow the world, which Christ inhabited through the presence of the Holy Spirit, to call God's people back to their true vocation. Soon, Wickham had built an ecumenical team of missioners around himself, interacting with the industrial life of the city at many levels although, as it turned out, impacting much less on the life of the Church in the diocese (Atkinson, 1985).

Hunter left Sheffield in 1962 and his successor was a bishop of the old school. Wickham had already moved on in 1959 to be Bishop of Middleton (as he put it, 'blackballed into the episcopacy'), and Michael Jackson was appointed in his place to lead the IM team.[3] But despite continuing Wickham's work for some years, Jackson experienced a personal theological crisis. In 1966, he published a lengthy article in *Theology* which repudiated the whole Hunter/Wickham experiment and reasserted a traditional ecclesiology in which the Church exemplified God's Kingdom and existed to draw the world to itself (Jackson, 1966). Wickham's 'secular theology', devoted to uncovering the presence of God in the mundane, was deemed heretical. In the ensuing conflicts between Jackson, his team and Sheffield IM's supporters, the Bishop took Jackson's side without qualification. IM did survive in Sheffield, going through many phases of structure, activity and rationale until its final demise in 2016. But the first lasting effect of the crisis was to create a diaspora as Sheffield-trained missioners migrated to other parts of the country and established comparable operations or inspired others to do so. The second major impact perhaps sowed the seeds of IM's eventual disintegration decades later in that, in reaction to the exercise of naked episcopal power (the Bishop even dismissed Free Church team members who were not under episcopal discipline) and the reassertion of a church-centred theology of mission, a climate of suspicion and rebellion developed against the institutional Church, its priorities and its leadership, which hindered future cooperation, severed IM from important trends in church life and, ultimately, offered no viable alternative ecclesiology.

For Wickham and his team, as for Hunter, the Church's captivity to middle-class values, oblivious to the economic foundations on which they depended, was an apostasy to be confronted. Instead of calling people out of a corrupt and corrupting world into a Church that stood as the simulacrum of the Kingdom of Heaven, Hunter and Wickham had delved into the lives of Sheffield's steelworkers in a bid to uncover the activity of the incarnate God who had always been present long before they arrived. Later, Mostyn Davies was to describe IM in terms of uncovering, in Wesley's phrase, the 'prevenient grace of God' (Davies, 1991). The realignment under Jackson in the 1960s reasserted the primacy of the Church and explicitly contrasted it with the fallenness of the world and its cultures.

So the struggles within IM are reflected in the huge theological shift that John mapped out in *Public Theology for Changing Times*, as what he called the Age of Atonement and Voluntarism (Atherton, 2000, pp. 66ff.) began to give way, in the early twentieth century, to an Age of Incarnation and the state. On this reading, Jackson's challenge to the

Hunter/Wickham model represented a throw-back to the late nineteenth century when the task of the Church was to call individuals out of a sinful and damned world and to use all their efforts to redeem their fellow men and women by offering a better way than the values that a newly urbanized culture could offer. The Age of Atonement saw God as apart from the world, apart from human society, and the Church as a kind of ark in which the faithful would be saved through the redeeming work of Christ on the cross.

In contrast, the Age of Incarnation which Atherton suggests dominated the Church of the twentieth century grew out of 'the arrival of great corporations and mass media, and of explosive population increases, accompanied by the struggle for democracy and labour movements' (2000, p. 75). Instead of regarding life on earth as a journey through a 'vale of tears to an eternal home', it was seen as a 'calling to transform God's world for the better' (2000, p. 79). If Christ had deigned to come among us, as one of us, who could say that the material world was not at least in the process of being hallowed by God? And so the task of the Church in an Age of Incarnation focused on the everyday as something beloved, something potentially sacramental, somewhere where we might expect to encounter the Holy Spirit. So, for example, on the basis of this incarnational theology the Church's national work on 'moral welfare' was transformed into 'social responsibility' (note the shift of emphasis from correcting sin in others to the duties of the disciple in the world).[4] By investing the everyday with a godliness that was not conferred by the Church but flowed from the love of God for the creation, human labour of hand or brain became a matter of interest rather than indifference. Hunter and Wickham's vision and practice epitomized precisely this Age of Incarnation.

Atherton's typology is not, of course, simplistically binary. As he notes, 'typologies are never tidy. There is always overlap between different ages and the regulatory principles of different ages always continue to exercise influence, even though no longer dominant' (2000, p. 68). That is evident in the history of IM. An incarnational theology was widely felt, within IM circles, to be at the theological cutting-edge, while Jackson's repudiation of it was an irrelevant throw-back. But, especially for those in the Church of England, the tension also reflected a fault line at the heart of Anglican theology, which continues, between world-affirming theology on the one hand and, on the other, a brand of evangelicalism in which the Age of Atonement has always dominated. And for all that IM made great efforts from early in its history to be an ecumenical movement, its underlying theologies remained shaped by Anglican assumptions, the majority of its personnel were Anglicans, and the divisions within Anglicanism were instrumental in introducing division into the IM movement.

However, IM received a significant boost in the mid-1980s – and John helped bring this about, although his purposes went much wider than sustaining IM. It grew out of urban disturbances in Brixton, Toxteth and elsewhere, in which a combination of poverty, racism and heavy-handed policing created a well of anger in the community that exploded in the face of provocations. The radical nature of Conservative Party policy from 1979 was not initially comprehended in 'middle England', and the Church was no exception to this general lack of insight. Just as, in the 1940s, Hunter had struggled with the gulf between the Church's strongholds and the experiences of working-class communities, so, 40 years on, the Church hierarchy took much convincing that urban riots were attributable to structural inequalities rather than just personal wickedness. Only an intervention by local clergy church people from the riot-torn areas persuaded the Archbishop of Canterbury, Robert Runcie, that not only the mission of the Church but government policies required urgent attention.

The result was an Archbishop's Commission on Urban Priority Areas (ACUPA). The Commission's report, compiled after numerous visits and hundreds of conversations in inner-city areas, was a model of careful research, plotting not only the social and economic conditions of the Urban Priority Areas (UPAs) but the state of church life in the cities. The title, *Faith in the City*, was a classic in an era when punning titles were in fashion – the Commission wanted to convey simultaneously that they had discovered the Christian faith active and present in UPAs, and that its members had faith in the communities of the inner cities. Of the main recommendations, 38 were addressed to the Church of England and only 23 to the government and nation. Understandably cautious about directly criticizing a democratically elected government, the report was nonetheless castigated by Conservatives who treated dissent as akin to treason. But most of all, it called for the Church to reorientate its priorities and stand for and alongside the communities that were bearing the brunt of the government's economic and social programmes.

The ACUPA project could have been designed to appeal to, and draw upon, John's interests and strengths. As a director of the William Temple Foundation, he ensured that the Foundation, through his own involvement, was among a small group of official resource bodies and advisors. And while it is not easy, in such a report, to spot an individual's fingerprints, it is interesting to reflect on where John's influence might have been most acute.

First, the focus on engaging with evidence from across the relevant disciplines is quintessentially Athertonian. It stems from his early engagement with Tawney and deepened through his close association with Ronald Preston. And this is very typical of a theological approach in an Age of Incarnation in which the study of the created order can lead to insights about the nature of God, salvation and so on, rather than all knowledge being moulded into a framework determined by doctrine.

Second, the clarity with which *Faith in the City* linked social conditions to economic policies was unusual in a church report at that time. True, after six years of market reforms and monetarism, the economic nature of the Thatcher governments' crusade could hardly be ignored – but John's presence behind the Commission helped keep the economic dimension in focus and ensured that a careful critique of economic ideas played a large part in the report's structure.

And, third, the report's emphasis on renewing and reforming the Church itself reflects John's simultaneous love for, and embeddedness within, Anglicanism, and his rigorous critiques of the Church of England's failures to live up to its vocation of serving all people and leavening national life.

But the main theological chapter of *Faith in the City* does not echo John's characteristic style at all – although its comments on 'intermediate action', which blend something like middle axioms with the kind of intermediate institutions promoted in the early twentieth century by Figgis (Figgis, 1914), cohere with some of John's interests while being expressed very differently. Its account of the Christian social tradition lacks John's characteristic historical breadth and insight. It has no mention of Temple or Tawney, let alone Maurice or Gore, all of whom figured large in John's own sense of the inherited tradition (Atherton, 1994). Read today, the theological chapter feels pedestrian and unremarkable. But it contained the trigger that drew sharp criticism from Tory supporters by introducing ideas derived from liberation theology, thus opening the door to the accusation that this was a Marxist report.

At the William Temple Foundation, on the Board for Social Responsibility and, most of all, in IM, John encountered many enthusiasts for liberation theology. Politically, he had considerable sympathy for its commitments and (in its Latin American modes) rootedness (Atherton, 1994, Part II). But he never embraced it for a British context and, if we assume that his typology around atonement and incarnation – developed further, as we shall see, to illuminate a coming Age of Partnership and Reconciliation – was developing in his mind by the mid-1980s, we can understand why.

Not surprisingly, the end of consensus politics and the sudden impacts of radical market ideology exposed divisions within IM in ways that even the local crisis in Sheffield had not. *Faith in the City* ensured that similar tensions ran through the Church as a whole. An essentially ameliorative approach to social change exemplified in South London IM challenged, and was challenged by, the belief that the end of political and economic consensus required a clear choice between two sides – a choice on behalf of the poor, the exploited and the vulnerable. The vocabulary of liberation theology was on hand at just the right moment to encourage and inform the next phase of the movement. While many retained the basic activity of factory visiting (whether, like Wickham, to discover God at work or, as in South London, to offer helpful ethical insight – and the two were not wholly incompatible), other practitioners found that the workplace was no longer a viable gateway for addressing issues like unemployment, poverty and injustice and so spent their time building alliances for change across the cities or regions where they worked (for example, Eagle, 1984a; 1984b). Indeed, with a newly bullish approach among management in some industries, some missioners found themselves unilaterally barred from visiting anyway. Although many long-lasting personal friendships transcended the theological divisions, a serious political gap had opened, which needed to be understood as the industrial and economic context shifted rapidly into forms that none of the existing models of IM really addressed.

Through the years of turbulence from 1979, IM's main site of serious reflection was the Theology Development Group, a floating membership of practitioners from around the country who met regularly to discuss issues and share papers, many of which were published by the William Temple Foundation under John's oversight (IMA TDG, 1983; 1984). His was much the most theologically informed voice in the discussions, digging beneath the then-fashionable approach to narrative theology, which rarely got behind the story to the theology, and challenging other members to portray their work on a much larger intellectual canvas.

In the Age of Incarnation, the point of discipleship is to be attentive to the presence of the Holy Spirit in the ordinary fabric of time and place. But there are dangers in that approach if it focuses primarily on the local and neglects the global economic and political contexts that shape local realities. As John noted in an IMA TDG paper of the early 1980s:

> I see (a) great need to rewrite the justification, theory and practice of factory visiting. We cannot simply carry on with the splendid Sheffield model in the light of [the] great changes occurring in Industrial Mission and in British society. If we do not do this, then I fear for Industrial Mission, and the possibly intolerable tensions which might arise between those involved in factory work, and those involved in issues like race and South Africa whose origins and *raison d'être* may well lie outside factories. (Atherton, 1983, p. 106)

Of course, factories as a 'central determining reality', as industrial missioners used to say, did not long survive that essay. Apartheid ended in South Africa some years later, but equivalent global and local injustices and oppressions continued – and continued to be ignored or glossed over in both national and church life. As John noted, it was the rationale for the workplace-based mode of IM that needed careful rethinking as people's experience of work fragmented (zero-hours contracts started appearing in the late-1980s) and technology rendered invisible much of the physical activity that had been the entry point for IM's engagement with people at their work.

Sadly, that rethinking never really happened. The sense of IM as mission to the Church, calling the Church out of its torpor through engagement with everyday working life, slid into a kind of extension of parish visiting applied to workplaces, apparently unaware that the model of the 'visiting parson' itself lacked much theological or even pragmatic rationale (Burgess, 2000). Even the more evangelistic framework that had been the rationale behind IM in South London faded. The catchword of the day, in IM and among those most passionately inspired by *Faith in the City*, was 'prophetic'. IM's history had begun with a prophetic ministry to the Church: now, along with UPA activists and other sector ministries, the focus turned to prophetic action and words directed to a government seen as waging class war against the poor. Often, the objective of prophecy was, tacitly, about both at once. By neglecting to think through and express this tension, an ecclesiological gap emerged. Following *Faith in the City*, the Church of England was frequently being described as the unofficial opposition to Thatcherism (Clark, 1993; Filby, 2015). But for practitioners in IM and beyond, that did not reconcile them to the institutional Church of sceptical or unreliable bishops and introspective parochialism.

John's roots in IM's story were among the influences that prevented his typology from becoming historically simplistic. He discerned the broad sweep in the Church's history that allowed him to speak of an Age of Atonement giving way to an Age of Incarnation, but IM's experiences showed him that this remained a live struggle between competing doctrinal emphases – one in which each offered a corrective to the other, and in which there would always be hybrid models. As he never regarded the two ages as the only alternatives, he was constantly looking forward to an age that would take their place, which he identified as the Age of Partnership and Reconciliation (Atherton, 2000, pp. 82ff.). He described this as an age in which we must find 'ways of holding together often profound differences for our own self-sufficiency and for future living on earth' (2000, p. 84). He saw change happening at such a pace, and across so many aspects of life at once, that no single analysis, no existing framework of understanding, was adequate to give humanity a grip on the way everyday life is shifting under our feet.

Liberation theology, despite its political commitment and practices of reflection on the realities of community experience, retained unmistakable features of the Age of Atonement and showed few signs of fitting an Age of Reconciliation. A version of Marxist dialectics pitted the gospel against the evils of the world and, although the temporal Church was part of the problem, the Church to come, exemplified in humble base communities, was celebrated as the embodiment of Christ in the world. Part of the difficulty for English Christians, in IM or inner-city ministry, who found deep inspiration in liberation theology, was that the conditions of Latin American base communities were not easy to replicate, even in UPAs. Respectful as he was to the founding voices of the liberative theological tradition, seeing it as a distinct strand in the broad tradition of social Christianity, John never invested it with a serious potential for a more developed and engaged theology of public life in Britain.

Many in IM, on the other hand, found liberation theology very much to their taste. The legacy of Sheffield ensured that the institutional Church was seen as a problem to be disowned or skirted around: the advent of Thatcherism added capitalism to the cast of villains.[5] This contributed to the sharp movement away from workplace visiting (although it remained a major activity) towards practical action like job-creation schemes or welfare advice, in partnership with secular allies such as trades unions and community groups, in which IM and post-*Faith in the City* projects became indistinguishable. The 'I' in IM was weakening and, with it, something of the open exploratory attitude that had characterized Wickham's journey into the steelworks. Now, the Church was being restored to pre-eminence as the moral arbiter and judge of the world's institutions – not, to be sure, as the empirical and compromised Church that actually existed, but as an idealized and sanctified Church of the poor that was yet to come. Unanswered was the great ecclesiological question of how the Church this side of the cross relates to, and can grow into, the Church on the other side of the cross (Lash, 1992).

It was not only IM's ecclesiology that was deficient. In general, the Age of Incarnation did not develop a missiology adaptable to changing times. In the same collection of essays as Atherton's comments on IM, Margaret Kane could note:

> Industrial Mission's involvement in and conversation with people in industry is only theological insofar as it relates to Christian tradition. It is in this respect that Industrial Mission is at its weakest ... When conversation starts with people's experience there is a danger of getting trapped in the categories of a secularised world. (Kane, 1983, p. 30)

This was a clear call for rapprochement with aspects of the theology and missiology that would have been seen as typical of the Age of Atonement. Kane could see, as John Atherton saw, that these were not questions that could be answered in crudely binary terms.

It is, perhaps, one of the contemporary tragedies of Anglicanism that the binary tension between those for whom the incarnation is the fundamental theological motif and those for whom the atonement is the pivotal truth about God's relationship to the world, continue to battle it out in a kind of zero-sum game where the achievements of one party are automatically taken to be blows against the other. In many ways, the Church of England makes most sense if it is seen as emerging from a temporary truce between the two sides of the Reformation struggles and later between the two sides of the English Civil War – a truce in which loyalty to place became elevated above differences of doctrine, and old theological rifts were subordinated to a coherence around nation and parish. It is a truce that is becoming less and less sustainable, as people's loyalty to place weakens in a footloose globalized world.

But John did not stop at a binary typology of atonement versus incarnation. He was well aware that both are orthodox and central Christian doctrines and that a church that seeks to embody one to the neglect of the other has got something seriously wrong. Systematic theology is often about holding together doctrines that, looked at in isolation, appear to be in tension if not in contradiction. The task of the Church is to work with doctrinal tensions that will not be finally resolved until God's Kingdom is completed on earth. All discipleship, all mission, takes place in the theological interim, between Pentecost and the Parousia – where the presence of the Holy Spirit and of God's grace among us are realities, but so is the persistence of sin. So neither the Age of Atonement nor the Age of Incarnation can be the last word.

To some extent, John identified a swing back towards a new Age of Atonement as the twentieth century ended, confidence in the nation-state faded in the face of global corporatism, the liberal narrative of human improvement faltered and the churches in the West found themselves beleaguered, declining and mistrusted. But rather than succumb to the fatalistic idea that the pendulum simply swings back to where it started, he looked hopefully forwards to a coming Age of Partnership and Reconciliation. John's later work, which continued into the last weeks of his life, was devoted to engagement in partnership with disciplines well beyond theology and, although his penultimate published work, *Transfiguring Capitalism* (Atherton, 2008), is not, in my view, completely persuasive, the posthumous publications of John's last writings should press that agenda further.[6]

At first sight, the word 'reconciliation' is not the most obvious term to describe the early twenty-first-century context of the economy, society or the churches. That may be because the word still conjures up ideas of peace divorced from justice, and comfortable people despairing at the rage of those whose sacrifices support their comforts. True reconciliation often comes through processes of discomfort and negotiating the conflicting claims of different perspectives on justice. The partnerships that John believed would grow towards reconciliation are partnerships between people whose experiences and perspectives are, at first sight, utterly at odds. They are partnerships between the world views of shaken people that cannot encounter each other authentically and still remain intact (Shanks, 1995). They emerge from what Alasdair MacIntyre calls 'epistemological crises' – moments when the frameworks we trust to tell us how the world works prove to be inadequate and we have to develop a new, enlarged, narrative to make sense of what is going on around us (MacIntyre, 1989, p. 140).

It was IM's tragedy that, just as the traditional concept of 'industry' began to disappear, along with all the romance of production and the celebration of skills that it entailed, to be replaced with the kind of economic activity that takes place mainly on a screen or in service delivery, so the search for a theological framework – for a missiology – was largely abandoned. While John could see the pressing need for such a framework in the early 1980s, neither the movement nor the churches took up the task in subsequent years. Instead, the churches in this country are, as John feared they might be, tending to see the world once again through the prism of the doctrine of atonement, and although this may be a necessary corrective to an excessively incarnational emphasis in the last century, it is far from adequate to address the context of complexity, connectedness and dislocation that characterizes everyday life today.

But while IM struggled, and the whole Church continues to struggle, with inadequate missiologies, there is a lot of activity in an area that IM neglected but that cannot be ignored today. One great problem for Anglicans in this country is that the Church of England has seemed immovable in its permanence: exasperating, often wrong, but ever-present and mainly taken for granted. Industrial missioners were able to talk crossly about 'the Church' without taking any serious responsibility for its maintenance or survival.

Yet the permanence of the Church, at least in a recognizable form, can no longer be taken for granted. The Church of England, with its mandate to serve all the people of the nation – the self-professed 'Christian presence in every community' – is not only exceedingly fragile but acutely aware of that fragility. The erosion of industrial mission – partly as diocesan finances tightened and partly as a result of theological and ideological incomprehension in the churches – was made easier by its theological stagnation in later years. But the privileging of parochial ministry over sector ministries, which justified cutting resources to IM and others, came down ultimately to the fact that parishes attract a congregational membership and can generate resources to ensure their own survival and flourishing – and sector ministries give no convincing account of how they contribute to an ecology of mission. At stake was, and is, the deep character of the Church of England as something more than a sect, and it was ultimately upon this deep character, this ecclesiology, that the whole venture of IM depended (despite its ecumenical aspirations). Crudely, when the Church of England abandons the parish system and the ministry to the whole people, it will de facto have abandoned the rationale that sustained ministries like IM as well. And that commitment to the parish system really is under threat not only from sectarian strands of Christianity, which are building their Arks with no allegiance to place but only to doctrine, but from the sheer cost of maintaining a viable ministry to all communities. The Church is not alone in this. Any institution that aims to serve the whole population, such as the Royal Mail or the BBC, faces similar problems. But it is ironic that IM, which ought to have gained a rudimentary sense of how businesses work, should have been caught and largely destroyed by the basic economic realities facing the Church.

Another facet of the tragedy is that most of those who have a story about how the Church's survival might be secured are those who still live, mentally, in the Age of Atonement. They are not wrong – but their story is inadequate. The countervailing story from the Age of Incarnation, still being told, appears oblivious to the resource question. Maybe that is understandable, given the affinity between the Age of Incarnation and the age of the state, in Atherton's typology, with the Church standing in for the benevolent state that is always there to ensure the welfare of its people. But that too is inadequate to the age we inhabit now.

So was John right to foresee an emerging Age of Partnership and Reconciliation offering a theology that reflects the pressing questions of today – including questions about human work and economic structures – and avoids the crude binaries of much Anglican polity?

Faith in the City generated a flood of church-sponsored anti-poverty programmes and projects and established the Church Urban Fund (CUF) in order to embed this work in the life of the Church. CUF continues, but social action has never taken root as an essential in the Church's mission. But since the financial crash of 2008, a new phenomenon has been the burgeoning of social action projects among evangelicals – crossing denominational boundaries but including many Anglicans. As Jonathan Chaplin notes (Chaplin, 2014), this activity currently lacks a coherent social theology, and may manage without one, but if the roots of an Anglican evangelical social theology that Chaplin outlines develop as he suggests, the possibility for bridging the 'Anglican binary' in new partnerships, accompanied by theological reconciliation, is tantalizing.

On a national canvas, the Church of England has, in Archbishop Justin Welby, its first primate whose background allows him to speak on economic issues with authority and whose priorities include reconciliation as a major theme of his archiepiscopate.[7] Welby, like his predecessor Rowan Williams, continues to struggle with Anglican divisions over human sexuality and, although this was a sphere of ethics where John trod reluctantly and seldom, it is noteworthy that Welby has deployed all his powers of persuasion and organization to see behind the presenting problems and understand the dispute as fundamentally theological and ecclesiological. Hence, the focus on 'indaba' and 'shared conversations' laying the ground for the current mammoth project of constructing an Episcopal Teaching Document on sexuality through a deliberately inclusive and very extensive collaborative process. If one sees divisions on sexuality as reflecting John's twentieth-century typology of incarnation in tension with atonement, it could just be that Welby's approach exemplifies the hopes invested in the Age of Partnership and Reconciliation. Whether that approach will influence the way the Church addresses wider issues of social ethics, not least the economy and human labour, is an open question. At the time of writing, the Labour Party is busily proclaiming the collapse of the market liberalism introduced in 1979, while capitalism itself shows signs of being wounded but resilient. What happens next in UK politics may well determine the possibility of the reconciliatory approach impacting effectively on the shape of economic life. Now that it has emerged that a few Labour Parliamentarians worked closely with Conservatives on aspects of the 2017 Tory manifesto, promoting the kind of communitarian politics that were espoused by the Church of England's bishops in 2015 (House of Bishops, 2015), it is at least conceivable that the next turn in political life will fit very closely with the age that John foresaw.

Typologies are, indeed, never tidy. They do not explain or describe everything and can sometimes bring a spurious order to genuine chaos. But typologies that make sense of the past and tell a convincing story about the future are few and far between. From his lifelong commitment to understanding economic life theologically, John Atherton was able to help many to understand complexity and confusion and make sense of the times they inhabited. 'Bloody clever' indeed!

Notes

1 Author's email correspondence with Mike Atkinson, 2016.

2 John's tour of Manchester and its environs, with his commentary on the history and implications of various sites, was a superb introduction to the meaning of urban and industrial contexts that remained ever-memorable to those who experienced it.

3 As Bishop of Middleton, and in retirement, Wickham was to become a close associate of John Atherton. Wickham left his large and eclectic collection of books to Manchester Cathedral to form the Wickham Library. John at one time intended his own, even larger, collection to sit alongside Wickham's, suggesting that, in some sense, he saw himself as Wickham's successor, perhaps in a school of northern industrial practical theology.

4 The Church of England's Council for Moral Welfare became the Board for Social Responsibility in 1958, later merging with other work to become Mission and Public Affairs in 2003. John was a long-standing member of the BSR and its Industrial and Economic Affairs sub-committee.

5 In the 1980s, the IMA's Theology Development Group split into a number of sections, one of which styled itself as the 'Anti-Capitalist Group'.

6 *Transfiguring Capitalism* is a tour de force in interdisciplinary reflection. But John's wide reading in alternative economics that informs the book led him to contradict – but without deep explanation of the arguments for and against doing so – some of the principles he had formerly taken to be axiomatic. For example, he is sympathetic to the view of some alternative economic theorists that the basic concept of scarcity that underlay all conventional economic theory is not fundamental after all. As John had been one of the most forceful critics of Christians who wanted to have their economic cake and eat it (i.e. who ignored the notion of opportunity cost), this shift required a great deal more exploration and explanation than he gave it. His old friend and mentor Ronald Preston would have seen the rejection of axiomatic scarcity as a fundamental error.

7 Welby and others have credited Temple with a similar economic competence, but Temple's understanding of economics derived mainly from his association with Keynes rather than direct experience of the business world, and, as Temple himself notes (Temple, 1942), he and his fellow churchmen got short shrift when they attempted to discuss economics and labour relations with Prime Minister Stanley Baldwin, whereas Welby was widely celebrated for his role on the post-crash Banking Standards Commission.

References

Archbishop's Commission on Urban Priority Areas (ACUPA) (1985), *Faith in the City: A Call for Action by Church and Nation*, London: Church House Publishing.

Atherton, J. R., 1983, 'The Contribution of Theology to Industrial Mission', in *Thinking in Practice: Theology and Industrial Mission*, IMA Theology Development Group.

Atherton, J. R., 1994, *Social Christianity: A Reader*, London: SPCK.

Atherton, J. R., 2000, *Public Theology for Changing Times*, London: SPCK.

Atherton, J. R., 2008, *Transfiguring Capitalism: An Enquiry into Religion and Global Change*, London: SCM Press.

Atkinson, M., 1985, 'A Sort of Episcopal Fly on the Wall of British Industry', in G. Hewitt (ed.), *Strategist for the Spirit*.
Bagshaw, P., 1994, *The Church Beyond the Church: Sheffield Industrial Mission 1944–1994*, Sheffield: IMSY.
Brown, M. (ed.), 2014, *Anglican Social Theology*, London: Church House Publishing.
Burgess, N., 2000, 'A Home-going Parson ...', *Theology* 103(811) (January/February), pp. 37–45.
Chaplin, J., 2014, 'Evangelical Contributions to the Future of Anglican Social Theology', in M. Brown (ed.), *Anglican Social Theology*, pp. 102–32.
Clark, H., 1993, *The Church Under Thatcher*, London: SPCK.
Davies, M., 1991, *Industrial Mission: The Anatomy of a Crisis*, Manchester: The William Temple Foundation.
Eagle, J., 1984a, 'Some Evaluation of the Role of the Institutional Church in the South African Liberation Struggle', in Industrial Mission Association Theology Development Group (IMA TDG), *Spirituality and Necessity*.
Eagle, J., 1984b, 'Focus on Liberation and the Industrial Mission Presence', in IMA TDG, *Spirituality and Necessity*.
Figgis, J. N., 1914, *Churches in the Modern State*, London: Longmans, Green & Co.
Filby, E., 2015, *God and Mrs Thatcher*, London: Biteback Publishing.
Hewitt, G. (ed.), 1985, *Strategist for the Spirit: Leslie Hunter, Bishop of Sheffield 1939–62*, Oxford: Beckett Publications.
House of Bishops, 2015, *Who is My Neighbour? A Letter from the House of Bishops to the People and Parishes of the Church of England for the General Election 2015*, London: Church of England.
Industrial Mission Association Theology Development Group (IMA TDG), 1983, *Thinking in Practice: Theology and Industrial Mission*, Manchester: The William Temple Foundation.
Industrial Mission Association Theology Development Group (IMA TDG), 1984, *Spirituality and Necessity*, Manchester: The William Temple Foundation.
Jackson, M., 1966, 'No New Gospel', *Theology* 69(558), pp. 539–44.
Kane, M., 1983, 'Characteristics of Industrial Mission's Theology', in IMA TDG, *Thinking in Practice*.
Lash, N., 1992, 'Not Exactly Politics or Power', *Modern Theology* 8(4), pp. 353–64.
MacIntyre, A., 1989, 'Epistemological Crisis, Dramatic Narrative and the Philosophy of Science', in S. Hauerwas (ed.), *Why Narrative? Readings in Natural Theology*, Grand Rapids, MI: Eerdmans.
Shanks, A., 1995, *Civil Society: Civil Religion*, Oxford: Blackwell.
Temple, W., 1942, *Christianity and Social Order*, Harmondsworth: Penguin.

7

Economic Activity, Economic Theory and Morality

IAN STEEDMAN

To write on questions of economics and morality in honour of John Atherton is, for me, inevitably to recall vividly the various occasions on which we discussed such matters face to face. John's long-standing interest in economic history, in economics and in Christian social ethics made him a fascinating conversation partner for someone who knew more about economics but less about both economic history and social ethics than he did. He was always ready to teach and to learn and did so with warmth, friendliness and enthusiasm. I miss him.

In our discussions, John was always insistent that criticism of the market, whether from inside or outside the Church, needed to be well informed and measured. He was well aware both that his generation were far better off than his grandparents and that the capitalist market system had contributed enormously to this. He thus had no time for cheap slogans about the immorality of the market. This did not, of course, stop him from being concerned about the inequality of the distribution of income and wealth; but he was much too canny to jump from that concern to any suggestion that only equity matters and that economic efficiency should be ignored. This chapter, therefore, will first consider whether economic activity is necessarily immoral or amoral. It will then move on to discuss what economic theory assumes about the motivations of economic agents, before emphasizing welfare economics and, in particular, the relations between efficiency and inequality. Traditional welfare economics assesses efficiency in terms of how well consumers' given preferences are satisfied. A fundamental difficulty arises, therefore, if producers use some resources to *change* consumers' preferences; this will be the final subject of the chapter.

The morality of economic activity

It will not be argued here that economic actions are always of a moral nature, whether by 'moral' we refer to intentions, to consequences, or to character and the virtues. It will simply be pointed out that economic actions *can* be of a morally positive nature and that some common ideas to the contrary are misguided.

A good starting point is provided by Alfred Marshall's *Principles of Economics* (1920 [1890]), *the* great economics text of the late Victorian/Edwardian period. On his opening page we read that 'man's character has been moulded by his everyday work, and the material resources which he thereby procures, more than by any other influence unless it be that of his religious ideas.' Working, for Marshall, is often a matter of working for the wellbeing of one's family, since 'the family affections' are among the leading motives to action. It can also involve striving to do one's work well, to achieve excellence in one's calling. It will often involve cooperation with and respect for one's fellow workers.

The spending of income can also have significant moral aspects, since it can be wise or unwise. It can be directed to the health and education of children, for example, or to ostentation and the demon drink; it can go to charity or to self-indulgence. It can be 'invested' in enhancing one's skills or in deepening one's culture. Self-reliance, prudence and a readiness to postpone gratification can all be embodied in one's patterns of expenditure and of savings.

Saving and lending too have a moral aspect, both via the prudence already mentioned and because lending can make it possible for borrowers to put to good effect their initiative and enterprise.

More generally, Marshall writes that 'money is a means towards ends, and if the ends are noble, the desire for the means is not ignoble. [Money] is sought as a means to all kinds of ends, high as well as low, spiritual as well as material' (Marshall, 1920, p. 22).

John Wesley said much the same in his 1744 sermon on 'The Use of Money', which contains the famous words, 'Gain as much as you can; save as much as you can; give as much as you can.' (Note that by 'save as much as you can' Wesley meant 'be as frugal as you can' and that one can 'give' by choosing *not* to earn as much as possible and by working in the voluntary sector.)

We now leave Marshall and Wesley to consider more fully some of the issues they have already raised for us, at least by implication.

Exchange

It is sometimes supposed that economic actions are always motivated by selfishness. Yet it is a normal, everyday experience that millions of individuals earn and spend with the intention of doing good for their children, for their elderly parents, or for the charities/churches/parties and so on they support. The idea that economic actions *must* be driven by selfish motives is, quite simply, a stupid idea.

Now consider the fallacy that, in an economic exchange, one of the two parties must be gaining *at the expense of* the other. In truth, *both* parties can be gaining, the exchange conferring a *mutual* benefit. The economist and Unitarian minister P. H. Wicksteed liked to refer at this point to 1 Corinthians 12 and its picture of differing gifts and mutual service; a division of labour combined with exchange of goods and services can be viewed in this light. Under certain conditions, indeed, neither party can be harmed by the exchange. That must be so if each party both understands fully what is involved in the exchange *and* is free not to enter into it. Why would either party engage in the exchange, knowing that they would be better off not doing so?

Faced with this simple but powerful argument, people sometimes resort to an abuse of the English language, saying that one of the exchangers 'had no choice but to engage in the exchange' (for example, to take a dangerous job at low pay). Such Humpty-Dumpty use of language achieves nothing. It is far better to say, for example, that 'this worker was faced by a nasty choice'; or even that 'no one should ever have to face such a choice'. But one must not pretend that there was no choice.

Note that if someone is badly off after making an exchange, it does not follow that the exchange has *made* them badly off. In fact it will often be the case that in the absence of the exchange they would have been still worse off. As the Cambridge economist Joan Robinson once remarked, for the worker in a capitalist society without social benefits, the one thing worse than being exploited is – not being exploited! It may be perfectly proper to criticize the conditions under which certain exchanges take place but it is empty rhetoric to say that some of those exchanging 'had no choice'.

Lending and borrowing

It seems commonly to be supposed, wrongly, that lending and borrowing at a positive rate of interest *must* be unjust to the borrower. Now it is of course a fact that *sometimes* rich and powerful lenders can and do place very onerous terms on poor borrowers, driving these latter into great distress. (An example often given is that of some Indian money-lenders and poor peasants.) But just as with the matter of exchange in general, one must not confuse objectionable conditions of exchange (now, conditions of lending and borrowing) with the fantasy that exchange (now, lending and borrowing) *must* benefit one party at the expense of the other.

Let A and B be two agents of broadly similar wealth; neither has any power over the other and each is free both to enter a lending/borrowing transaction and, equally, to refrain from doing so. Their roughly equal wealth notwithstanding, it so happens that A is relatively 'flush' now but expects to be 'short' in a year's time; B is in exactly the opposite situation. A may consider it advantageous to lend £1,000 at 5 per cent for one year, while B may consider it advantageous to borrow £1,000 at 5 per cent for one year. If so, the corresponding loan from A to B makes *both A & B better off* than they would have been in the absence of the loan.

To say that A, the lender, has gained 'at the expense of B' would be utter nonsense; B is made better off, as is A. The gain is mutual (as in other cases of well-informed and freely entered exchange). Of course, they may not always be well informed; for example, unforeseen inflation may occur between the granting of the loan and its repayment. The lender may then *lose* in real terms by lending.

Work

As already noted, waged and salaried work can have aspects of mutual service, of seeking to benefit others and of cooperation. (The firm/business enterprise is, in part, an exercise in cooperation among the employees.) Material incentives, along with other motives, can of course influence which employment is taken up, how many hours are worked, how hard one works, and so on. It is sometimes implied that material incentives are morally suspect, or even to be despised. But Wesley, Marshall and simple common-sense thinking show such 'ideas' to be merely muddle-headed. There is nothing inherently ignoble (to use Marshall's term) in responding to pecuniary incentives.

Turning now to such specialized forms of working as invention, innovation, risk-bearing and entrepreneurship, we note that they can have much to do with freedom, creativity, independence and initiative, which would generally be thought to have significant moral aspects. Note, too, that these dimensions of human activity can easily have a competitive aspect to them – and that that is not self-evidently a criticism of them. Some new methods of working and some new products may not be morally superior to those they replace, but that is no reason to deny that some results of market activity improve our lives. When would you rather do the weekly wash, or need medical treatment, or require dental surgery – now or in 1910? Moreover, business activity often creates employment and this can be a virtuous thing to do.

The firm

We cannot here consider all the many moral dimensions of profit-maximizing activity but one dimension can readily be noted. A profit-maximizing firm is *ipso facto* a cost-minimizing firm. But to minimize costs is to avoid waste and to use as carefully as possible various scarce resources, including minerals and non-renewable energy sources; this is a virtuous activity. (Issues of under-priced resources etc. would need more detailed consideration – but they do not destroy the general thrust of the point being made.)

To speak of entrepreneurship, profit-maximizing and so on is inevitably to evoke questions relating to cooperation and competition. It has already been noted that there is cooperation within firms. It must now be noted that competition between firms may well be *morally superior* to cooperation between them. When firms 'cooperate' to form monopolies or cartels they are not always doing this in order to benefit others! Such cooperation can be a selfish exercise in increasing the benefits of exchange to those firms and reducing the benefits of exchange to their customers. The slogan 'Competition is bad, cooperation is good' is a morally irresponsible slogan. Matters are far more complicated than that.

Is there the slightest reason to be surprised by the fact that economic actions can give expression to morally positive intentions and virtues? Only if we are silly enough to suppose that real flesh-and-blood economic agents are hypothetical 'economic men', concerned only to maximize wealth. But, of course, they are not. Over one century ago, in 1910, Wickstead published his brilliant *Common Sense of Political Economy*. Throughout that long work, above all in Chapter V, 'Business and the Economic Nexus', he both demolished the idea of 'economic man' and, more positively, showed that there are no distinct, separable 'economic motives' but only ways of choosing and deciding that apply to *all* kinds of action and reflect all our purposes, aspirations and values. It would thus only be surprising if economic actions did not have moral aspects! And there is no reason at all to expect them always to be morally negative aspects.[1]

It has not been said, or implied, that economic activity can never have amoral or immoral aspects. To say that economic actions can be virtuous is not to say that they always are so. They are, after all, the actions of human beings, who sometimes act virtuously and sometimes do not.

What economic theory assumes about agents

Much economics seeks to be explanatory, not prescriptive – and there is nothing wrong in this, of course. There is no reason why economics should all be normative in its thrust. Even here, though, there can be connections to moral issues.

Explanatory economics takes agents to be however they in fact are, with *all* their beliefs, goals, dispositions, ethical values and so on. As Lionel Robbins famously put it, 'Our economic subjects can be pure egoists, pure altruists, pure ascetics, pure sensualists or – what is much more likely – mixed bundles of all these impulses' (1935, p. 95). Or as Bishop Butler said somewhat earlier in 1726, rational behaviour 'may as well be directed towards the well-being of others as towards one's own well-being' (see Atherton, 2003, p. 154). There is no need to suppose narrow egoism/selfishness, or to exclude benevolence, malevolence, the desire to give to charity, to make gifts and so on. As Wicksteed explained (1910, ch. V), 'non-tuism' is the key assumption, not egoism; the buyer and the seller may each be aiming to benefit someone other than themselves – all that economic theory need assume is that neither aims to benefit the other. Nor is there any need to exclude virtue-ethics considerations, or Kantian rights-based issues. In fact economic theory *presupposes* that many personal and property rights are respected, albeit for instrumental reasons rather than intrinsic ones (Sen, 1987, p. 49), that the law is upheld and that judges' decisions are *not* for sale.

Economic theory in the 1870s, say, certainly had strong connections with utilitarian philosophy – think of Jevons, Edgeworth and Sidgwick. But it must be emphasized that by the 1890s Alfred Marshall was warning his readers *not* to suppose that economic reasoning presupposed that philosophy. Then Pareto's *Manuale* (1906) and Wicksteed's *Common Sense* (1910) made it crystal clear how the results of such reasoning could be presented without any reference to utilitarianism. In the 1930s Lionel Robbins explicitly rejected (rightly or wrongly) the possibility of making interpersonal comparisons of utility. (Unfortunately, economists still use the term 'utility function', even though Pareto advised them not to do so over 110 years ago, but it is now merely a term of art and economic theory is *not* a part of utilitarianism.)

Some explanatory theory, such as the theory of income distribution, bears directly on issues that concern many people from an ethical angle. And while it is not the job of economists, per se, to support or to oppose, say, a Rawlsian concern with the position of the worst off, or a Basic Income Policy, it is certainly proper for them to consider the possible consequences of such concerns and policies – whether or not their conclusions please the supporters or opponents thereof. Explanatory theory certainly can be morally relevant.

Welfare economics, efficiency and inequality

Turning now to more directly normative aspects of economic theory, we inevitably come first of all to the concept of Pareto Efficiency. While economists themselves have noted limitations and alternatives to this central construction, it continues to play a major role in their contributions to normative economics. An allocation of resources is said to be Pareto Efficient if and only if it is not possible to change that allocation without making at least one person worse off, in their own estimation. It can readily be seen that such an allocation can be a very unequal one: for example, if one person has everything (and everyone else has nothing) that will be a Pareto Efficient allocation, unless the person with everything *prefers* not to have everything.

While the traditional Pareto Efficiency approach to 'welfare economics' may at first sight appear to be very thin stuff in terms of ethical judgement, it is not in fact ethically innocent. Thus it presupposes that only the welfare of the various households in the economy matters (welfarism); that households are the best judges of their own welfare; that economic processes do not matter for their own sake (but only for their results); that no inter-household comparisons of welfare are to (can) be made. Clearly, questions can be raised about each of these matters – and they have been, by economists among others. To query whether households are the best judges of what promotes their welfare is, of course, to plunge into the problems of 'paternalism'. To ask about individuals' commitments to principles, and about their capabilities for functioning in various objective ways (à la Amartya Sen), or to consider Rawlsian primary goods, is to move well beyond welfarism. And so on. Yet one should not therefore despise the traditional Pareto Efficiency arguments, for they teach us a lot. For example, they lead straight into discussion of various kinds of 'market failure', where markets may not lead to efficient outcomes and hence to consideration of what policies might perhaps correct such failures and thereby contribute to economic welfare.

A major topic within welfare economics is that of Efficiency and Equity, which is covered in some detail in any half-way-decent microeconomics textbook. Okun (1975), indeed, devoted an entire brilliant monograph to this matter. The broader scope of his discussion is the conflict between democracy's promotion of equality and the market's acceptance – and perhaps creation – of inequality, but here we must focus on the more specific tension between economic efficiency and economic (in-)equality.

It has already been noted that Pareto Efficiency is compatible with great inequality of income; more fundamentally, it is compatible with great inequality in the distribution of wealth (assets of various kinds), which is a major determinant of the distribution of incomes (the flows of current purchasing power). Okun suggests, though, that in the USA at least unequal outcomes are not what is most resented; rather, it is inequality of opportunity and discrimination that are found most objectionable (1975, p. 34). He argues that reducing inequalities of opportunity can increase *both* economic efficiency *and* equality of incomes. This is naturally of particular importance with respect to children, in terms of their nutrition, health, education and so on (pp. 76, 80–1), but as long as most children grow up within family households, complete equality of opportunity is always going to be a mirage.

If an economic system is sufficiently competitive to be Pareto Efficient, the given distribution of the ownership of assets – in the form of both commodities and skills – will often lead to a decidedly unequal distribution of income. If it is then judged to be politically and/or morally necessary to change that income distribution, without much changing the underlying wealth distribution, the question will arise of how any proposed system of taxes and welfare payments is likely to change economic incentives (Okun, 1975, pp. 109–11). Could the proposed income transfers damage incentives so severely that total output falls – and falls sufficiently that *everyone* ends up, after the taxes and welfare payments, worse off than in their absence? This is clearly a very stark way of posing the problem – but there is an issue to be faced, even when it is less dramatic. And it is an issue on which judgements may well be swayed by more general political and moral attitudes rather than by evidence. For what it is worth, Okun, who was quite strongly egalitarian in outlook, judged that 'cash grants to the deprived pose genuine and difficult problems of efficiency' and observed that avoiding disincentives to work for poor households versus providing food for their children is 'a particularly nasty tradeoff' (1975, p. 111). Overall, he suggested, 'the conflict between equality and economic efficiency is inescapable' (p. 120).

Some non-economists might be tempted to suppose that while equity is important, efficiency is not – but this would certainly be mistaken, as Atherton rightly insisted (1992, pp. 58, 96, 213; 2003, p. 156). In everyday language, Pareto Efficiency is about avoiding avoidable waste; and how could anyone who thinks *seriously* about helping the poor, or protecting the environment, or safeguarding natural resource availability for future generations pretend that waste does not matter? Thinking about scarcity and about efficiency is a necessary part of serious choosing and deciding (Walsh, 1961).

Efficiency and equity are not the same thing (as Atherton emphasized:

1992, pp. 118, 121, 212). What is required by considerations of equity is not directly an economic question; nor is it an economist's particular responsibility to pronounce on the relationship between equity and economic inequality. (Though equity and equality are certainly not synonyms.) As the philosopher Nagel, among others, has pointed out (Nagel, 1987, ch. 8), perfectly legitimate decisions by millions of households on how to spend their money, or naturally arising interpersonal differences in skills and talents, can lead to very high incomes for some and very low incomes for others. Is this wrong? No one, we may suppose, has acted wrongly. Some people will argue that, since no one has acted badly, *nothing* should be done; the unequal outcomes are 'just life'. Others will insist that the outcome is wrong, even though the processes leading to it are not, and that the state should introduce taxes, benefits, public expenditure on education, health and so on, to bring about a more equal 'post-tax/expenditure' situation. Economists have no particular right to speak on the moral issues involved here, of course, but they can contribute to careful consideration of how different kinds of tax and various sorts of expenditure may alter agents' behaviour, for example through changing the incentives to earn, to consume and to save. Their conclusions *may* help to improve policy and hence lead to a morally superior outcome.

The above discussion is essentially static but the capitalist market system is, of course, an ever-changing and fundamentally restless system. Schumpeter captured this well in his phrase 'creative destruction' (as noted by Atherton, 1992, pp. 49, 59). In the endless process of introducing new commodities and new methods of production, while abandoning old ones, those who gain (both consumers and producers) will rarely compensate those who lose, which raises questions of equity. Moreover, any policy designed to enforce such compensation may well destroy the incentives to invent and to innovate. Since the introduction of new commodities may sometimes involve the creation of new wants (Atherton, 1992, p. 211), this leads us into our final topic.

Advertising, welfare economics and ethics: producing wants

One of the most fundamental weaknesses of the market system is the use of persuasive influence by sellers upon buyers and a general excessive tendency to produce wants for goods rather than goods for the satisfaction of wants. (Knight, 1982, p. 39: see also Knight, 1935, pp. 41–2, 46, 52, 59)

If Frank Knight, an acute observer of economic affairs, was even approximately correct in the remark just quoted, then it is disappointing that over the more than 80 subsequent years the 'persuasive influence [of] sellers upon buyers' has not acquired a central place in standard economics. The use of resources to change preferences over goods and services is a fact of economic life and therefore 'preference-shifting' uses of resources ought to be incorporated within our standard analyses of production, exchange and consumption and within welfare economics. Sales promotion can take many forms. It may simply announce the existence of some particular commodity, bringing it to the public's attention or just reminding them of it. Advertising may announce prices, including discounts or special offers. Yet other sales promotion may seek to foster false beliefs about commodities among potential purchasers. We shall not consider here any such kinds of sales promotion. Rather, thinking in terms of Lancaster's 'characteristics' model, we shall consider, first, sales promotion that gives true information about commodities (in place of potential purchasers' vague or false beliefs about them) and, second, sales promotion that seeks to change the public's preferences *over characteristics*. In both cases, of course, preferences over commodities can be expected to change but it is not immediately obvious that one must evaluate both kinds of sales promotion in the same way. It is to be noted that, in the first case, we refer to giving true information – and not merely to giving 'more accurate' information – because it has been shown, in Currie and Steedman (2000), that more accurate but still inaccurate information can have surprising implications for consumer welfare.

Provision of true information

How is one to make an ethical comparison of two alternative economic equilibria that differ because in one of them resources are being used to make some of the agents' preferences different from what they would have been in the absence of such resource use? By definition, one cannot adopt a straightforward Paretian Welfare Economics approach; the very nature of the difference between the alternatives renders that approach inapplicable. One could assess the two alternatives from *both* the perspective of the unchanged preferences *and* that of the altered preferences, hoping that the two rankings will be the same. But they may not be.

More fundamentally, there is a problem *even if* the two rankings agree. Suppose that sales promotion activity has led the 'new' preference ordering over commodities to be based on true beliefs about commodities and characteristics, while the 'old' ordering was based on (at least partly) false beliefs. Griffin (1986) has argued, plausibly enough, that the satisfaction of 'well-informed preferences' is more valuable than that of ill-informed preferences. Does this mean that only the 'new' ranking of alternatives is to be reckoned into one's overall assessment? Suppose that situation P is *marginally* better than situation Q, according to the well-informed ordering, but *far* worse than Q, according to the ill-informed ordering; how are the two rankings to be combined into an overall judgement?

Be that as it may, there is a further type of question to be asked, one that lies well beyond the boundaries of Paretian Welfare Economics. As McPherson (1987, p. 402) pointed out, when changed preferences are at issue, procedural questions come to the fore and one must ask not only what preferences happen to be but also *how* they came to be as they are. Does it matter (ethically), for example, that the sales promoters have provided correct information *because* it is in their interest to do so? Can they properly be criticized for 'acting selfishly'? Or is this rather a matter in which *everyone* is made better off – the sales promoters by increasing their levels of preference satisfaction and others by becoming better informed? In so far as the answer is 'Yes', does this offset, partially or fully, any reduction in the preference satisfaction levels of the 'others'?

A failure to provide true information, on the part of sales promoters, can sometimes provoke strong criticism, the *caveat emptor* notion notwithstanding. Think, for example, of the fierce arguments that raged around the issue of cigarette promotion and the (statistical) relationship between smoking and certain kinds of illness. Yet it is impossible (logically impossible) to provide a 'complete' description of any commodity, so that sensible criticism can only be to the effect that 'significant/relevant' true information has been withheld. How is this to be defined and by whom? Such issues are commonplace in both popular thought and the law courts; should they not also be standard fare within welfare economics? A resource owner, for example, may have an *obligation* to use resources in providing true information to others.

Important as it may be to consider how well pre-given preferences over commodities are satisfied, responsible assessment of economic systems cannot be *confined* to such consideration, since resources are in fact used to change preferences. It is true both that a more ambitious welfare economics will go against the grain of economists' traditional caution in such matters and that that caution has a defensible (anti-paternalist) background. But it hardly furthers the cause of anti-paternalism simply to refuse to recognize that resources are being used to influence the preferences of others.

Influencing deep-level preferences

We now consider sales-promoting activities that change not beliefs about the relations between commodities and characteristics but, rather, preferences over characteristics. It is probably not that difficult, in many cases at least, to identify *true* beliefs about commodities and characteristics. But how far could even a determined moral realist go in maintaining that there is a *true* ranking of states of being and of actions and hence, derivatively, of characteristics? How far is there an analogue here to 'well-informed' preferences? Such questions might appear to be overblown in the present context; not a great deal of sales promotion refers to the relations between Goodness and Beauty, or between Justice and Mercy! Nevertheless, they should not be brushed aside too easily. As Wicksteed (1910), for example, made very clear, there is no sharp dividing line between the deepest ethical questions and the query, 'What ought I to be doing with my time?', or between that query and the modest, 'What shall I buy?' The world of practical reason is not ultimately compartmentalized, even if we do tend to focus our attention on one level at a time. While sales promotion does not commonly give lectures on ultimate values, it often suggests that some emphases in life are of great importance, while leaving equally or even more valuable emphases unmentioned. Is there anything wrong with this? *If* 'strong moral realism' is correct *and if* we can know the moral truth, then the answer is, presumably, 'It is wrong to endorse moral falsehood – just as it would be to purvey false information about commodities.' Perhaps the satisfaction of vicious preferences is no better than that of ill-informed preferences? (There are, of course, ethical traditions according to which 'bad' actions are always 'ignorant' actions.)

How do matters stand, though, if we do not *know* what would be a 'correct' preference ordering over characteristics? Can there be anything wrong with influencing a deeper-level preference ordering, if there is no such thing as a known correct or true deeper-level ordering? Some will say that there can, on the grounds that such influence violates the autonomy of preference-holders (or the authenticity of their actions). Thus Crisp (1987), for example, insists that many have – and all ought to have (p. 415) – 'a strong second order desire not to be manipulated by others without our knowledge, and for no good reason' (p. 414). Persuasion is not necessarily wrong, and if we attend a film, a play, a sermon or a lecture we may be glad to be persuaded. But persuasive advertising, Crisp argues, is not always comparable to these cases and can involve an assault on our (Kantian) autonomy, in which we are treated simply as means and not at all as ends. 'It seems, then, that persuasive advertising does override the autonomy of consumers, and that, if the overriding of autonomy, other things being equal, is immoral, then persuasive advertising is immoral' (Crisp, 1987, pp. 416–17). We may ask whether consumers are all innocent dupes whose values can be led this way and that *without their conscious participation* in the value-changing process. The answer to this last question may of course be, 'No, not all. But some are more easily swayed than others.' In so far as this is true, with respect to which consumers is the acceptability or otherwise of value-changing sales promotion to be assessed? And do consumers themselves have a *responsibility* to appraise – and where appropriate reject – such sales promotion?

If and when it is wrong to attempt to influence the deeper-level preferences of others, can making such an attempt be harmful to those who make it? Does it, or can it at least, encourage in *them* a cynical, manipulative mentality, with the result that the activity in question harms them ethically even as it is profitable to them?

Such questions may not be easy to answer. But that does not make them non-questions. Their answers are *relevant* to assessment of the use of resources to affect others' preferences – and the familiar armoury of Paretian Welfare Economics provides only limited help in finding those answers. We shall have to move beyond its cautious constructions if we are to build a welfare economics capable of dealing with the type of resource use at issue here.

Concluding remarks

Economic activities can be virtuous and economic theory can suppose agents to be virtuous. Yet, since resources are sometimes employed to change others' preferences over commodities, economic theory should attempt to deal with that issue. Hence a responsible welfare economics, able to guide the assessment of real world economic processes, has to go beyond Paretian Welfare Economics and to grapple with more difficult – and more contentious – ethical questions than welfare economists have been in the habit of facing. John Atherton was right to insist both that effective policy intervention and criticism must not be based on ill-informed moralizing about economic matters and that a concern for equity must not lead to a dismissal of efficiency. The best way to honour John will be to follow his advice.

Note

1 For further comments on Wicksteed's analysis of rationality, see Steedman (1989), ch. 10.

References

Atherton, J. R., 1992, *Christianity and the Market*, London: SPCK.
Atherton, J. R., 2003, *Marginalization*, London: SCM Press.
Crisp, R., 1987, 'Persuasive Advertising, Autonomy and the Creation of Desire', *Journal of Business Ethics* 6, pp. 413–18.
Currie, M. and Steedman, I., 2000, 'Consumer Perceptions of Commodity Characteristics: Implications for Choice and Well-being', *Manchester School* 68, pp. 516–38.
Griffin, J., 1986, *Well-being: Its Meaning, Measurement, and Moral Importance*, Oxford: Clarendon Press.
Knight, F. H., 1935 [1923], 'The Ethics of Competition', in *The Ethics of Competition and Other Essays*, London: Allen & Unwin.
Knight, F. H., 1982 [1934], 'Social Science and the Political Trend', in *Freedom and Reform: Essays in Economics and Social Philosophy*, Indianapolis, IN: Liberty Press.
Marshall, A., 1920 [1890], *Principles of Economics*, London: Macmillan.
McPherson, M. S., 1987, 'Changes in Tastes', in J. Eatwell, M. Milgate and P. Newman (eds), *The New Palgrave: A Dictionary of Economics*, vol. 1, London: Macmillan, pp. 401–3.
Nagel, T., 1987, *What Does It All Mean?* Oxford: Oxford University Press.
Okun, A. M., 1975, *Equality and Efficiency: The Big Tradeoff*, Washington, DC: Brookings Institution.
Pareto, V., 1906, *Manuale d'Economia Politica*, Milano: Società Editrice Libraria.
Robbins, L., 1935 [1932], *An Essay on the Nature and Significance of Economic Science*, London: Macmillan.
Sen, A. K., 1987, *On Ethics and Economics*, Oxford: Blackwell.
Steedman, I., 1989, *From Exploitation to Altruism*, Cambridge: Polity Press.
Walsh, V. C., 1961, *Scarcity and Evil*, Englewood Cliffs, NJ: Prentice-Hall.
Wicksteed, P. H., 1933 [1910], *The Common Sense of Political Economy*, London: George Routledge & Sons.

8

Faith, Finance and the Digital

JOHN READER

Introduction

In an article written in 2016 for the World Economic Forum, Klaus Schwab, its Founder and Executive Chairman, argues that the world is now entering the Fourth Industrial Revolution (Schwab, 2016). Its scale, scope and complexity will be unlike anything that humankind has experienced before. The First Industrial Revolution was that of water and steam power being deployed to mechanize production; the Second used electrical power; the Third electronics and information technology to automate production. This latest one is down to the digital revolution that is bringing together a fusion of technologies and blurring the boundaries between the physical, digital and biological spheres. If this is correct, one might question which philosophical and theological frameworks or concepts might now be appropriate for interpreting and framing ethical responses to these developments. Having proposed the notions of blurred encounters (Reader, 2005) and then entangled fidelities (Baker, James and Reader, 2015) as ways forward for a public theology and now entered the even less familiar territory of new materialism and its theological counterpart of relational Christian realism (Reader, 2017), I will suggest that this Fourth Industrial Revolution requires a new conceptual framework developing ideas from this vein of thought.

· Are Schwab's claims justified though, and what makes this a revolution? He argues that the pace and depth of the changes now underway are unprecedented. The possibilities of billions of people being connected by mobile devices alongside previously unheard of processing power, storage capacity and access to knowledge are characteristic of these changes. Ally this with the emerging technologies in the fields of artificial intelligence, robotics, the Internet of Things, driverless vehicles, 3-D printing, nanotechnology, biotechnology, materials science, energy storage and quantum computing, and we are indeed entering into a very different and largely unknown world. It is so much more than these individual developments that creates that context; it is the potential interaction between each of them that makes the future exciting and unpredictable. The science fiction of a generation ago is now becoming science fact, or at least possibility. All of this, of course, is to ignore the wider economic, political and social context in which this is happening, and that brings its own dangers of growing inequalities, disruption on a major scale even for established business and companies, let alone the risk that these developments are running so far ahead of the human capacity to adapt and absorb that time itself is being reconfigured in ways we are yet to understand. At the most basic level we need to ask who is going to benefit from this, who is in control of these innovations and their application, and under what circumstances are they likely to lead to a more positive future? Along with new possibilities run new vulnerabilities and dangers: how can these be evaluated and monitored?

As Schwab himself concludes, it will all come down to people and values. How are we to avoid the frightening scenario of a world where the majority of humans become effectively enslaved or marginalized by an elite society that controls the new developments for their own ends at the cost of the rest? He suggests that there needs to be a new collective and moral consciousness building on the best aspects of humanity – creativity, empathy and stewardship – which will then construct a shared sense of destiny. Hence a vision that appears to embed at least some religious values and concepts – but will they be enough?

Crossing boundaries, blurred encounters

My first encounter with John Atherton took place when I was a curate in Manchester and studying for the Diploma in Social and Pastoral Theology at the university. I recall a conversation with him about Paul Tillich, which set the tone for our relationship then and in later years. As John's own commitment beyond theology was to economics, so mine was to philosophy and sociology. We shared the concern as to how theology could engage more openly and effectively with other disciplines and cross boundaries into other intellectual sources. This commitment to interdisciplinary working became a strong bond even though our particular interests differed.

Another boundary that I was eager to cross and in which John encouraged my efforts was that between theory and practice. In the 1980s, Manchester diocese was at the forefront of church engagement with community work projects and I subsequently took this example with me into the rural contexts where I have served most of my ministry. My theoretical pursuits have always emerged from direct practical engagements, although those have changed over the years, and John's guidance in constructing what might be termed a public theology based on empirical research and interdisciplinary work has been a constant until his death in 2016. The themes of blurred encounters and then entangled fidelities have been my way of describing the complex and messy nature of a realist theology that attempts to remain grounded in the activity of creating those alternative spaces that also relate to the practices and insights of the Christian tradition. For John, this led him into religious studies, while my work has become more closely associated with philosophy of religion.

Before John suffered his series of heart attacks and was unable to participate fully, we were part of a group meeting in north Oxfordshire to look at the subject of faith and finance. Although this never got beyond initial discussions with some representatives of the banking and finance world, it did lead John to identify some issues that exist only in note form. I now want to refer to these in response to the challenges of the Fourth Industrial Revolution and, in particular, the impact of the new technologies upon the world of finance. One of John's comments was that many issues that seem purely technical are actually complex amalgams of technical and ethical judgements, so ethics must be acknowledged as natural parts of economic affairs (always John's primary interest). From the philosophical sources that I brought into the discussion, notably the work of Bruno Latour (Baker, James and Reader, 2015, pp. 45ff.), I would add that values are always already deeply embedded in what are often presented as simply technical issues, and that Latour helpfully proposes that we abandon the language of 'matters of fact' and replace it instead with 'matters of concern'. In this way we can take account of the values and begin to both articulate and challenge them. If ethics come too late to the party then they are likely to be simply a convenient gloss upon a position already taken.

What this demands though is a careful and interdisciplinary empirical study of the factors involved, something that theologians are notoriously bad at doing. This is another of John's reflections during those discussions, that church leaders and theologians are very good at making grand sweeping statements on such matters without ever doing the hard miles of serious study. That has to be left to the 'experts' and we only intervene once those matters of fact have been established, bringing some Christian ethical perspective to bear when it is already too late! In fear of being 'out of our depth' we retreat from the detailed investigations that are required of us.

John's third point – and the other with which I agree – is that theology has been at its strongest when addressing the pastoral and individual level of contemporary society, probably because this has always been the heart of parochial ministry and the level at which we are (or have been) trusted to engage or intervene in the lives of others. Our capacity or willingness to engage at the structural or collective level of social, economic or political life is much more limited, therefore when it comes to the context as described above, we are as at sea with addressing the issues of the Fourth Industrial Revolution as we have been with the previous three. With a few notable exceptions from within the public theology and perhaps Manchester tradition going back to Tawney, Temple, Preston and Atherton himself, the Church of England has made a poor job of engaging with these significant social changes. What I hope to do in this chapter is point to some issues and resources that may assist in addressing the area of finance and how it is being affected by the digital in particular.

Financial services and the digital

In due course I will examine in greater detail one of the innovations that, it is claimed, will change the face of financial services and even be as ground-breaking as the internet itself, that of what is called 'blockchain'. But to set that in context I will summarize a recent document produced by PriceWaterhouseCoopers, one of the primary financial service providers in the UK. The document is entitled *Technology 2020 and Beyond: Embracing Disruption* (PriceWaterhouseCoopers, 2016) and identifies ten areas or forces where the industry will need to organize itself and get up to speed in applying and adapting to technological change. What they call Fintech (presumably financial services technology) will drive the new business models and will enable new and smarter businesses to enter the market and challenge the current incumbents or large groups that currently dominate the scene. Then the document argues that the sharing economy will become embedded in every part of the financial system – this reminds me of the language of flat hierarchies or even flat ontologies with which I am familiar from the philosophical discourses of new materialism. So instead of vertical infrastructure, the predominant mode becomes horizontal and potentially much more open. Blockchain will shake everything up – and the details of this will come shortly.

The digital will become the mainstream in terms of regular operations. 'Customer intelligence' will be the most important predictor of revenue growth. I presume this relies upon the existence of Big Data and the algorithms that collate and predict customer behaviour. Advances in robotics and artificial intelligence (AI) will start a wave of re-sharing and localization, so it will matter less where the organizations are located, which I imagine would present a threat to the dominance of the City of London, for instance. The public cloud will become the dominant infrastructure model, so once again challenging the need for large organizations based in the traditional global financial centres. Cyber security will become one of the top risks facing financial institutions and there have already been examples of these being hacked into and data stolen. Asia will emerge as a key centre of technologically driven innovation, and, finally, the regulators themselves will have to turn to the technology in order to keep abreast of all these developments and the rapid pace of change. All of this is placed under the heading of disruption as the previous models of operating will rapidly be overtaken by the technological innovations.

So let's look in more detail at blockchain and its implications, acknowledging that the financial services industry is only one sphere where this new technology is claimed to have a major impact. Blockchain is essentially a digital ledger technology and operates through links between networks of computers that become the nodes of this new system. Drawing on a recent document produced by Goldman Sachs, its key characteristics are as follows (Goldman Sachs, 2017). The system gathers data into blocks and then chains them together securely. So each block is time stamped and, in theory at least, no changes can be made once this has happened. Any attempt to interfere with a chain once it is established will set off alarms, hence security is guaranteed. This will change the way in which we buy and sell goods and services, and even impact upon the way in which we interact with government. The central issues here are therefore of trust and security. Within the financial field, blockchain will establish a paperless way of establishing the ownership of money, information and objects, and will therefore obviate the need for the current mediating institutions who handle these exchanges for us, such as banks. It will also remove current bottlenecks in markets where, although agreed transactions can function rapidly, actually following these through and putting them into action can often take much longer periods of time while everything and everybody is monitored and validated. So exchanging assets and payments can take days, involving multiple banks and clearing houses, all of which increases both the risks and the costs of the transactions. Blockchain will replace all of this by smart contracts and reliance upon digital identities verified within the system.

As we can see, the central issues at stake in this are those of trust, speed, security and even the status of knowledge itself, let alone the question of who exactly will benefit from this. It is essentially a new and different way of hard-wiring trust into the system that bypasses more traditional means of establishing it. Is this, however, necessarily a good thing? A document produced by the World Economic Forum raises questions about this new technology and the claims being made for it (World Economic Forum, 2017). Apart from the fact that there is a great deal of hype around this and that in these early days when the most obvious application for the technology has been in the area of bitcoin and this itself is under examination, the authors question whether this system of cryptographic verification can be made permanently secure and indeed whether this is the best means of establishing trust within these exchanges. As trust is supposedly hard-wired into the architecture of the network it means that trust between individuals and institutions is bypassed. Is this something that is desirable at all, and what would be the implications of this for wider social and political relationships where trust is already at a premium? Should we not be putting more time and energy into building those relationships of trust rather than delegating them to this technology? Will it not further erode the very relationships that we should be working harder to foster? Then, on a more overtly political level, does not this decentralizing and distributing of information further fragment and undermine democracy itself?

So it can be seen that the blockchain technology has to be examined in proper detail not only in terms of how it operates but also in relation to its implications for behaviour within the financial services industry *and* for the wider society. As will be seen as we draw upon some more theoretical sources for assistance in the ethical evaluation of the system, there is more to this than simply looking at a new technological fix, as certain values are already built into it and it is necessary to draw those out and even challenge them.

The values of blockchain: trust or fidelity?

The next step is to examine the individual values behind this developing technology to decide to what extent they are to be adopted and endorsed. A major claim is that blockchain creates trust within this system of exchanges and thereby also enhances levels of security. How is such a claim to be assessed? In a moment I will draw upon the work of the philosopher of technology Bernard Stiegler, as I have argued elsewhere that this provides some vital elements of the new conceptual framework that is now required (Reader, 2017, pp. 121ff.). One can immediately question though whether the use of the term trust is appropriate in this context. It could be argued that trust is only established within human-to-human relationships and does not apply to technology. To be able to trust someone depends upon a depth of relationship built up over time and carries the connotation that moments of suspicion or mistrust have been dispelled as a result of direct experience of a continuity of encounter. Can this be applied to encounters either with or between machines within this network of computers? Reliability seems to me to be a much more appropriate term for this type of relationship. Machines are reliable – or not – and therefore to be trusted or relied upon to perform certain limited tasks, but I am not convinced that one can then claim that trust itself has been created.

Stiegler's position on technology is complex and beyond the scope of this chapter to describe, but one of the cornerstones of his approach is his use of the term *pharmakon*, which he derives from Plato and then Derrida. *Pharmakon*, according to those sources, is both remedy and poison, and, as Derrida suggests, there is no such thing as a harmless remedy. In other words, the technology has the capacity to be both beneficial and detrimental to human development and wellbeing and one has to evaluate each case on its merits. It is also the case that the technology is not to be reduced to purely instrumental value, but we need to understand that the technology shapes us and how we behave as much as we shape the technology and simply employ it for our own purposes. One only has to review the ways in which the responses of young people to social media have potentially damaging impacts as they become increasingly addicted to the machines, and others would exploit them by gaining access to children and teenagers via their smartphones. There are also clearly beneficial impacts of access to the internet in terms of both knowledge and communication, although those also have to be carefully assessed. Hence each technological development, including blockchain, has the capacity to change human behaviour in both positive and negative ways. What then is to be said about the issue of trust, or, as Stiegler prefers to term it, fidelity?

One of his ways into this debate is to use the concept of transitional objects, which Stiegler adopts from the work of the psychotherapist Donald Winnicott. The transitional object is that which allows the infant gradual detachment from its mother and to gain a greater sense of independent identity and autonomy. So it is not so much the object itself that is of importance, as a whole range of objects can perform this function, but the role that it plays in human development. The risk is that particular transitional objects can themselves become a source of addiction rather than enabling a further process of detachment. So we switch our attachment to objects or other people and get stuck at that stage rather than letting go and moving on. Stiegler argues that current developments in technology create a new infidelity as many of those technical objects operate in such a fashion and at such a speed that it is not possible to create new forms of fidelity or trust. He believes that each society attempts to construct a rule of fidelity or trust, and that since 'the death of God' (Stiegler is an atheist of course) our society has been based on a developing infidelity. The impacts of marketing and mass consumption have undermined that element of constancy in relationships that is required for fidelity to develop. Most things are instant and then expendable as we are encouraged to move swiftly on from one purchase and attachment to another.

The question that Stiegler attempts to address is that of what now guarantees the trustworthiness of transitional objects. When most aspects of our lives are now subject to calculation, often according to financial criteria, he suggests that this leads to the liquidation of fidelity, friendship, love, the arts and even knowledge itself, in fact all the things that make life worth living (Stiegler, 2013, p. 64).

Going into more detail on this process, he proposes that what is happening now is a process of adaptation rather than adoption. So adoption is the unconscious desire directed towards the transitional object, a projection beyond the self that through this takes care of transitional space, affirming the independent existence of the object itself. Reason is a matter of this desire, whereas adaptation is a process of short-circuiting this relationship and prevents the possibility of critical thought and questioning as it undermines the appropriate distance between the individual and the object. Stiegler wants to see a new politics of adoption and fidelity. He also employs concepts taken from the work of the philosopher Simondon, who talked about the processes of individuation or what we might understand as different stages of human development. In parallel with Winnicott perhaps, he argued that an appropriate relationship with both others and objects requires trust in intermediaries (formerly priests even, but now possibly therapists), which itself relies upon time for interaction, networks within which intensities circulate and can be experienced and questioned, whereas the operations of the new technology move us on so rapidly that these processes are short-circuited. A relationship of care is like an apprenticeship where we have the opportunity to learn by mistakes without too much harm being done. In this way we learn to move with confidence from one transitional object to another, realizing that each has to be respected in its own right but without developing an unhealthy attachment to anything or anybody. Long circuits produce that care and appropriate attention. Short circuits lead to regression and addiction and inhibit the development of trust and fidelity.

If this is the case, then there is a danger that blockchain presented as some sort of substitute for these processes of care and attention could undermine further trust as it needs to develop in human relationships. As one of the articles examined earlier suggests, is this an appropriate means of constructing relationships of trust when the process is short-circuited and delegated to the machines rather than built into and upon face-to-face encounters? On the other hand, perhaps there are also benefits in other areas of human conduct.

The value of speed and time

These arguments have been taken further by Hui, another scholar researching in this area and whose work draws upon that of Stiegler as well as Heidegger and Simondon (Hui, 2016). Hui looks in finer detail at the operation of algorithms, which are essential to the new digital technologies. The dynamic involved is that logical knowledge as mediated by algorithms cuts through the time-consuming process of assessment and assimilation conducted by humans, working instead on the basis of mechanical rules and logic gates, which reduce all impurities or deviances to the minimum. What results is a standardization that cannot recognize anything that deviates from what is already embedded within the system. For instance, a customer of a bank, because he had lived at the same address since 1987, well before the systems were computerized, had to go through the process of proving his identity because the new system did not recognize him, despite being with the same bank for over 30 years. As Stiegler says, the normal operations of care and attention cease to function once this level of standardization and depersonalization take over.

Little scope is left either for the imagination or for the development of human relationships. Technics offer a storage function, and the emergence of the visual domain allows for a different kind of inspection, a reordering and refining of meanings that eliminate other more human dimensions. It has to be recognized that this is not a neutral or passive process but embodies certain values that short-circuit the operation of others. Algorithms are the means by which Big Data are processed and then yield determinate results or suggestions. For instance, they generate the recommendations for new purchases that appear on our computer screens on the basis of items that we have previously viewed online. This is a making present or bringing forth into the present a future that might or might not be of interest to us, but inevitably has the impact of shaping our future purchases as a marketing tool. We are made aware of a possibility that had not even occurred to us as our future behaviour is predicted in advance by the use of these algorithms. In this way, the future – but a very specific future, determined by those employing these algorithms for their own financial benefit – is brought into the present. It is as if time itself is being reconfigured, but only in order to convince us that our next purchase should be this rather than that.

Is this short-circuiting of the process of discernment and judgement of benefit or not? Both Stiegler and Hui would argue that the time and space for critical thought and reflection is being undermined by the speed at which the technological systems now operate. So although speed of exchange and the removal of the supposed blocks created by the intermediaries of humans in banks and legal offices may well be the result of the operation of blockchain, perhaps something important for the functioning of human relationships is in danger of being destroyed. Time itself is being conflated, and that has its own risks and costs of another sort.

Knowledge and the alternatives

Are there then viable alternatives or antidotes to the most damaging impacts of the technology? For this I return first to Stiegler and his more recent work. His starting point is that the 24/7 infrastructures never stand still and thereby eliminate the time for decision-making and critical thinking, keeping us continually connected to the online resources in a manner that short-circuits everyday life and standardizes and anonymizes it. This in turn removes the capacity for what he calls states of sleep and daydreaming that are the intermittences that could provide alternative ideas and visions of the future. Stiegler wants to argue that the technology itself, though, can be employed to enable this process to happen as it potentially creates more thinking space because tasks can be carried out through the increasing automatization of society. There needs to be a massive redistribution of thinking time on the basis of these temporal benefits. So the reconfiguring of time can enable a different and more creative response, but this will require quite deliberate social and political organization. He refers to the religious practice of keeping Sunday as a day of rest and refreshment, and as an otium of the past that helped people sustain their energies in the midst of the business of normal life (Stiegler, 2016, p. 75). The keeping of religious festivals and special times of celebration was vital to this rhythm and dynamic of everyday life and needs to be rediscovered in an appropriate contemporary format. Perhaps, therefore, the religious life that still includes these elements has something of value to offer? So he suggests:

> We will try to show in the following chapters that there is still time to think – to dream the conditions of the realization of dreams – in the contemporary world, and that this possibility passes through a new thinking of automatisms and dis-automatization, whereby automatons will come to serve dis-automatization, which is a matter of conceiving systems and infrastructures founded on digital tertiary retention. (Stiegler, 2016, p. 79)

This, then, will be Stiegler's *pharmakon*, where the poison or potentially harmful consequences of the digital technology can be turned against itself into something positive and creative, a means of creating more thinking time rather than a mechanism for short-circuiting critical thought. This depends upon a particular understanding of knowledge itself. Knowledge – like relationships and trust – takes time: time to learn, reflect, experiment, to dream and deliberate and to play around with ideas, often with others in open discussion and debate. It is in the intermissions, interstices, spaces or gaps in the business of life that this happens most effectively, and it is these that must be either protected or recreated. They are what I have elsewhere called 'spaces of faithful dissent' (Reader, 2017).

Are there practical examples of this that Stiegler can offer? In a way that parallels my use of Latour, where he argues that our relationship with technology should not be that of creating more distance but of engaging more intimately, and my own approach of entangled fidelities, Stiegler proposes that this involves not trying to escape the disruption but becoming more closely engaged. He presents the idea of an economy of contribution as a practical example of this. This involves creating a contributory income, remunerating or augmenting the incomes of those who agree to contribute to civil society. So, with others, he is in the process of creating a Chair of Contributive Research in the Seine-Saint-Denis district of Paris in partnership with universities and businesses. This will encourage those selected to innovate and to develop their practical as well as intellectual skills in a way that will be of benefit to the wider community. So the forms of knowledge created will be practical know-how as well as the life skills now required. Rather than rejecting or retreating from the disruption resulting from the new technology this is a way of embracing and working with it to construct not only the time for reflection but the knowledge that requires the time to develop and function. Hence this is a deliberate social and political strategy to counter the worst effects of developments such as blockchain.

Spaces of faithful dissent

The example above raises the question of what, if anything, faith groups might have to offer to this process. Do we create or protect those spaces for critical thought and reflection, let alone the building-up of trust and knowledge that seem so crucial if we are not to be overwhelmed by the impact of new technologies? One might argue that both the liturgies and symbols of the faith do indeed create exactly those opportunities to stand back, to take time and to be in a consistent and stable context that can still offer alternatives to the fast-moving and pre-emptive impacts of the internet and social media generally.

However, it is also the case that churches as institutions adapt and participate in the very culture that is being criticized, for instance through the use of emails, online forms and surveys, and other forms of impersonal communication that work against the means by which we develop relationships of trust and knowledge. By operating increasingly according to a business model we undermine the strengths we have in areas such as contemplation and silence. Or do we? Certainly there are examples of the use of video and social media, not only to communicate elements of the faith but also to institute those opportunities for faithful reflection that emerge from church-based social gatherings. Catholics for Faith Exploration (CaFE), organized at the behest of the Vatican, is an interesting instance of this as a type of post-Alpha course based on pastoral and ethical issues. To what extent, though, does the medium add to or detract from the message? Then there are the regular events such as parish gatherings, although these are becoming ever more difficult to sustain in the 24/7 culture. One must not forget times of celebration that still occur, notably weddings and baptisms, and the opportunities they present to create pastoral contacts and even an alternative experience of time. As we have discovered, the offering of food and hospitality is so often vital to other gatherings, which may draw people together across and beyond faiths in order to address issues of local concern. All of these are spaces of location and time that must be encouraged and supported. At a time when social interaction is at a premium, and it is too easy to reduce external commitments and contacts by using technology rather than face-to-face contact, faith groups need to value their alternative means of operating. Perhaps, as Stiegler suggests, it ought to be possible to use the technology to relieve people of certain tasks in order to create more time for silence and other reflective activity.

Conclusion

This chapter set out to make a contribution to an ethical evaluation of the digital from a faith perspective, so it is only right that it concludes with a proposed framework for this.

By drawing on both new materialism and relational Christian realism, as in *A Philosophy of Christian Materialism* (Baker, James and Reader, 2015) and *Theology and New Materialism* (Reader, 2017), it is possible to establish a new conceptual framework for an ethical faith-based engagement with questions relating to technology and, in particular, the growing significance of the digital. Which particular faith values could play a part in the matters of concern that are to be reassembled in these areas? A starting point for this is that technology and the digital are not to be reduced to the purely instrumental – a means to an end – but themselves participate in and contribute to the shaping of the assemblages of the human/non-human in this field.

Concepts drawn from new materialism and relational Christian realism relevant to the discussion are:

- local or mini transcendences (namely rejecting the idea of an overall hierarchical model of transcendence for instead a 'beyond in the midst' development of the immanent, one that refers to time as well as space);
- assemblages of the human and the non-human, thus rejecting the established concepts of human autonomy and bringing the digital into direct relationship with the human;
- plastic autonomy or metastability, which emphasize the malleability and change-driven nature of those assemblages;
- distributed agency (so not denying any role for the human but setting that in the wider content of the agencies of the non-human/digital);
- *pharmakon* in its interpretation as both remedy and poison, but also acknowledging the undecidability of the concept;
- the disjunctive synthesis between the relational and the apophatic (within contemporary theology, where the relational approaches are contextual and the apophatic represents those aspects that lie beyond articulation);
- the need for care, trust and attention; the tension and relationship between the otium and the negotium (spaces of rest and contemplation against places of activity, business and commerce).

So how and where does an ethical approach begin to develop? It requires reassembling each instance with care and attention, paying proper regard to detail and the question of who will benefit, rather than making sweeping judgements. It also means acknowledging the plastic autonomy and scope for new forms of human (and non-human) development within the distributed agencies that are now evident – such as patterns of behaviour in individual and social life shaped by the new technologies (do faith groups collude or collide?). Is there still space and scope for alternative patterns of behaviour and values related to the apophatic, the sublime, what Catherine Keller and Richard Kearney call *chora* (Reader, 2017, p. 128; Kearney and Zimmermann, 2015), which might be a different experience of both time and space itself? Is there a growing risk of total control of the human by those manipulating the digital to their own commercial advantage – Matrix world? Do we have an understanding of what it is to be or become human in this new dispensation that is adequate to these challenges?

An ethics of non-appropriation might be a starting point – so the other exists for themselves not as they are for me (Reader, 2005, p. 107) – but is this ever possible? Can we avoid being 'eaten' and 'eating', or appropriating, others, and is the task to eat and be eaten well? What might this mean in specific instances? What is life-enhancing and what life-denying within this ethical pragmatism? Is there something to be said for a strategy of deliberate non-engagement – for example, Bartleby the Scrivener's 'I would rather not' – rather than a direct contradiction and challenge? What are our understandings of fellowship, relationship, community, which run counter to the tendencies to elevate the individual that appears to be at the heart of the advance of the digital? So new materialism and relational Christian realism must continue to pursue these matters of concern, employing faith-based local transcendences but with due attention to the apophatic as well as the relational.

References

Baker, C. R., James, T. and Reader, J., 2015, *A Philosophy of Christian Materialism: Entangled Fidelities and the Common Good*, Farnham: Ashgate.

Goldman Sachs, 2017, *Blockchain: The New Technology of Trust*, available at www.goldmansachs.com/our-thinking/pages/blockchain/.

Hui, Yuk, 2016, *On the Existence of Digital Objects*, Minneapolis, MN: University of Minnesota Press.

Kearney, R. and Zimmermann, J. (eds), 2015, *Reimagining the Sacred*, New York: Columbia University Press.

PriceWaterhouseCoopers, 2016, *Financial Services, 2020 and Beyond: Embracing Disruption*, available at www.pwc.com/gx/en/industries/financial-services/publications/financial-services-technology-2020-and-beyond-embracing-disruption.html.

Reader, J., 2005, *Blurred Encounters: A Reasoned Practice of Faith*, Vale of Glamorgan: Aureus Publishing.

Reader, J., 2017, *Theology and New Materialism: Spaces of Faithful Dissent*, New York: Palgrave Macmillan.

Schwab, K., 2016, *The Fourth Industrial Revolution*, Geneva: World Economic Forum.

Stiegler, B., 2013, *What Makes Life Worth Living: On Pharmacology*, Cambridge: Polity Press.

Stiegler, B., 2016, *Automatic Society: Volume 1, The Future of Work*, Cambridge: Polity Press.

World Economic Forum, 2017, *Four Reasons to Question the Hype around Blockchain*, available at www.weforum.org/agenda/2017/07/four-reasons-to-question-the-hype-around-blockchain/.

9

Bending It Like Atherton: Doing Public Theology in an Age of Public Anger

WILLIAM STORRAR

Public theology stands or falls in the headwinds of the public sphere. It aims to influence public opinion on public issues. It offers an appropriately translated theological contribution to the public conversation. It seeks to make common cause to challenge and change public policy and practice in the public interest. It does so at all levels of society from the local to the global, and always in solidarity with the poor and the least. In the opening decades of the twenty-first century a fierce wind of public anger is blowing through the public sphere around the world, as the dispossessed of post-industrial and authoritarian nations turn in despair to the false promise of populism and terrorism. It is into this headwind of public anger that theologians, religious leaders and faith communities must speak a public word in season. No one did it better than John Atherton. Inspired by his thinking and friendship, this chapter reflects on the challenge of doing public theology in a time of public anger, arguing that we must bend it like Atherton.[1]

John Atherton was an outstanding exemplar of that modern Anglican tradition of social ethics associated with the Manchester School of William Temple, Ronald Preston and the William Temple Foundation. He made his own original contribution to that tradition, writing a series of books on religion and economics, including his last major publication on the wealth, wellbeing and inequalities of nations, *Challenging Religious Studies* (2014). John's late thought on these public issues was deeply influenced by Angus Deaton, the Princeton economist who won the Nobel Prize in 2015 for his own work on measuring inequality. The appreciation was mutual. Deaton endorsed John's book with these words:

> Relations between economics and religion have long been fractious, to the detriment of both. While economists have broadened their interests,

the centrality of religion to human wellbeing is rarely recognized. On the other side, many theologians brand economics as a soulless doctrine of materialism. Such polarized views hurt both economics and religious studies, and have long been due for change. John Atherton's *Challenging Religious Studies* is a splendid bridge across the divide and lays out a path for a richer, more productive, and more sympathetic collaboration. Bravo! (Atherton, 2014)

With this eminent commendation of Atherton's gift for bridging worlds, we can justifiably claim that public theology came of age as a credible dialogue partner in the wider academy. Such is the measure of John's achievement.

I first met John Atherton when taking part in a conference at Manchester University to honour the work of his late mentor, Ronald Preston. I had just been appointed to the chair in Christian Ethics and Practical Theology at Edinburgh University, and to the directorship of its Centre for Theology and Public Issues. John beamed at me after I had given my paper (Storrar, 2004) in unfashionable defence of Preston's advocacy of middle axioms in ecumenical social ethics: 'We wondered what the new lad in Edinburgh would be like – most acceptable, you'll do!' With that typically Athertonian imprimatur, it was the beginning of a warm friendship and collaboration on common theological concerns that continued right up to his final illness, with John's last emails characteristically focused not on his own health but on the work in hand and encouragement to take it forward.

The work in hand was nothing less than understanding the role of religion in economic life and developing a theology of the economy and society that took seriously the transformative impact of first industrialization and then globalization in improving humanity's wealth and wellbeing over the past two centuries. This shift was something John felt theologians had too often failed to acknowledge in theorizing about the economy with the redundant assumptions of a pre-modern age of scarcity. At the heart of his endeavour to renew the tradition of Christian economic thought was a metaphor I first heard John use in delivering the John Baillie Memorial Lecture at Edinburgh University's New College on the theme of the global economy. We must bend the forces of globalization, he argued, in order to ensure a more humane world order, where the evident benefits of a deeply connected world do not come at the cost of rising inequality and environmental collapse. In bending globalization towards Martin Luther King's arc of justice, John believed religion and religious communities had a key contribution to make. In this chapter in memory of my mentor on engaging global issues, I wish to apply his metaphor to the challenge of doing public theology in an age of public anger. I shall argue in what I trust is an authentically Athertonian way that we must bend that anger toward hope, not hate.

From hope to wrath

With the fall of the Berlin Wall, the Rio Declaration on the environment and sustainable development, the end of apartheid and leadership of Nelson Mandela, the adoption of the UN Millennium Goals, the Arab Spring's call for democracy, and the election of Barack Obama, our global public life seemed hopeful by the opening decade of the twenty-first century. But now our public life around the world is characterized by public anger, whether among voters in the 2016 presidential election in the USA and the referendum on EU membership in the UK, or among protesters against austerity and racism on the Left and against migrants and elites on the Right. In such a climate of anger in the global public sphere, what does theology have to say?

The sources of the anger in all these instances, and many more, are different and complex, and must be treated as such. But in developing a public theology for these times, we must understand the significance of this public anger, which is bringing our earlier hopes for social justice through democratic institutions into scorn and derision, not only in younger democracies like South Africa, Hungary or the Philippines but also in older democracies like the United States or the United Kingdom. Let me suggest a different way of thinking about this public anger.

As a public theologian, I stand on an invisible meridian line that runs between two Capes, the Cape of Good Hope at the southern tip of Africa, and Cape Wrath in the far north of Scotland, where the Atlantic meets the North Sea in one of the angriest stretches of water in the world. My professional and personal life runs between these two Capes, not only because my work as a public theologian is now based in South Africa as an extraordinary professor of the University of Stellenbosch, but also because my own values as a citizen are rooted in the sense of social justice, commitment to democracy and love of Jesus that I inherited from my maternal grandparents. They were lifelong exiles from their beloved North, the land of Cape Wrath, as economic migrants in search of work after the First World War. It is this iconic place name from the land of my ancestors that helps us to rethink the meaning of public anger in countries around the world like South Africa, with its recent Fees Must Fall protests, and to see how to bend it like Atherton.

The name at the northern end of my theological meridian line does not mean Cape Anger. In the Old Norse language of the Vikings, who named this Cape in their voyages around the Scottish coast from Scandinavia, a 'wrath' meant a 'turning point'. Cape Wrath was a navigational point where the Vikings would turn their ships. Standing on this meridian line between these two symbolic capes in my moral imaginary, can we see public anger as a turning point on a new political voyage to hope again around the world? I think we can, in three practical ways.

The gospel of anger?

Before considering these three ways in which to see public anger as a turning point to hope, however, it is important to acknowledge how problematic anger is as a human emotion, not only for Christianity but also in many other philosophical and religious traditions. Ancient philosophers like Galen and Seneca thought of it as a form of madness.[2] Buddhists see it as an addiction underlying human suffering. As Robert A. F. Thurman has argued, it is 'one of the three root poisons (along with greed and delusion) that constitute the real cause of the life of suffering, the *samsara*, or endless lifecycle of unenlightened frustration' (Thurman, 2004, p. 11). Going against these common negative assessments of anger, Thomas Aquinas offers a rarer philosophical defence in his writings on the passions in his *Summa Theologiae*, echoing his master, Aristotle. Robert Miner expounds Aquinas' understanding of anger among the passions in this way:

> In the course of treating anger itself, Aquinas positively connects anger to reason, nature, and justice. Though anger may distort our perception of what is required by each of these things, its primal connection to these things is divinely intended and, as such, good. (Miner, 2009, p. 269)

Miner goes on to argue:

> While attentive to the negative and destructive effects of immoderate anger, Aquinas emphasizes that anger, like other passions, is part of human nature and has an appropriate role to play in the human pursuit of good when directed by reason. That Aquinas takes this view of the matter is confirmed by examining [his] treatment of Christ's anger. (2009, p. 269)

In light of Aquinas' account, then, Miner wishes to claim that 'Anger in itself – anger as a passion – is not a sin.' Indeed, a *lack* of anger can be sinful for Aquinas, in situations where anger is merited; constituting what Alasdair MacIntrye calls a failure of practical rationality (Miner, 2009, p. 286).

Aquinas' distinction between anger as a human passion and as a sin would seem to be borne out in the New Testament, where Jesus is portrayed as both angry and without sin.[3] The Letter to the Ephesians allows us to be angry with two qualifications: we must not make our anger an occasion for sin, nor prolong it beyond sunset.[4] Does that mean there can be occasions for being angry without sinning or being trapped in endless cycles of destructive fury? Can we bend public anger into a positive global force, as Atherton would have us do? I would argue so.

My initial receptiveness to thinking of anger as a positive as well as a negative emotion was prompted by my teacher in pastoral theology at Edinburgh University, Alastair V. Campbell. In his book, *The Gospel of Anger*, Campbell writes:

> We are familiar – perhaps too familiar – with the idea that the Christian gospel is the good news of love and that our response to this gospel should be to love God and our neighbours as ourselves. But could Christianity also be a gospel of anger? And could being angry with our neighbours and with God also be a part of the Christian life? These ideas sound strange, but ... anger and love are not as far apart as we might at first imagine, and in pastoral situations anger can be a potent influence for good. (Campbell, 1986, p. xi)

Campbell's gospel of anger is especially relevant in addressing complex public issues:

> Thus the gospel of anger in the face of political injustice is that we can use our anger to expose falsehood and hypocrisy, reject the compromise that seeks peace at any price, demand the truth, even though to do so means a risk to self, speak honestly about our own uncertainty in the midst of the complex political issues of our day but demand the same honesty from others ... Thus, in taking seriously the anger of whole groups of our fellow humans, we can learn how the pastoral ministry of truly listening leads to the prophetic ministry of truthfully speaking. For, in the Christian gospel, truth, love and justice are all aspects of the one reality. (1986, p. 102)

This openness to seeing anger as a potent influence for good in certain pastoral and political situations finds further biblical support in Lytta Basset's book on the notion of *Holy Anger*, her study of anger in Jacob, Job and Jesus. She writes that holy anger is healthy anger: 'It is not an end in itself; its function is to restore health in the full sense [shalom]' (Basset, 2007, p. 217). Or, as the South African practical theologian Cas Wepener describes the current waves of public anger in his own country,

'To feel angry when things are not right is not wrong – it is an expression of the fact that you still care' (Wepener, 2015, p. 25). Their theological defence of a healthy and caring public anger finds a secular parallel in the essay of the French Resistance veteran and humanitarian activist, the late Stéphane Hessel, written when he was 93 years old: *Indignez-vous!* or *Time for Outrage*. Despairing at the global financial crash in the opening decade of the twenty-first century, he writes:

> The basic motive of the Resistance was indignation. We, veterans of the French Resistance and the combat forces that freed our country, call on you, our younger generations, to revive and carry forward the heritage and ideas of the Resistance. Here is our message: It's time to take over! It's time to get angry! (Hessel, 2011, p. 6)

Having made the case that it can be a force for good as well as destructive and sinful, we now return to seeing public anger as a turning point in the restoration of healthy and just societies.

Seeing public anger as trauma – turning it into pastoral care

First, we must see public anger not only as a political protest but also as related in many instances to the experience of trauma, with its bodily and emotional, psychological and biological, medical and social dimensions. Two recent case studies of public attitudes and of public health in the United States bear this out. In research on the rage expressed in authoritarian and discriminatory public attitudes, for example, there is a consistent correlation between oppressive attitudes to others as adults and the experience of physical violence and emotional abuse as children and young people. In their introduction to the 2016 edition of their book, *Raised to Rage: The Politics of Anger and the Roots of Authoritarianism*, Michael Milburn and Sheree Conrad described their earlier research on this phenomenon:

> Twenty years ago, with the publication of *The Politics of Denial*, we presented our initial research supporting what we now call 'affective displacement theory.' Our results suggested that attitudes towards some political issues might be determined, in part, by emotion rather than reason. We found, specifically, that men with a history of being brutalized in childhood seemed to both deny the pain of their own experience and their anger at the perpetrators, while simultaneously displacing that anger onto political issues that involve an element of punishment – the death penalty, the use of military force, punitive policies towards

women seeking abortions – attitudes with a large symbolic component of power, toughness and retribution. (Milburn and Conrad, 2016, p. xxi)[5]

As the researchers state presciently in the same Introduction:

> As we write this, Donald Trump has become the presumptive nominee of the Republican Party ... Mr. Trump and his followers represent exactly the destructive processes we described in *The Politics of Denial* ... Whether Trump wins or loses, the underlying psychological processes driving the success of his campaign along with the appeal of authoritarian prescriptions in response to the problems facing the United States are important to recognize and confront in the decades ahead. (Milburn and Conrad, 2016, p. xxi)

The scale of this trauma behind the public anger that leads people to vote for punitive policies and politicians has been shown in recent research on public health in the United States by Princeton economists Anne Case and Angus Deaton (whose earlier work on measuring poverty and inequality profoundly influenced John Atherton's thinking on religion and economics). In their pioneering 2015 paper on mortality and morbidity data in US public health figures, Case and Deaton exposed a hidden American tragedy among the communities who voted for Trump:

> This paper documents a marked increase in the all-cause mortality of middle-aged white non-Hispanic men and women in the United States between 1999 and 2013. This change reversed decades of progress in mortality and was unique to the United States; no other rich country saw a similar turnaround. (Case and Deaton, 2015, p. 15078)

What are the causes of falling life expectancy among these midlife white Americans? Case and Deaton have identified addiction to legally prescribed opiates as a major factor among a community in distress:

> Self-reported declines in health, mental health, and ability to conduct activities of daily living, and increases in chronic pain and inability to work, as well as clinically measured deteriorations in liver function, all point to growing distress in this population. (Case and Deaton, 2015, p. 15078)

They cautiously connect this human distress to structural changes in the economy:

> Although the epidemic of pain, suicide, and drug overdoses preceded the financial crisis, ties to economic insecurity are possible. After the productivity slowdown in the early 1970s, and with widening income inequality, many of the baby-boom generation are the first to find, in midlife, that they will not be better off than were their parents. (Case and Deaton, 2015, p. 15081)

If this kind of psychological and physical trauma in response to economic change is one factor behind the public anger driving contemporary populism in the United States, and elsewhere, then what is an appropriate response? Milburn and Conrad recognize the scale of the public and therapeutic challenge:

> Repairing the damage that the politics of denial has done to our society will not be easy, on a practical level or an emotional level. Overcoming denial as a nation ultimately begins with the individual, and the personal costs of relinquishing it are high. Part of that price is confronting complex problems for which there are no easy answers – a distressing prospect. Hasselbach ... discovered that when he left the neo-Nazi movement, 'It was as though I had stepped out of a cartoon universe into real life and was seeing it before me in its staggering complexity.' (Milburn and Conrad, 2016, p. 236)

Beyond complexity, argue Milburn and Conrad, those escaping the politics of denial must face painful feelings of loss and grief about their own early experiences of mistreatment, for so long repressed and displaced in anger not against the original perpetrators but against later, imagined scapegoats in society. When this happens, then that anger can be turned to hope:

> The hopeful message is that there is another level. Individuals and societies both use large amounts of energy maintaining denial. When denial is no longer necessary to protect us from the pain of our experiences in a punitive society, individuals, and the nation, too, will have access to that energy for creatively solving problems. The first step, we are convinced, is to develop empathy for one's own suffering; those who can empathize with themselves can begin to have empathy and compassion for others too. (Milburn and Conrad, 2016, p. 237)

This sounds very familiar for faith communities in the Abrahamic traditions: loving our neighbour *as we love ourselves*. Churches have an opportunity and a responsibility to be places where angry people can experience such a turning point in their suffering. In Wepener's words:

> I am convinced ... that the theme of anger needs to be aired in our country and that churches and other faith communities in South Africa should not focus only on the negative aspects of anger. Anger can also be viewed as a God-given emotion and the churches should be a safe place where we can voice our anger in meaningful ways, where we can say 'damn it' when we need to and not feel guilty about the fact that we have reached boiling point. To feel angry when things are not right is not wrong – it is an expression of the fact that you still care. (Wepener, 2015, p. 25)

A public theology in an age of public anger must first be a pastoral theology of care in this double sense: offering care to those emotionally and bodily damaged by de-industrialization, or indeed de-colonialization; and caring enough about these systemic causes of despair to do something to repair them by civic action. Doing public theology in an age of public anger means first developing pastoral practices of various kinds, individual, institutional and communal, that offer care for the embodied trauma of angry neighbours and damaged children. Such pastoral care could be a turning point for democracy, countering the populist politics of denial and hate. As Alastair Campbell has argued, 'In taking seriously the anger of whole groups of our fellow humans, we can learn how the pastoral ministry of truly listening leads to the prophetic ministry of truthfully speaking' (Campbell, 1986, p. 102). This leads us to our second way of seeing public anger.

Seeing public anger as trigger: turning it into political organizing

On our meridian line between hope and wrath, we can now see public anger not as indiscriminate rage against the other but as a moral pilot light, firing the commitment of ordinary citizens to work with one another through democratic practices in their locality and the wider world. That is certainly how the community organizers that I know in the United States see public anger: not as a threat to the civil order but as a trigger to action for the public good. The organizing movement that began with Saul Alinsky on the South Side of Chicago in the 1930s took self-interest, face-to-face meetings in local communities, leadership training and the calculated use of power against power to achieve winnable victories as its public engine for social change (Alinsky, 1946; 1971). His heirs today in the Industrial Areas Foundation identify those issues in local communities that cause public anger at particular injustices, and around which the natural leaders of those communities can be trained to organize their neighbours in public actions to achieve tangible benefits for their communities – better social housing, decent sanitation, improved schooling or safer streets. The power is that of ordinary citizens to bring about real change through channelling their moral anger at specific social injustices into civil, non-violent, effective political action for the common good.

It is here in the organizing movement at local level that we see the transformative power of religion and faith communities that John Atherton thought had the 'necessary but not sufficient' capacity to bend globalization. As John wrote in the Introduction to *Transfiguring Capitalism*: 'This book [and I would add, John's whole *oeuvre*] tests a hypothesis – that religion has a necessary if not essential place in our world, historically, contemporarily and in the future, in terms of contributing to the necessary maintenance and transformation of our world' (Atherton, 2003, p. 1). The best way to make John's point about religion and the global economy is to adopt his preferred method of providing empirical evidence for this claim, as he was so careful to do in his own work. Having cited the data-based analysis of Milburn and Conrad, Case and Deaton, on the root causes of public anger as physical and emotional distress, let me quote two social scientists who contributed to the volume I co-edited on faith-based organizing in the United States, *Yours the Power*. Richard Wood and Brad Fulton have conducted research on interfaith community organizing in the United States. Here is how they describe their research into this example of what John called the place of religion in maintaining and transforming the world:

> [Our research] profiles the characteristics and dynamics of a particular type of interfaith work, done under the rubric of 'broad-based', 'faith-based' or 'congregation-based' community organizing. For reasons detailed [in our work], we term this form of interfaith and religious–secular collaboration 'institution-based community organizing'. By drawing on results from a national survey of all local institution-based community organizations in the United States in 2011, [our research] documents the significance of the field, its broadly interfaith profile, how it incorporates religious practices into organizing, and the opportunities and challenges that religious diversity presents to its practitioners and to North American society. (Fulton and Wood, 2013, p. 17)

Wood and Fulton offer data to support the continuing significance of religion in institution-based community organizing (IBCO) in the United States:

> Despite the field's tendency to de-emphasize religious differences and the growing proportion of member institutions and organizers that are

secular, drawing on religious faith continues to be an integral part of the IBCO ethos. Sixty percent of ICBO offices contain objects with religious references and eighty percent of ICBOs reported that their promotional material contains religious content. Furthermore, the directors of ICBOs are, on average, more religious than the general US population (that is, they pray, read sacred texts, and attend religious services more often than the average US adult). (Fulton and Wood, 2013, p. 33)

Their analysis of such survey data leads Wood and Fulton to conclude that congregations involved in community organizing across different religions in the United States – churches, synagogues, mosques and temples – are well placed to make an impact on public life:

Although ICBO culture commonly distinguishes between congregational life and public life, a better way to think about the relationship of organizing and religion recognizes that 'public life' includes every setting in which people come together to reflect on their shared life in society. Thus, congregations themselves represent part of the public arena, and 'public life' spans both the religious and political dimensions of ICBO work. (Fulton and Wood, 2013, p. 39)

This is a conclusion about the significant political role of local congregations in public life that I think John Atherton would have welcomed. In analysing the importance of civil society for doing public theology in a global context, for example, he cites his beloved William Temple:

Actual liberty is the freedom which men [sic] enjoy in these various social units ... for it exists for the most part in and through those intermediate groups – the family, the Church or congregation, the guild, the Trade Union, the school, the university, the Mutual Improvement Society. (Temple, 1942, p. 70, quoted in Atherton, 2000, p. 96)

It is therefore through the intermediate group of the local congregation that public anger about local and global injustices can be safely expressed and constructively turned into a trigger for mobilizing its power to bring about political change. However, Atherton never lost sight of the contribution of religious transfiguration to any movement for social transformation:

For *unless* [it] is reinforced through being connected to the transfiguration narrative, to the religious-ethical dimension of the religious field, then it simply lacks the spiritual substance to perform the role [ascribed to it]. The transfiguration narrative precisely offers that possibility, essentially and profoundly as supreme *gift* to the secular. (Atherton, 2003, pp. 288–9)

As the Nobel Laureate Angus Deaton has written, John's work in religious studies was just such a gift to secular economics. And so, as Atherton reminds us, we can turn public anger towards the common good through congregation-based community organizing, but only if we retain the necessary religious narrative. And yet, as John also formulated in his hypothesis on the relationship between religion and public life, while necessary, a religious contribution is not sufficient to bring about social transformation: 'Of course, this is not to argue that such transformations can be achieved only by religion, or even more so by only one religion. It can only be by involving a variety of contributions from faiths, governments and civil societies' (Atherton, 2003, p. 1).

This brings us back to our first meeting in the Manchester conference where I defended the late Ronald Preston's advocacy of middle axioms. It is precisely the middle-axiom method in ecumenical social ethics that invites a variety of contributions in bending globalization from wrath to hope. It is also my third way of turning public anger towards the global good.

Seeing public anger as transition – turning it into provisional goals

The one thing we can assert with certainty at this moment in global political history is that there is no certainty about the future direction and welfare of the planet. The international order established by Western states after the Second World War is now unravelling with globalization, technological change and the emergence of the new economic powers of Asia, especially China and India. We are in a period of profound transition to an uncertain future, where humanly caused climate breakdown is the greatest threat to our planetary survival. The public anger of those enduring the direct effects of such a time of transition is evident around the world. The young populations of the Near East are living without prospects under tyrannical regimes and turning in their anger to political violence. The forced migrants and refugees fleeing civil wars or droughts and floods around the world despair at having no prospects at home. And the old working-class populations of the West and former Communist East now live without prospects under the impact of de-industrialization and are turning in their anger to electoral populism.

In such a global context of uncertain transition, I believe that a new case for middle axioms can be made by drawing on one unlikely source among Atherton's invited variety of contributions to social transformation,

Immanuel Kant. The American philosopher Elisabeth Ellis has shown that Kant is one of the few political thinkers who has taken seriously the politics of transition:

> Connecting all of Kant's political interests, the project of enlightenment – of escaping moral, intellectual, and political tutelage – moved Kant to think about what we now call regime change. The problem of how to escape absolute rule and make progress towards republican self-rule dominated Kant's political thought. These days we use the language of democracy to justify nearly every variety of political order, but our problems are still problems of transition. Instead of clashes between ostensibly perfect representatives of different regime types, we have a universe of in-betweens and halfway-to-who-knows-wheres cooperating and competing in unpredictable ways. Kant, among political theorists, is uniquely comfortable with the provisional and uncertain politics of transition. (Ellis, 2005, p. 1)

What guidance does Kant offer us, as those who now find ourselves tossed back and forth in the angry and uncertain global politics of transition to who-knows-where? One can of course find in Kant writings that set out his notion of an ideal state in the fairly conventional terms of moderate Enlightenment thinkers. What is original and often missed in Kant's full range of political writings, according to Ellis, is his 'concept of publicity as a motor of progress towards an ideal state', which she sees 'as among his most important contributions to modern political theory' (Ellis, 2005, p. 12). Here are the roots of a Kantian *public* theology for a time of transition:

> Though Kant explicitly places some of his political work in the long tradition of imagining and justifying perfect political systems, the more interesting and original aspects of his writing deal not with the ideal state per se but with the transition from the current, imperfect 'provisional' state towards political perfection. Scholarly attention to Kant's political philosophy has focused on his theory of the ideal state, at the expense of the far more interesting account of transition via the mechanism of publicity. Kant is rightly honored for his defense of human rights, the rule of law, and the cause of international peace; in short for his attempt to devise a political system that would protect human freedom at every level of interaction. Nevertheless, what is interesting and original in each of these achievements of Kant's comes not from his doctrine of the ideal state, which is fairly typical of moderate enlightened political thought of the time, but from his theory of the conditions of the gradual approximation of that state in practice. (Ellis, 2005, p. 13)

What are the key elements in Kant's account of political transition from the provisional to the ideal state? Unlike thinkers such as John Locke, Kant rules out violent revolution as a means of transition from despotic rule to self-rule. Kant wishes to progress slowly towards his ideal republic of self-determining and free citizens, avoiding the chaos of revolution but also escaping royal absolutism. His mechanism for gradual reform is publicity, the slow formation of opinion and citizenship through disinterested interaction in the public sphere, leading to eventual change in a political order that reflects such discourse in civil society. Ellis suggests this is not an exercise in abstract theorizing for Kant but based on his participant observation of the actual republic of letters operating in eighteenth-century Prussia and Europe:

> Kant, then, had ample opportunity to model his image of the public sphere on the rich intellectual exchange going on around him. Part of the appeal of this 'world of readers,' in fact, was its cosmopolitan nature. Writers addressed each other's arguments according to their persuasiveness without regard for social distinction, geographic location, or any other particular personal quality. By the time Kant published 'What is Enlightenment?' (1784), he had incorporated a number of the qualities of the actual public sphere into an early version of his concept of the ideal public. (Ellis, 2005, p. 32)

In his political writings, not least in his more popular essay, 'An Answer to the Question, What is Enlightenment?', Kant holds up the disinterested and civil exchange among scholars as an empirical model for interaction in this emerging public sphere. As Ellis notes:

> Though the details of his theory vary, Kant remains interested in the power of public reason as the driving force behind concrete institutional change. As early as the first *Critique* (1781), Kant writes about the need to protect an enlightened realm of inquiry that would remain free of all but the interests of reason. (Ellis, 2005, p. 13)

In *The Conflict of the Faculties*, for example, Kant develops his earlier concept of the public sphere into the notion of the judging public. As Ellis observes: 'Though the specific solutions to a number of ongoing problems vary, the main lines of Kant's argument remain the same: progress towards the just state results from comparisons made by some human agents between rational ideals and empirical reality' (2005, p. 13).

Such comparisons can only be made in the freedom of the public sphere in ways that are not possible in the regulated 'private' realm of institutions and the state which are 'necessity-governed' and 'legitimately regulated' (Ellis, 2005, p. 19). In 'What is Enlightenment?' Kant offers the concrete example of the clergyman who must subscribe to official doctrine as an officer of the Church but is free to be true to his conscience and the disinterested demands of critical reason when participating in the public sphere as a scholar. While Ellis doubts this neat distinction will hold in practice, she highlights how Kant goes on to propose 'concrete institutions for regular consultation with actual members of the public on religious matters', as a way of 'how official church doctrine might rightly be instituted' (Ellis, 2005, p. 21). Ellis concludes:

> Kant does not explicitly propose the creation of institutions for public enlightenment with regard to legislative matters, as he does for spiritual ones. He identifies religious dependence as the most dangerous kind of immaturity, from which it follows that freedom of discussion about matters of conscience matters more than other forms of free speech. However, he also mentions more than once that the sovereign would do well to allow public discussion on political topics. The comparison between a free realm for discussion of religion and one for discussion of politics becomes more explicit as the essay progresses. (2005, pp. 21–2)

Kant hopes that an enlightened king will allow such a disinterested public sphere on questions of religion to flourish in the short term, even though its eventual and inevitable politicization will lead to the demise of absolutist monarchical rule in the long term. The realms of religion and politics are therefore connected for Kant in his theory of the public sphere as the motor of progress for reform, not revolution.

Kant also analyses his mechanism of publicity for political reform in terms of his classic distinctions between the noumenal and the phenomenal, the a priori and the empirical. In Kant's politics we are always in transition from the actual and empirical state of things towards an ideal state conceived in a priori terms:

> In the first place, Kant applies his distinction between phenomena and noumena to the sphere of politics, breaking all possible knowledge of political life into actual (phenomenal) and ideal (noumenal) spheres. Manfred Riedel has translated this distinction into modern terms as a break between facts and norms. Different standards of inquiry apply to possible knowledge of each of these spheres: whereas knowledge of phenomena relies on useful but ultimately uncertain deductive reasoning, knowledge of noumena – of unchanging, 'categorically true things' – is reached via deductive reasoning. Accordingly Kant's *respublica noumenon* serves as a sort of model for the actual *respublica phenomenon*. Such a theory necessitates a mechanism whereby this ideal model

(*respublica noumenon*) would be applied to practical politics. (Ellis, 2005, pp. 33–4)

For Kant these distinctions form the conceptual basis for his politics of transition; and the public sphere and civil society provide the historical mechanism for applying his ideals to practical politics. As Ellis notes, 'Thus Kant's theory of publicity constitutes an odd, early version of our modern sense of civil society: the public judges state action and thus provides or withholds legitimacy to the state' (2005, p. 35). Here we are close to Atherton's citation of William Temple's case for the importance of having a public of intermediate groups like congregations and trade unions between the individual and the state in ensuring democratic freedom.

But *publicity* is not the only concept that Kant develops in his political writings to show how progress in practical terms from the actual state of things towards his ideal might be possible. Kant's notion of *provisional right* is the other key concept that Elisabeth Ellis identifies as central to his political thought. Ellis considers this aspect of Kant's politics in a succinct summary:

> The concept of provisional right applies to institutions that imperfectly mirror their own normative principles; since all existing political institutions do this, pragmatic politics must follow a rule of provisional rather than conclusive right. A general formulation for provisional right in Kantian language is: 'Always leave open the possibility ... of entering a rightful condition.' (Ellis, 2005, p. 112)

We have seen how publicity, or free and public deliberation on matters of common interest, is the mechanism Kant chooses to connect politics and ethics 'in the transition from the actual phenomenal state of things towards the ideal noumenal state' (Ellis, 2005, p. 114). But how is justice to be maintained amid the vagaries of transition from the actual to the ideal state? As Ellis graphically describes it, the journey to the ideal state is an extremely long one for Kant, 'But travelers on that road do not have to endure a Hobbesian nightmare of lawless insecurity until the dawn of the ideal republic. En route, the rule of provisional right applies':

> While Kant's concept of the public sphere provides a historical agent of progress towards [his ideal of] republican governance, his concept of provisional right provides the standard of justice applicable during the transition. Provisional right exists, Kant argues in the *Rechtslehre*, in the intermediate stage between the absence of civil order (the state of nature) and the advent of the ideal republic (the civil condition). Since

all actual societies on earth occupy such an intermediate position, provisional right is the rule that applies to them. Simply put, Kant's notion of provisional right requires that the norms of the ideal republican state be respected as far as possible without violating current civil order: this boils down to acting in such a way that one does not render the eventual realization of the ideal state impossible. Those on the way to the ideal republic find themselves in the provisional state between the perceived realms of freedom and nature, in this case represented by the ideal and actual political states. (Ellis, 2005, p. 114)

Classic ecumenical middle axioms from J. H. Oldham to John Baillie and Ronald Preston are close to Kant's notion of provisional right, I would argue. They all recognize the political context of our public engagement as a time of transition. They all set provisional goals between the ideal and the actual in public life that a 'variety of contributions' can support from their different ideal sets of convictions, including the 'transfiguration narratives' of religious traditions so eloquently expounded by John Atherton in his work on capitalism in a global context. They are all concerned to keep the possibility of political, social and economic progress open in the most hostile of circumstances by setting achievable goals rather than demanding impossible ideals. Middle axioms subscribe to Kant's maxim: always leave open the possibility of entering a rightful condition. That is the purpose of the provisional goals for particular societies and historical periods that are developed through the middle-axiom method of ethical reasoning.

What does a Kantian renewal of the middle-axiom method as 'provisional goal-setting' have to do with turning public anger towards hopeful political action for the common good? Quite starkly, at the root of much public anger in this time of global transition is the loss of trust in democratic states, governments, politicians and expertise by millions of people who rightly feel abandoned by such institutions and elites. In that public desert of political and economic abandonment, seven demons worse than the one cast out of the world in 1945 have now taken possession of the global body politic. If we are to 'turn it like Temple' and 'transfigure it like Atherton', then we need to rebuild public trust in the transformative capacity of civil societies, public spheres and democratic states to act wisely and deliver concretely for such abandoned communities of anger. The way to do so is to set and achieve provisional goals that keep open the possibility of entering a rightful condition – a more equal and just society, a sustainable planetary future, God's coming reign on earth as it is in heaven.

Bending it like Atherton

As we are reminded by the health data analysers and pastoral responders to the physical and emotional trauma of authoritarian childhoods and de-industrialized neighbourhoods, the way to rebuild such public trust is to provide safe places and resources for the hurt to be healed without self-harm or scapegoating the other. Congregations are one such place. Religion is one such resource. As the community organizing movement exemplifies, the way to build such public trust is to win realistic political victories in the rightful self-interest of local communities for a decent and dignified life. Religious leaders are at the forefront of such organizing. As the Mancunian advocates of middle axioms and Kantian defenders of provisional right remind us, we must turn the present towards the ideal, always keeping open the possibility of entering a rightful condition in a transitional time of public anger. Doing public theology as provisional goal-setting in collaboration with a variety of contributors is the best way to turn public anger towards hope in the global public sphere. No one 'bended it better' than John Atherton.

Notes

1 The allusion is of course to Gurinder Chadha's 2002 film *Bend It Like Beckham*, a celebration of women's soccer in a multiracial English local team from the kind of urban community that John served all his life.
2 See, for example, Seneca, *Dialogues: On Anger*, Bk III.
3 See Mark 10.4 and Hebrews 4.15.
4 Ephesians 4.26.
5 See also Milburn and Conrad, 1996.

References

Alinsky, S., [1946] 1989, *Reveille for Radicals*, New York: Vintage Books.
Alinsky, S., 1971, *Rules for Radicals: A Practical Primer for Realistic Radicals*, New York: Vintage Books.
Atherton, J. R., 2000, *Public Theology for Changing Times*, London: SCM Press.
Atherton, J. R., 2014, *Challenging Religious Studies: The Wealth, Wellbeing and Inequalities of Nations*, London: SCM Press.
Basset, L., 2007, *Holy Anger: Jacob, Job, Jesus*, Grand Rapids, MI: Eerdmans.
Bretherton, L., 2010, *Christianity and Contemporary Politics: The Conditions and Possibilities of Faithful Witness*, Oxford: Wiley-Blackwell.
Campbell, A. V., 1986, *The Gospel of Anger*, London: SPCK.
Case, A. and Deaton, A., 2015, 'Rising Morbidity and Mortality in Midlife among White Non-Hispanic Americans in the 21st century', *PNAS* 112(49) (December 8).
Ellis, E., 2005, *Kant's Politics: Provisional Theory for an Uncertain World*, New Haven, CT: Yale University Press.

Fulton, B. and Wood, R. L., 2013, 'Interfaith Community Organizing: Emerging Theological and Organizational Challenges', in W. Storrar et al. (eds), *Yours the Power: Faith-based Organizing in the USA*, Leiden: Brill.

Gecan, M., 2004, *Going Public: An Organizer's Guide to Citizen Action*, New York: Anchor.

Hessel, S., 2011, *Time for Outrage <<Indignez-vous!>>*, New York: Twelve/Hachette Book Group.

Milburn, M. A. and Conrad, S. D., 1996, *The Politics of Denial*, Cambridge, MA: MIT Press.

Milburn M. A. and Conrad, S. D., 2016, *Raised to Rage: The Politics of Anger and the Roots of Authoritarianism*, Cambridge, MA: MIT Press.

Miner, R., 2009, *Thomas Aquinas on the Passions: A Study of* Summa Theologiae *1a2ae 22–48*, Cambridge: Cambridge University Press.

Storrar, W., 2004, 'Scottish Civil Society and Devolution: The New Case for Ronald Preston's Defence of Middle Axioms', in Esther Reed and Elaine Graham (eds), *The Future of Christian Social Ethics: Essays on the Work of Ronald Preston 1913–2000*, Studies in Christian Ethics 17(2), London: T&T Clark Continuum, pp. 37–46.

Stout, J., 2013, *Blessed are the Organized: Grassroots Democracy in America*, Princeton, NJ: Princeton University Press.

Temple, W., 1942, *Christianity and Social Order*, Harmondsworth: Penguin.

Thurman, Robert A. F., 2004, *Anger*, New York: Oxford University Press.

Wepener, C., 2015, *Boiling Point: Reflections on Anger – A Faithful Reaction of a Disillusioned Nation*, Wellington, South Africa: Biblecor.

10

Flourishing and Ambiguity in UK Urban Mission

ANNA RUDDICK

As the nature of the 'urban' in the UK changes, complicated by high-density populations, gentrification and precarious livelihoods, so too must the responses of Christians involved in urban mission. John Atherton's concern for the wellbeing of humanity began with his experiences as a parish priest in Salford and Glasgow. From exposure to the realities of poverty and marginalization in these urban communities, Atherton developed his understandings of poverty and wellbeing and the appropriate Christian response to the urban. This chapter seeks to situate Atherton's work on wellbeing and Christian responses to poverty back into current trends in urban mission. I argue that Christianity, as it is expressed in contemporary urban mission, contributes to wellbeing through community rather than church-centric perspectives and practices.

In response to the changing dynamics of poverty in UK society, urban mission is increasingly shaped by a methodological and practical commitment to listening to people experiencing poverty and seeking to be alongside to learn and build community together. This entails vulnerability and the willingness to be changed by the 'other', insights that constitute a significant contribution for urban mission to offer to the wider Church. Beginning with an exploration of these commitments, I go on to illustrate them, drawing on research into the incarnational urban mission of the evangelical Eden Network.[1] In this case study, urban mission aims for human flourishing understood as a stronger love of self, a more positive approach to life choices, an increased ability to act, increasing awareness of a good God, and mutuality. Alongside this, however, come elements of loss and ambiguity, highlighting the vulnerability of building mutual missional relationships in situations of marginalization. Using Atherton's modelling of the relationship between Christianity and wellbeing (Atherton, 2014), I will evaluate the contribution of the Eden Network's urban mission to the wellbeing of participants and suggest that it addresses the wellbeing of people experiencing marginalization by offering both an affirmation of personhood and practical opportunities for participation.

Through his commitment to interdisciplinary work between theology, religious studies, psychology, sociology and economics, Atherton demonstrates the task of those engaged in urban mission – to understand the varied forces at play in the urban context and to seek to navigate them alongside others for our shared flourishing. This chapter suggests that a central part of this task is to draw together the experiences of urban mission practitioners and people in urban communities and engage them in interdisciplinary and theological reflection alongside wider theoretical frameworks and denominational hierarchies.

Partnership and reconciliation: emerging threads in UK urban mission

In *Challenging Religious Studies*, Atherton concludes that Britain may be entering a season of partnership and reconciliation in which the binaries of individual and crowd and qualitative and quantitative methodologies are overcome; and interdisciplinary working becomes the norm, preventing intellectual and practical siloes (Atherton, 2014, pp. 185–6). While acknowledging that the path is unclear, he considers the renewed role for faith groups in society and the acknowledgement of participation as a contributor to individual wellbeing to be positive signs for the future (2014, pp. 188–90).

Moves towards such positive partnership are evident in recent developments in UK urban mission. Urban theology as it emerged in the 1970s and 80s was largely focused on inner cities and social housing estates. However, as Baker describes, urban spaces are increasingly complex and characterized by a hybrid world view in which identities are blurred and local issues are impacted by global forces. He argues that this hybridity is ambiguous: 'it works in ways that are exciting and creative while simultaneously reinforcing marginalization and poverty' (Baker, 2009, p. 8). The static inner city or outer estate is now complicated by gentrification and development on one side and transient and precarious gig economy, refugee and migrant communities on the other. Entrenched and generational poverty still exists in some areas, exacerbated by the additional challenges of adapting to religious and cultural diversity and experiencing the sharp end of austerity, and leading to disenfranchised communities. Baker describes the combination of global forces, hyper-mobility and post-colonial culture creating an environment of contested space and marginalization, the underside of the market-created, consumer-orientated 'city-lite' (2009, pp. 35–41). Such rising inequality, austerity and hybridity mean that areas historically seen as 'estate' or 'urban' are not the only places in which there is local poverty, calling into question an exclusively 'urban' mission.

A focus on those who find themselves excluded from the marketplace of global cities has been a defining feature of urban theology, and, as the context shifts, the concept of *marginality* may have more resilience to adapt than that of the urban. Pears sees 'marginalization' as usefully combining 'both geographical and social exclusion', 'physical poverty and multiple forms of deprivation' (Pears, 2016, p. 37). A focus on marginalized people, groups or communities enables a flexible and capacious response to contemporary poverty and theologically refocuses on the margins, rather than the centre, as the source of divine revelation (Veling, 2005, p. 70; Kilpin and Murray, 2007, p. 10).

A focus on marginality has developed alongside two other themes within urban mission and Christian responses to poverty more broadly: attending to direct experience of poverty, and a focus on presence and mutuality in relationship with people in poverty summarized by Sam Wells as 'being with' (Wells, 2015, p. 23). Together these represent significant progress towards the kind of partnership and reconciliation envisaged by Atherton.

Prioritizing direct experience of poverty

While urban theology has been deeply influenced by a liberationist perspective of a preferential option for the poor, this has not always led to foregrounding the voices of people with direct experience of poverty. In fact, the majority of urban theology has been written by Christian leaders, incomers to deprived communities, seeking to process their experiences and reinterpret their inherited traditions in the light of their new and challenging contexts. Recent initiatives in urban mission practice seek to reorientate the conversation towards amplifying the voices of people for whom silencing is a part of their marginalization. For example, the Poverty Truth Commission works regionally, bringing those with direct experience of poverty together with those in positions of power, facilitating conversations designed to build empathetic personal relationships and to enable shared action for structural change in the area.[2]

Another feature of this shift is a rise in broad-based community organizing with the growth of Citizens UK and its regional counterparts. This is exemplified by the work of the Centre for Theology and Community in London and the renaming of the Urban Theology Unit in 2016 as the Urban Theology Union, with, as its new Director Keith Hebden describes, a desire to 'build the collective and personal power of our members to transform their work' (Hebden, 2016). This focus on elevating the voices of people experiencing marginalization is an important step in allowing urban theology to develop along with the changing experience of poverty and marginalization.

'Being with' not 'working for'

Complementing the focus on the voices of people experiencing poverty is a conversation which challenges the role of the non-poor in response to poverty. The language of doing 'with', rather than 'to' or 'for' has been a part of the vernacular of urban mission for many years. But it is now gaining further clarity through a renewed emphasis on community development and is helpfully explored in the work of Sam Wells.

In *Living Without Enemies*, Wells and Owen describe four possible responses to poverty, distinguishing between 'working' as a task-orientated approach to solving problems, and 'being' as concerned with presence and celebration of a person in the midst of their situation (Wells and Owen, 2011, pp. 44–7). 'Working for' involves 'tackling obstacles' on behalf of the person in poverty; 'working with' is more collaborative, still working, but in partnership, respecting the agency of the person in poverty. Third, 'being for' does not involve activism or direct relationship but is rather an orientation of one's life towards the wellbeing of the poor. The fourth response is 'being with' which, elsewhere, Wells describes as about stillness and disposition, receiving the gift of the person in poverty (Wells, 2015, p. 23).

Wells argues that 'while there is a place for working for, working with and being for, it is being with that is the most faithful form of Christian witness and mission.' In this he draws on Jesus' invisible 'Nazareth years' as God's 'being with' humanity, and emphasizes a view of creation as something to be enjoyed, not as a problem to be solved (Wells, 2015, p. 23). This provides a helpful corrective to the dominance of solution-focused and service-orientated responses to poverty that define people by their needs. Organizations such as Church Urban Fund and Livability are working to promote mutual, community-building approaches to marginalization, and alternative models such as Asset-based Community Development, Co-production and Local Area Co-ordination are gaining momentum within churches as well as in the statutory sector (Eckley, Ruddick and Walker, 2015). These emerging trends within urban mission demonstrate a methodological resonance with Atherton's work and point towards the ways in which Christianity contributes to the wellbeing of society. To explore this contribution in more detail, the following case study presents the findings of research into the incarnational urban mission of the Eden Network, which exemplify the themes identified above.

Case study: the Eden Network's contribution to wellbeing

The Eden Network is a national, and newly international, initiative of the Message Trust, which places incarnational mission teams into local churches in urban communities identified as among the most deprived in the country. From my position as a participant observer, both employed in a national developmental role by the Eden Network and living in an Eden community, I sought to research the relational dynamics between Eden teams and the urban community members they encountered. My hope was to understand what kind of outcomes were arising from this activity and how they were coming about. I identified a new model of mission emerging between Eden team members and community members, which I call missional pastoral care. This model is characterized by mutual meaning-making and results in a complex good, involving both flourishing and ambiguity. Before assessing missional pastoral care as a contribution to wellbeing, I first consider the ways in which Atherton's methodological approach is expressed in my analysis of urban mission practices.

Methodological keys

Atherton suggests that certain specific methodological commitments are necessary in order to address an issue as wide ranging as human wellbeing. First, he affirms practical theology as an important step forward in its interdisciplinary approach and in its ability to integrate the theoretical with the experiential (Atherton, 2014, p. 18). In this practical theological study, sociological and ethnographic research tools blended with work on pastoral care, religious identity and evangelical theology. The interdisciplinary nature of this project was necessitated by the real-world locatedness of the research and my desire to generate insight that could be translated back into the practice of urban ministry. Taking an ethnographic approach meant observation as well as interviewing, and a focus on analysing observed experiences alongside narratives of experiences. As a result, it is the practices of Eden teams and urban community members that have formed the basis for my conclusions, aligning with Atherton's emphasis on practice rather than belief and revealed rather than expressed convictions as being more significant in understanding the realities of people's lives (Atherton, 2014, p. 76).

Second, Atherton highlights the difference between institutional and practitioner understandings of religious faith and advocates a focus on the 'ordinary church' (2014, p. 75). My commitment to an 'ordinary' account of urban mission was motivated by an awareness of a dissonance between the narrative that was told about the work and its outcomes by the Eden Network as an organization and the reality of the work and its outcomes as experienced by those involved. Eden team members found themselves in the crux of this dissonance and many expressed confusion and disappointment when their expectations for their ministry were not realized. Atherton's approach to issues of human wellbeing is rooted in his experiences of ministry among people in poverty. Likewise, by starting with the experiences of Eden team members and urban community members I consider them as 'an interpretative context which raises new questions, offers challenges and demands answers of the gospel' (Swinton and Mowat, 2006, pp. 6–18).

In my doctoral research into the activities of the Eden Network I questioned who defines mission and ministry and prioritized the perspective of Eden teams and urban community members as practitioners and so-called 'recipients' of ministry models (Ruddick, 2016). By inviting Eden team members to share their experiences of ministry I addressed the theological and organizational superstructures of evangelicalism from the perspective of ordinary practitioners. Furthermore, by drawing on the experiences of urban community members I enabled the working-class recipients of middle-class evangelical mission to define it for themselves, undermining the power relations inherent in social class and between missioner and missionized. In doing so I acknowledged the liberative potential of attending to experience, allowing those traditionally objectified to tell their story (Skeggs, 1997, p. 27).

A final methodological challenge issued by Atherton is the need for religious studies to hold together the personal, national and global scope of wellbeing (Atherton, 2014, p. 18). In his work, Atherton traversed from the deeply personal engagement of urban ministry as expressed in the stories he includes in his first book, *The Scandal of Poverty* (1983), to his use of cliometric studies of long history in *Challenging Religious Studies* (2014, pp. 105–20). While in my research the 16 qualitative interviews and period of participant observation make the study personal in scale, in the work that follows I draw my data alongside Atherton's model for evaluating the contribution of Christianity to wellbeing and in doing so begin to connect my study with his quantitative survey of indicators of wellbeing.

Missional pastoral care as a contribution to wellbeing

Eden teams began their urban ministry with an inherited and top-down missional narrative, strongly influenced by Western, middle-class, evangelical social norms, which set expectations of conversion and life change. What in fact took place was an emergent form of missional living: missional pastoral care. In this new model, a way of life characterized by difference, locality, availability, practicality, long-term commitment, consistency and love, brought about a process of meaning-making for both Eden team members and urban community members. The relationships they built together involved the mutual sharing of experiences and life stories, and over time the world views of each began to change. Of central importance in missional pastoral care is the combination of difference and love, expressed as an affirmation of the personhood of the 'other'. These elements together create safe space in which new meanings can be experimented with and life changes established.

To consider missional pastoral care as a contribution to wellbeing I begin with more general perspectives on wellbeing and its contributory factors. Atherton articulates the trajectory of human wellbeing along three strands: material wellbeing ('Do I have enough money?'), life expectancy and health ('What is the length and quality of my life?'), and subjective wellbeing ('How happy am I?'). The first two inevitably impact the third. He notes the correlation between economists (primarily Layard's big seven) and psychologists (drawing on Diener and Biswas-Diener) in their assessment of what contributes to wellbeing: life satisfaction and happiness, spirituality and meaning, positive attitudes and emotions, loving social relationships, engaging activities and work, values and life goals to achieve them, physical and mental health, and material sufficiency to meet our needs (Atherton, 2014, p. 51). Following Atherton's approach, I can assess the contribution of missional pastoral care to wellbeing by noting the ways in which it promotes these elements.

The result of missional pastoral care is a 'complex good' containing multiple elements, some of which are experienced positively as flourishing, resonant with the work of Grace Jantzen (Jantzen, 1998, pp. 156–8), and others which are experienced as loss, ambiguity and limitation (Gerkin, 1984, p. 65). In the experiences of my participants I identified five interconnecting effects of missional pastoral care which constitute the positive aspects of the complex good: a stronger love of self, a more positive approach to life choices, an increased ability to act, increasing awareness of a good God, and mutuality. Across the stories of my participants these five effects were consistently present, constituting both a part of the process of missional pastoral care practice as well as the result of it. They demonstrate clear resonance with economic and psychological perspectives on enabling wellbeing, as the story of Paul, a community member from Manchester, illustrates:

> I'm not a Christian now but I spend a lot of me time with the Christians ... I do a lot of voluntary work ... I do get a lot of responsibility off 'em and obviously I appreciate that 'cos it's trust and I am a trustworthy guy ... it does make you feel good because someone's trusting you with all their property ...

... say if I carried on on the streets ... half of us probably be in jail now ... but knowing these and starting getting into all more activities and helping out ... I see my change ... obviously we still went back to do our own stuff while we was with them but instead of just climb one ladder causing trouble I was climbing two. So I was still messing about causing trouble but also climbing the ladder to gain respect you know ... cos I was being with them and then ... things move on like so I was climbing two instead of one and obviously you only want to climb one ladder and I just jumped back on to the good ladder to go the good way.

God in a way does help you [find] your way through everything if you think about it but I wanna see something before I believe in him ... God's probably that one rung ahead of me, you know until actually something happens and I meet up with him, and until that day I'm always going to be one behind him.

I could stay away from [the church] for a long time ... but obviously if I still got to see the people because they're good friends now ... obviously your friends come and go but these people I've had for eight, nine, ten, some of them ... twelve years so you build a good friendship with 'em cos you know they're always going to be around, so you can trust 'em.

In Paul's account, the correlation between the effects of missional pastoral care and his own wellbeing are clear. He describes loving, long-term social relationships which involved responsibility, through his volunteering at the church, and mutuality. These relationships enabled Paul to develop stronger self-esteem and to make positive life choices in accordance with his self-perception as a 'trustworthy guy'. He describes feeling good and his words demonstrate a satisfaction in his choice to go 'the good way'. While Paul does not consider himself a Christian he articulates a developing spirituality based on a helping, if elusive, God with whom he expects one day to meet up. While not directly addressing health or income it is expected that the mutual community of care enabled by missional pastoral care is supportive of good mental and physical health. Furthermore, while missional pastoral care does not cancel out the real structural and entrenched poverty experienced by some participants, it can begin to address it at a personal and local level. Paul's choice to 'go the good way' led, as he described in the rest of his interview, to his current job and the qualifications he has achieved, which have enabled him to secure a regular income.

A further step in this case study is to consider in what ways missional pastoral care demonstrates the contribution of Christianity to the subjective wellbeing of its adherents and that of wider society. In this respect Atherton develops a model comprising seven features of Christianity, which, he notes, are identified by secular sources as promoting wellbeing among practising Christians (2014, pp. 64–9). They are:

- comforting beliefs which generate positive emotions;
- transcendence, or connection to realities greater than the self;
- personal and corporate experiences of ritual;
- regulating lifestyle and behaviour, including ethics and acquiring skills to better participate in society;
- churchgoing as social support and networking;
- nurturing children;
- generating and sustaining personal values and meaningful philosophies of life. (Atherton, 2014, p. 65)

Holding these features alongside my analysis of missional pastoral care highlights areas of correlation and of difference. The starting point for Eden team members is the local community rather than the church; and while Eden teams are rooted in a local church context this may be unconventional, adopting an experimental planting approach. Equally, the primary focus of Eden teams is not to enculturate others into a normative Christian 'churchgoing' life, and experiences of ritual such as worship are not foregrounded within missional pastoral care. Churchgoing is also not the primary focus for social support; instead, the neighbourhood becomes the locus of supportive networks. Correlation can be seen, however, in the way in which missional pastoral care relationships enabled Paul to develop his personal value system, including a transcendent element. Meaning-making is at the heart of missional pastoral care, in which life philosophies are communicated and new, shared values emerge between Eden team members and urban community members, shaping identity. From this base of affirmed identity, personal ethics and participation in society emerge.

Missional pastoral care is located in the community rather than in the Church and is orientated towards the affirmation of personhood among participants. This suggests that the contribution to wellbeing of contemporary urban mission may be conceived in terms broader than the seven elements currently acknowledged, while also questioning the sense in which missional pastoral care constitutes a *Christian* contribution to wellbeing.

To understand the incongruence between the features of Christian practice that promote greater wellbeing and the way of life described in missional pastoral care it is important to note two defining theological convictions: the incoming shalom or Kingdom of God in the world and *missio Dei*, the understanding of God's mission as being essential to his nature. Underpinning these is a positive anthropology resonant with that found in the work of Grace Jantzen. I construe the outcome of missional pastoral care as a kind of flourishing based on Jantzen's definition of the term as 'growth and fruition from an inner creative and healthy dynamic' (Jantzen, 1998, p. 161). Jantzen's flourishing is a process of thriving that begins with an affirmation of the world and the self; it is embodied, derived from our 'natality', and contains a necessary interconnection to other people and to ecosystems. It affirms the 'natural inner capacity [of humanity] ... being able to draw on inner resources and interconnection with one another' (1998, pp. 160–5). This accounts for the impacts on the inner lives of participants, relating to their sense of self and their way of understanding the world and their place within it, while also including the corporate and communal elements of shared meaning-making and mutuality.

Jantzen's flourishing requires God's immanence rather than distance as the 'divine source and ground' of all creation and as incarnate within humanity (Jantzen, 1998, p. 161). In missional pastoral care God's immanence is conceived in two related theological themes. First, that of the *missio Dei*, which states that 'mission is not primarily an activity of the church, but an attribute of God' (Bosch, 2011, p. 399). The implication of this theology is that God is going about his mission in the world, and the task of the Church therefore becomes finding ways to participate in this activity of God wherever he may be found. Second, the focus of God's mission is an incoming 'shalom', or Kingdom of God, defined by Nicholas Wolterstorff as 'the human being dwelling at peace with all his or her relationships: with God, with self, with fellows, with nature' (Wolterstorff, 1983, pp. 69–71). These two themes locate the practices of Christianity in the community of the world rather than that of the Church, and an acknowledgement of God at work among people outside of the Church leads to an affirmation of the context of the self and the urban community as sites of God's presence.

Baker's work on participation can help to situate this as a contribution to wellbeing. He argues that a central way for Christianity to promote wellbeing is in its capacity to generate and mobilize religious and spiritual capital to engage in wider society (Baker, 2011, pp. 181–2). Building on this he suggests a framework of *belonging, becoming* and *participation*, which traces the relational and identity-forming elements of faith and their relationship to engagement with the community. In this framework, *belonging* to a religious community leads to personal growth, a sense of *becoming*, which in turn results in *participation* in the wider community (Baker, 2013, p. 355). The focus on belonging and becoming account for the importance of relationships within missional pastoral care and for their central task of meaning-making, shaping the identities of those involved. Paul's story illustrates how this occurs alongside community participation, both as a part of the process of belonging and becoming as well as its outcome. Therefore, in missional pastoral care, Christianity can be seen as promoting wellbeing both within and beyond itself from a starting point of the community rather than the Church, and through the processes of identity-formation in relationships and in participation.

This case study demonstrates the way in which Atherton's engagement of the practices of ordinary Christians with statistical evidence can add to and nuance a practical theological project. As an ethnographic study with a small, qualitative sample, the significance of this research lies in its ability to provide resonance rather than in any conception of generalizability. Geertz describes the process of engaging the local detail of ethnographic research with global structures or concepts as 'dialectical' movement, a cyclical process in which they begin to explain one another (Geertz, 1999, pp. 61–2). By demonstrating the connections between my research findings and economic, sociological and psychological literature on wellbeing it is shown to provide an important 'ordinary' contribution to understandings of faith and wellbeing.

Implications and tensions

The themes of prioritizing direct experience of poverty and practices of being with rather than working for in urban mission are illustrated in my case study of the urban mission experiences of the Eden Network. In considering the practical outworking of these commitments by Eden team members a tension concerning the role of the local and national church becomes evident. In the analysis of Christianity's contribution to wellbeing offered by Atherton, church-based Christian practices generate increased wellbeing that flows via transmission processes to the wider society. My research complicates this in that the practices that are generative of wellbeing are not church-based, rather they are located in a neighbourhood with a more diffuse sense of Christian community embedded within the wider community. Relationships that affirm personhood and encourage meaning-making in words and in participative practices generate increased wellbeing among Christians and others, with the wider society benefiting from the process and the outcome as it is focused on building up the local community as a site of incoming shalom.

This tension is expressed in current Christian engagement with poverty as questions relating to power and the role of the Church. Is the Church to be understood as the provider of wellbeing or salvation, or as a participant in mutual receiving and giving, building shalom in communities? While, as I have shown, in the urban mission tradition mutuality and partnership have become defining values, with the diffusion of poverty from the exclusively 'urban' to the social and geographic margins of most communities, there has been a much wider engagement in issues of poverty among local churches, bringing these tensions out of the inner city to the mainstream Church.[3]

At a practical level there is a fresh recognition that much of the church activity that seeks to address poverty assumes that the Church's role is as provider. It therefore takes a 'service delivery' approach, in which 'service users' benefit from what is offered (emergency food, a night shelter, a parent and toddler group) without having a role in shaping or contributing to that provision. This approach establishes a client–provider relationship in which the service user becomes defined by their need and the Church as the source of help. The profusion of this type of intervention can be seen, in part, as due to the church response to political ideas of a Big Society, in which a robust voluntary sector steps in to shore up the gaps in a struggling welfare state. Many local churches perceive this as a way to make a positive contribution in their communities and to meet a real need. However, as Smith notes, particularly within evangelical Christianity, the tendency to understand poverty in individualized terms leads to a focus on 'handouts' rather than addressing the 'structural and political causes' of poverty (Smith, 2017, pp. 31–2).

Within debates on mission and evangelism the role of the Church is equally at the fore. Urban Life is an organic group 'collaborating to explore new approaches to mission and Christian presence among marginalised people groups and neighbourhoods in UK society' (Urban Life, 2017). As a new contribution to the urban mission tradition they have usefully explored the shifts from urban to marginality and are articulating contextual approaches to mission rooted in a post-colonial critique of the provider-church model of mission (Pears and Cloke, 2016, pp. 4–9). Others, such as the National Estate Churches Network, are seeking to ask afresh what is meant by 'good news' for those living on housing estates, as well as contributing an urban perspective to wider denominational concerns for church growth.

Tensions concerning the approach of Christians seeking to engage with poverty, the role of the Church in public life and in marginalized communities, and the need for growth within declining denominations, all complicate any moves towards partnership and reconciliation. Atherton's third age is emerging, but it is contested. With the presence of poverty in many more hybrid communities, and the involvement of the Church in addressing this, there is a need for the wider Church to listen to the learning of the urban mission tradition and be willing to undergo its own conversion to mutuality and community building.

This raises the question of how the insights of urban mission are communicated to the wider Church. Holding the tension between theoretical conceptions of marginality and mission and the ordinary experiences of both at the grass roots is, I suggest, a central task of urban mission. Atherton's concern was to effect change in communities, increasing wellbeing, because that was at the heart of his understanding of Christian faith. Bridging the gaps between the ordinary and the academy to ensure that practice and theory inform one another for the sake of learning and greater wellbeing is the way in which urban mission as a tradition can continue to enrich the understanding of marginalization and the missional practice of the Church.

Conclusion

Missional pastoral care produces a complex good in which loss and ambiguity are the counterpart to flourishing. Such ambiguity is found in vulnerability, and in the challenge to and breaking apart of aspects of meaning-systems, which occurs in the mutual relationships of missional pastoral care. Therefore, in this model, ambiguity is a necessary part of the process of flourishing without which the more positive outcomes described above would not be possible. Anxiety concerning vulnerability and changes in one's self-understanding can be seen in the institutional tensions outlined above. Entering into relationships of mutuality requires a relinquishing of power over, in favour of the affirmation of difference and personhood within the relationship. Christian denominations engaging with poverty and marginalization are being confronted by the need to change their world views of ascendency and domination, even goodness, in order to acknowledge the ways in which they have been complicit in impoverishing and marginalizing people through their theologies of us and them, their needs-focused social service provision and their colonial modes of mission (Pears and Cloke, 2016, p. 5).

Within UK urban mission, previous notions of urban places, urban people and urban missional engagement are being challenged by the social, economic, cultural and political changes in UK society. There is a consistent demand to keep paying attention, so that a once contextual theology does not stultify and find itself addressing a context that no longer exists. Atherton's work provides a methodology and precedent for such paying attention to take an interdisciplinary view of both the ordinary and the theoretical, the personal and the crowd, thereby creating a rich and robust understanding of changing contexts and the modes of engagement that can best promote human wellbeing. The emergence of the themes and practices explored above offer a hopeful future for Christian contributions to wellbeing, which arise primarily from within the community rather than the Church. In this, missional pastoral care, alongside other developments in contemporary urban mission, demonstrates positive steps towards Atherton's hope that theology and religious studies can take seriously the practices of ordinary people and engage them critically with denominational or theological narratives and a wide range of academic and theoretical discourses.

Notes

1 For more information on the Eden Network, see www.joineden.org.
2 For example see www.leedspovertytruth.org.uk/.
3 Statistics from the Church Urban Fund suggest that 90 per cent of Anglican churches are responding to at least one social need in their communities (Eckley and Sefton, 2015). Additionally, Greg Smith's survey of evangelical social action concludes that while the complexity of evangelicalism makes it difficult to quantify, nevertheless 'the available evidence does suggest a substantial level of evangelical social engagement in the UK today' (Smith, 2017, p. 28).

References

Atherton, J. R., 1983, *The Scandal of Poverty: Priorities for the Emerging Church*, Oxford: Mowbray.
Atherton, J. R., 2014, *Challenging Religious Studies: The Wealth, Wellbeing and Inequalities of Nations*, London: SCM Press.
Atherton, J. R., Graham, E. L. and Steedman, I., 2011, *The Practices of Happiness: Political Economy, Religion and Wellbeing*, London: Routledge.
Baker, C. R., 2009, *The Hybrid Church in the City*, London: SCM Press.
Baker, C. R., 2011, 'The "One in the Morning" Knock: Exploring the Connections between Faith, Participation and Wellbeing', in J. R. Atherton, E. L. Graham and I. Steedman (eds), *The Practices of Happiness: Political Economy, Religion and Wellbeing*, London: Routledge, pp. 169–83.
Baker, C. R., 2013, 'Moral Freighting and Civic Engagement: A UK Perspective on Putnam and Campbell's Theory of Religious-based Social Action', *Sociology of Religion: A Quarterly Review* 74:3, pp. 343–69.
Bevans, S. B. and Schroeder, R. P., 2011, *Prophetic Dialogue: Reflections on Christian Mission Today*, New York: Orbis Books.
Bosch, D. J., 2011, *Transforming Mission: Paradigm Shifts in Theology of Mission*, 2nd edn, New York: Orbis Books.
Eckley, B. and Sefton, T., 2015, *Church in Action: A National Survey of Church-based Social Action*, London: Church Urban Fund.
Eckley, B., Ruddick, A. and Walker, R., 2015, *Fullness of Life Together: Reimagining Christian Engagement in Our Communities*, London: Livability and Church Urban Fund.
Geertz, C., 1973, *The Interpretation of Cultures*, New York: Basic Books.
Geertz, C., 1999, '"From the Native's Point of View": On the Nature of Anthropological Understanding', in R. T. McCutcheon (ed.), *The Insider/Outsider Problem in the Study of Religion: A Reader*, London: Continuum, pp. 50–63.
Gerkin, C. V., 1984, *The Living Human Document*, Nashville, TN: Abingdon Press.

Hebden, K., 2016, *Why Urban Theology 'Union'?* (15 November), retrieved from utusheffield: http://utusheffield.org.uk/2016/11/15/why-a-union/.

Jantzen, G. M., 1998, *Becoming Divine: Towards a Feminist Philosophy of Religion*, Manchester: Manchester University Press.

Kilpin, J. and Murray, S., 2007, *Church Planting in the Inner City: The Urban Expression Story*, Cambridge: Grove.

Kuhrt, J., 2010, 'Going Deeper Together: Resisting Tribal Theology', in A. Davey (ed.), *Crossover City*, London: Mowbray, pp. 14–21.

Pears, M., 2016, 'Place and Marginality: The Formation of Redemptive Places', in P. Cloke and M. Pears (eds), *Mission in Marginal Places: The Theory*, Milton Keynes: Paternoster Press, pp. 33–56.

Pears, M. and Cloke, P., 2016, *Mission in Marginal Places: The Theory*, Milton Keynes: Paternoster Press.

Ruddick, A., 2016, 'Missional Pastoral Care: Innovation in Charismatic Evangelical Urban Practice', Doctor of Professional Studies dissertation, University of Chester, available at: http://chesterrep.openrepository.com/cdr/handle/10034/620322.

Ruddick, A. and Eckley, B., 2016, *Building Kingdom Communities: The Prophetic Role of the Church in Community Engagement*, London: Livability and Church Urban Fund.

Skeggs, B., 1997, *Formations of Class and Gender: Becoming Respectable*, London: Sage.

Smith, G., 2017, 'Evangelical Social Action in the UK', *Crucible: The Journal of Christian Social Ethics*, October, pp. 25–37.

Swinton, J. and Mowat, H., 2006, *Practical Theology and Qualitative Research*, London: SCM Press.

Urban Life, 2017, *Urban Life: The Journey So Far*, Bristol: Urban Life.

Veling, T., 2005, *Practical Theology: On Earth as It is in Heaven*, New York: Orbis Books.

Wells, S., 2015, *Nazareth Manifesto: Being with God*, Chichester: Wiley Blackwell.

Wells, S. and Owen, M. A., 2011, *Living Without Enemies: Being Present in the Midst of Violence*, Downers Grove, IL: InterVarsity Press.

Wolterstorff, N., 1983, *Until Justice and Peace Embrace*, Grand Rapids, MI: Eerdmans.

11

Alternative Possible Futures: Unearthing a Catholic Public Theology for Northern Ireland

MARIA POWER

The Roman Catholic Church is often described as fortunate to have the pre-packaged and unified body of social and political ethics that is commonly known as Catholic Social Teaching (CST).[1] As Malcolm Brown argues, 'Catholics, it is implied, know why they do what they do and can locate their actions within a developed tradition that both guides engagement and justifies it to others' (Brown, 2014, p. 4). According to this reasoning, there should be a flourishing body of Catholic public theology in Northern Ireland – a region in the UK that has more reasons than most to expect such an intervention in the public square from its religious institutions (Elliott, 2009). However, despite popular conceptions, CST and Catholic public theology are not the same thing. CST is not the unified body of thought that it is often assumed to be. Instead it is full of tensions. Take for example this passage from *Populorum Progressio*, Paul VI's encyclical on development, which, in the 50 years since its promulgation on 26 March 1967, has provided inspiration for many.

> Everyone knows, however, that revolutionary uprisings – except where there is manifest, longstanding tyranny which would do great damage to fundamental personal rights and dangerous harm to the common good of the country – engender new injustices, introduce new inequities and bring new disasters. The evil situation that exists, and it surely is evil, may not be dealt with in such a way that an even worse situation results. (Paul VI, 1967, §31)

The manifest tyranny of which Paul VI speaks is communism, and in this paragraph can be seen a compromise between the hawks and the doves within the Catholic hierarchy. These tensions and compromises inevitably bury the vision that is the very essence of any public theology.

Further, they highlight that while it is true that CST should feed into the development of a Catholic public theology, it cannot and should not be its only source. Merely falling back on CST as an uncontextualized body of teaching is not enough and it could be argued that the lack of a public theology for Northern Ireland is a direct consequence of the misunderstanding that CST is a systematic, cumulative and unified body of thought (Forrester, 2001, p. 196) that can be simply uncritically translated into any setting.

Using John Atherton's theological method, which is incarnational, dialogical and practical, which for Atherton meant engaging with the secular and empirical, I therefore intend to undertake the task of outlining the contours of what I call a Catholic public theology for Northern Ireland. This chapter represents a conversation between Atherton's aim to 'attempt to demonstrate the value of theology not just in its own world but in the world of politics, economics, government and civil society' and, crucially, making connections between the social, economic and historical context (Atherton, 2003, p. 6), and the principle of orthopraxis seen in liberation theology. Through it, I will begin to show how influential John Atherton's work will be in creating a bridge between the doctrinal focus of CST and the practice of a Catholic public theology.

The practice of theology by Atherton and liberation theologians

In creating a Catholic public theology, Roman Catholic theologians have much to learn from the Protestant tradition, especially from John Atherton. Most instructively his work teases out the interconnectivity between the secular and the religious, which, although hinted at, is never fully expressed in CST:

> It is the special vocation of the laity to seek the kingdom of God by engaging in temporal affairs and directing them according to God's will. They live in the world, in each and every one of the world's occupations and callings and in the ordinary circumstances of social and family life which, as it were, form the content of their existence. (Second Vatican Council, 1964, §31; cf. Second Vatican Council, 1965, §72)

For Atherton, public theology 'is a development based upon practical experience and reflective observation of contemporary secular and church life' (Atherton, 2000, p. 3). It thus needs to be grounded enough in contemporary realities, while remaining focused upon God's relationship to and desires for the world, to enable the vision presented to be realized. This crucial element was emphasized by Atherton when he argued that 'we cannot start again. I believe [Young (1990)] is right so we will reject all the radical alternatives symbolised say by radical orthodoxy, essentially returning to pre-industrial Christendom models. We should regard these as cul de sacs, however creative ... as terminal wistfulness' (2004, p. 26). Here, Atherton deftly prevents public theology from becoming utopian. Instead, he empowers it to proactively address issues such as marginalization and the democratic deficit, which have been at the centre of the conflict in Northern Ireland. Thus, building upon Atherton's work, it is my contention that a public theology for Northern Ireland needs to be based upon interaction between the local leadership of the Catholic Church and the laity working at the grass roots within both faith-based and secular structures. This engagement between clergy and laity is the key to the realization of its vision of an alternative possible future and is, as I have previously suggested, what is lacking in faith-based engagement in the resolution of the conflict and peace-building in Northern Ireland (Power, 2007; 2008). It will result in the development of a creative interdependence between the leadership, clergy and laity, with the Church forming a paradigmatic community that places peace and the preferential option for the poor at the heart of its vision for society and communicates this to the public square through dialogue and, most importantly, praxis.

While the Catholic Church offers guidance on the phenomena that should trigger action in the form of public theology and praxis (Second Vatican Council, 1965 §§1, 4, 9, 29, 34, 39), it does not offer a programme for such action. Like the Gospels, CST cannot be literally interpreted to create a blueprint for life. Instead, although these guidelines or moral principles come from the Magisterium's engagement with society, they require further refinement in the light of indigenous circumstances. Influenced by Atherton's focus on empirical data, context and engagement with the secular, this 'reading of the signs of the times' (Second Vatican Council, 1965, §4) should, I argue, take place at the intersection of three elements: the Gospels and tradition, empirical research and, crucially, dialogue. Such a combination is vital because, as Johan Verstvaeten points out:

> Judgements on the world cannot be made merely on the basis of faith propositions. Without social and economic analysis, the faith perspective loses touch with reality or leads to the construction of a world of pious ideas, which risks being an expression of social alienation rather than a solution to it. (Verstvaeten, 2011, p. 317)

Through the creative tension that emerges from such an interaction, a public theology will emerge that not only allows for consciousness raising, by alerting people to the injustices in their midst that they may be either blind or apathetic to, but also fuels the moral imagination allowing what the liberationist Leonardo Boff has called 'alternative possible futures' (Boff, 2011) to be envisioned and articulated. Public theology therefore provides people with an understanding of what they are working towards and the necessary nourishment for the journey.

While liberation theologians and others have used CST to create public theologies for their own particular contexts, with the notable exception of Cardinal Cahal Daly and one attempt by the Irish Inter-Church Meeting (Power, 2013; 2007; 2003), this has not happened in Northern Ireland. It is therefore incumbent upon Catholic theologians to take CST's systematic body of teaching and shape it into a public intervention designed to facilitate the coming of the Kingdom of God within that particular context. In the case of Northern Ireland, such a public theology needs to focus upon the development of a just peace, an outline of which is available in CST (Hrynkow and Power, 2017), and take the lead, sorely lacking in the political classes, in addressing the underlying causes rather than the consequences of the conflict, thereby promoting a 'preferential option for the poor'. Such a public theology should above all offer hope. It should provide a roadmap for society that challenges prevailing norms and values, which in the case of Northern Ireland are based upon long-held grievances dating back centuries rather than years, and socio-economic disparities. This chapter will begin to undertake such a task, referring to Boff's category of 'alternative possible futures' (Boff, 2011), combined with the framework for engagement offered by Atherton that seeks to reconnect the churches to the public sphere (Atherton, 2000; 2004).

Before going on to outline a public theology for Northern Ireland, in line with Atherton's approach, I will first provide a brief understanding of the political and social context from which this theology emerges.

The Northern Irish context

On 10 April 1998, Tony Blair, the UK's Labour Prime Minister, and Bertie Ahern, the Irish Fianna Fáil Taoiseach, emerged from Stormont to announce to the waiting media that a deal had been struck that brought an end to the armed conflict in Northern Ireland; a conflict that had cost 3,600 lives and was caused by competing constitutional claims and massive socio-economic inequality (see Tonge, 2006, for further information). This accord, known ether as the Good Friday (Catholic/ Republican/ Nationalist) or Belfast (Protestant/ Loyalist/ Unionist) Agreement was greeted with widespread celebration and support, with Bono's triumphant greeting to David Trimble (UUP) and John Hume (SDLP) at a concert to support the referendum's 'yes' campaign neatly summing up the elation that many (including myself) felt on hearing the news (BBC News, 1998).

In the ensuing referendum held on 22 May 1998, 71 per cent of the population of Northern Ireland agreed to the terms of the Good Friday Agreement and, in the Republic of Ireland, 94 per cent of voters agreed to the Nineteenth Amendment of the Irish Constitution (Irish Stationery Office, 2015), which allowed for the removal of the irredentist claims in articles two and three that had caused so much fear and consternation among the Unionists of Northern Ireland. Both the British and Irish governments hoped that the democratic deficit that had accompanied the years of violence in the region would be replaced with strong institutions that would eventually normalize into Western European models of political representation – a hope that Blair felt had been realized when confronted by anti-Iraq-war protestors on a visit to Stormont in 2007 (Blair, 2010, p. 199). The Agreement also supplied provision for dealing with controversial matters such as human rights, the decommissioning of arms, reconciliation and victims of violence, prisoners, and policing and justice (Northern Ireland Office, 1998). In short, it was a blueprint for peace in Northern Ireland in the fullest sense of the term.

However, 20 years after the 1998 Good Friday Agreement was signed into law, as I write Northern Ireland is once more under direct rule from Westminster as a consequence of disagreements between the Democratic Unionist Party (DUP) and Sinn Féin about the Irish Language Act (an issue specifically dealt with in the Good Friday Agreement), with a 'war of words' erupting over the issue along 'traditional community lines' (Young, 2017). This has left Sinn Féin and the DUP unable to form a power-sharing government together, thereby perpetuating the democratic deficit that dominated politics during the conflict and highlighting the problems caused by a consociationalist approach to government (Power, 2011, pp. 2–6). Furthermore, corruption among the political elite is endemic, the Renewable Heat Incentive or Cash for Ash scandal that led to the dissolution of the Assembly on 26 January 2017 being the latest in a long line of incidents.

Although armed violence is at an all-time low, the conflict continues but by other means (Power, 2011). Thus, in terms of CST's definition of peace, which sees a peaceful society as one in which all can fulfil their potential, Northern Ireland is in a situation of what Galtung has termed negative peace (1964, p. 2). Terrorist and state violence may no longer dominate, but structural violence is now the norm. The sites of conflict have thus now moved on to cultural issues, and the socio-economic inequalities that initially caused the conflict have not yet been addressed and indeed are worsening as a consequence of the Conservative government's policy of austerity (O'Hara, 2012). Furthermore, the expected peace dividend has not materialized in Northern Ireland: one person in six has been targeted by government intervention to alleviate their deprivation through the Neighbourhood Renewal Programme (Knox, 2016, p. 491); 22 per cent of Catholics and 17 per cent of Protestants live in households experiencing poverty (Knox, 2016, p. 489); unemployment currently stands at 5 per cent, 1 per cent above the UK average, with Foyle, West Belfast and North Belfast (areas that experienced intense violence during the conflict) making up three of the top ten jobless black spots in the UK (McGuinness, Brown and O'Neill, 2017). The Troubles have also left a legacy of poor mental health and increased rates of suicide (O'Connor and O'Neill, 2015) and domestic violence (Williamson, 2017), which have yet to be addressed.

Most challenging, however, are what have become known as the 'legacy issues', which can be broadly defined under the two headings of reconciliation and furthering economic development. The Flag Protests in December 2012 and January 2013 demonstrated that some communities still feel that there is a fundamental threat to their identity and constitutional status, with Brexit only serving to reinforce such fears. Concerns still linger regarding paramilitary and dissident activities, which on the whole threaten the security of the most deprived sectors of Northern Irish society. Sectarian attacks have been joined by an increase in racially motivated crime that shows that the othering (Jenkins, 2004, p. 4), scapegoating and victimization (Girard, 1989), which were some of the main drivers of the conflict, still remain active in society. Various attempts to deal with the past and the experiences of victims have stalled, with, for example, the Bradley Eames Report (Consultative Group on the Past, 2009) being rejected for, among other reasons, the suggestion 'that there is a moral equivalence between the paramilitary victim and the innocent victim' (BBC News, 2009). Finally, issues surrounding the passage of the Northern Ireland (Welfare Reform) bill in 2015 demonstrate that political parties are still willing to use the most vulnerable in society as political pawns, thereby invalidating any rhetoric surrounding the alleviation of deprivation that politicians may espouse (BBC News, 2015).

This context therefore demonstrates that in order to achieve peace and stability rather than the situation of suspended violence in which it now finds itself, Northern Ireland needs to confront and deal with the issues of communal reconciliation and socio-economic deprivation. Such a process requires deep-seated changes within society and the rebuilding of relationships that have until now been characterized by mistrust, antagonism and fear. This presents the Catholic Church in Northern Ireland with both a challenge and an opportunity which it has yet to embrace in any meaningful sense of the term. Catholic Social Teaching contains resources to deal with the two major issues facing contemporary Northern Ireland, and it is incumbent upon Catholics to create a moral vision of peace and reconciliation, alongside a preferential option for the poor, which will provide the roadmap necessary for an alternative possible future to emerge. Such a task cannot be left to the institutional Church alone. As the Second Vatican Council taught, the laity have an obligation to work in the social and political spheres to realize the Kingdom of God. What follows is the attempt by one lay Catholic theologian, whose work has been influenced by John Atherton, and in particular his emphasis upon full and truthful narratives of the context that such a theology seeks to address (which in Northern Ireland have been subsumed by a narrative proclaiming the success of the peace process) and partnership and reconciliation (Atherton, 2000), to commence the process of developing a public theology for Northern Ireland from which a moral vision of an alternative possible peaceful future can emerge.

A public theology for Northern Ireland

The foundation stone of such a public theology for Northern Ireland is the Sermon on the Mount (Matt. 5—7): Jesus' manifesto for the construction of a society in which human dignity and flourishing lie at the heart of all decision-making. Through this Jesus' promise that 'I have come that they may have life, and have it to the full' (John 10.10, NIV) can become more than an eschatological expectation. As Atherton rightly argues, 'public theology should elaborate a Christian anthropology which emphasises the profound equality of the human in creative interplay with the recognition of each individual person' (2004, p. 31). It is my contention that this can be achieved in Northern Ireland through the development of a preferential option for the poor (Luke 6.20–23), reconciliation (Matt. 5.38–48), and dialogue with the other (Matt. 5.46–47). However, in order to avoid this emulating the rhetoric of the past (Power, 2011), only by practising such elements within their own communities, both church and secular, can Christians become a paradigmatic community with a respected voice in the public square. The resultant dialogue between public theology and praxis has the potential to provide creative visions of alternative possible futures as long as it holds these two elements in tension with each other, and accepts that the secular sphere can provide excellent and innovative examples of practice. This was emphasized by Atherton when he said:

> The promotion of the human as the capabilities to be and to do provides a way of doing that is informed by this theological anthropology. As important, it then flows into the debate over what kind of social

arrangements are needed to support such understandings of human development. (Atherton, 2004, p. 32)

Through this, a moral vision of an alternative possible future will emerge that is underpinned by the concept of justice (Matt. 6.33), and through which the Kingdom of God can be realized within both religious institutions and secular society.

The conflict in Northern Ireland has left behind it a legacy of marginalization and deprivation, as well as strained community relations and a culture of fear best immortalized by Seamus Heaney in his poem 'whatever you say, say nothing' (1975, p. 52). If Northern Ireland is to achieve a peaceful future in which each member of society can achieve his or her potential, then issues of marginalization and deprivation have to be addressed. Here, CST provides useful concepts that can be deployed to tackle these issues, most prominent of which is the preferential option for the poor.[2]

As Francis's papacy has so vibrantly demonstrated, the Catholic Church is not neutral, rather it takes the view that 'God chose the foolish things of the world to shame the wise; God chose the weak things of the world to shame the strong. God chose the lowly things of this world and the despised things – and the things that are not – to nullify the things that are, so that no one may boast before him' (1 Cor. 1.27–29, NIV). The Church and its members should stand firmly on the side of the poor and the oppressed, seeking the development of a society in which

> those who are weak, poor, marginalised, or disadvantaged are privileged instruments of God ... This in turn indicates that the poor and the disadvantaged have a privileged role in the prior reading of the 'signs of the times', which enables people to discern God's will for themselves, for their communities, and for the wider world. (Dorr, 2016, pp. 4–5)

From such a stance, a peaceful society, epitomized by the parable of the workers in the vineyard in which Jesus tells us that 'the last will be first, and the first will be last' (Matt. 20.1–16, 16), where all have enough to fulfil their material needs (through, for example, a living wage), and the ability to fulfil their potential will emerge.

This parable brings to the fore two elements in CST that, when employed in a contextually sensitive and importantly non-bureaucratic and person-centred manner, foreground the preferential option for the poor in social arrangements and make the creation of a just peace in Northern Ireland possible. These are solidarity and subsidiarity. Although implicit in the teachings of the Church prior to John Paul II's election in 1978, solidarity was first made explicit in his second social encyclical,

Laborem Exercens (John Paul II, 1981, §8) and compels people to take into account the effect of their actions on others, asking them to strive to promote the common good, while standing and working *with* the poor and marginalized rather than myopically focusing on their own desires and needs. Through acting in such a manner, individuals thus come to see themselves as part of a community and organize its power structures accordingly. The term 'subsidiarity' was first used in papal teaching by Pius XI in *Quadragesimo Anno* (1931, §79). This element of Catholic Social Teaching affirms the idea that each person has the right to shape their own destiny rather than it being solely subject to external forces. When at all possible, therefore, power and decision-making processes should be exercised at the lowest possible level. Taken together, these two concepts act as a check upon one another, by ensuring that power is distributed fairly throughout society, thereby promoting social justice and the vision of the Kingdom on earth.

Fundamentally, these two teachings are about responsibility, both personal *and* communal, and it is this realization that enables us to translate these ideas from abstract theological and doctrinal documents into social arrangements and praxis. Examples of such arrangements already exist in Northern Ireland and demonstrate that if there is both the communal and political will to work together to allow a community to flourish, then peace in the most meaningful sense of the term can be achieved. As Atherton puts it, 'The active pursuit of a more just social order is an intimate part of the process of reconciliation in terms of rebuilding shattered communities and preventing the recurrence of conflict' (2000, p. 23). Take for example Farset Youth and Community Development Ltd, a secular organization based on the Springfield Road in Belfast. The predominantly Catholic/Nationalist/Republican Springfield Road was a major site of conflict during the Troubles and it still acts as an interface between the Protestant/Loyalist/Unionist Shankill Road and the Catholic/Nationalist/Republican Falls Road. During the early years of the conflict, it was the site of intense rioting, and the local RUC station housed a British Army barracks that was frequently attacked by the IRA. Loyalist paramilitaries, due to the IRA's prominent presence in the area, attacked and killed many of its residents.

Despite, or indeed perhaps because of, this physical and political environment, the Springfield Road has become a hub for groups aiming to express solidarity and foster the practice of subsidiarity within the community (Power, 2007, pp. 118–64).[3] Farset Youth and Community Development Ltd is one such group, the genesis of which came entirely from the local community and the success of which demonstrates the power of subsidiarity and solidarity (seen here between the working classes of some of the most deprived Protestant/Loyalist/Unionist and

Catholic/Nationalist/Republican communities in Northern Ireland). This group

> help[s] young adults to move away from anti-social behaviour through our RESPECT program. This enables Young Adults to make choices in their own life by self-discipline, good citizenship and to develop their physical, mental and spiritual capacities and grow to full maturity as individuals and members of society and to improve the conditions of life. (Charity Commission Northern Ireland, 2014)

The result has, among other things, been Farset International, a 38-bedroom conference and accommodation facility on what had previously been waste ground separating two communities, founded 'in response to local community needs for a neutral place for meetings, [and] discussions' (Farset International) and Farset's former position as the largest Action for Community Employment scheme (1981–1999) employer in Belfast. These programmes train young people for employment and provide them with the support to gain the qualifications that in some working-class communities of Northern Ireland remain elusive. They show how government and philanthropic funding (of which there is a great deal in Northern Ireland) can indeed be transformative if the impetus and management of the process comes from *within* communities and adequate support is provided for those dealing with the bureaucracy inherent in such processes.

Both of these schemes therefore demonstrate a strong and lasting commitment to human flourishing and equipping people with the skills to fulfil their potential. Above all, however, this cross-community scheme was conceived through a process of dialogue which shows the practical power of Jesus's call to perfection in the Sermon on the Mount:

> If you love those who love you, what reward will you get? Are not even the tax collectors doing that? And if you greet only your own people, what are you doing more than others? Do not even pagans do that? (Matt. 5.46–47, NIV)

Peace can be achieved if people accept the diversity of viewpoints within society and come to embrace these as a form of empowerment and partnership that will allow them to harness resources to deal with the community's most pressing problems, thus creating a society in which human dignity and flourishing are put above all else.

However, such things are easier said than done – especially in a society that has experienced a violent conflict based upon diverse political aspirations that has led to intense competition for resources between different identity groups. This competition has, despite independent evidence proving otherwise (Buchanan, 2014, p. 135), led to some Protestant groups feeling discriminated against in favour of Republican paramilitary groups. The Democratic Unionist Party (DUP) MEP Jim McAllister accused Peace II of 'rewarding those who were perpetrators of heinous acts of violence [which] merely serves to undermine the confidence of mainstream society in the entire Peace II programme. The ongoing and institutionalised discrimination in funding against the Unionist community must end immediately' (Buchanan, 2014, p. 135).

Paul VI's famous axiom 'if you want peace, work for justice' (1971) cannot therefore be fully achieved without the communities in Northern Ireland entering into a process of reconciliation with one another. It is only through undertaking what is both a process and a goal that members of Northern Irish society can accept that the diversity that was so threatening during the period of conflict and its aftermath could actually be a strength in the active pursuit of a more just social order in which human dignity and flourishing are the norm. By overcoming such differences these communities would be creating a society reminiscent of Paul's first letter to the Corinthians in which all parts of humanity accept their interdependence upon one another, seeing this as a strength that can yield excellent results (1 Cor. 12.12–31).

The social arrangements needed to put such a vision in place centre on dialogue. As reconciliation needs to be a collective as well as individual process, it can only be achieved by open and honest communication that reverses the process of othering (Power, 2007, pp. 203–4). However, such a process can take years rather than months to build up the trust necessary for people to overcome their fear and animosity and work together to secure a just and peaceful society. The virtue of patience must therefore be built into the process. One of the main problems facing reconciliation is the conceptual confusion surrounding the term (Buchanan, 2011, p. 189), which has prevented progress in this area. To overcome this, I will use Duncan Morrow's definition:

> Reconciliation in Northern Ireland ultimately describes the possibility that violent enemies in the past might have a future marked by partnership, civic equality, and the rule of law or even trust and friendship ... Reconciliation carries a positive vision of sustainable peace as transformed political and social relationships. It involves a future-orientated commitment to good relations as well as drawing a line under the conflict and violence of the past. (Morrow, 2016, p. 39)

ALTERNATIVE POSSIBLE FUTURES

In the realization of such a vision, CST can be particularly instructive to the process of reconciliation, especially through its teachings on inter-religious dialogue, which I will now contextualize for Northern Ireland.

The Pontifical Council for Inter-Religious Dialogue (PCID) (1984) has developed a fourfold schema for contact between different cultures, two elements of which are particularly useful in the Northern Irish context. These are the dialogue of specialists, which, if successful, should lead to the dialogue of deeds and action. The usefulness of these elements is that they are specifically aimed at the laity, who in the terms of Northern Ireland are the ones who should be driving reconciliation. This position 'draws primary inspiration from the teaching presented in *Gaudium et Spes* that each member of the laity should employ their specialist training and learning in the service of society, which in this case translates into contributions to' reconciliation based upon each person's unique experience of the conflict (Hyrnkow and Power, forthcoming, p. 28). Through the dialogue of specialists, therefore, the participants confront the differences between them in a respectful manner, seeking to understand the origin stories of the myths and stereotypes that abound in a Northern Irish context. This is because 'The path of dialogue is a path of discoveries, and the more we discover one another, the more we can replace the tensions of the past with bonds of peace' (John Paul II, 1986a).

I have described the various methodologies for achieving this elsewhere (Power, 2007; 2011), but the most important element for developing an alternative possible future is that the participants come to trust one another enough to work together to secure a just peace, the result of which will be a society that places human dignity and flourishing at the heart of its decision-making processes. This will ultimately be manifested through the dialogue of deeds and action (PCID, 1984, §31), whereby previous enemies work together to achieve a mutually agreed-upon goal, be it political, cultural or social. The power of such processes can be seen in the work of Farset described above and in the numerous faith-based social action projects that exist in Northern Ireland (Power, 2007, pp. 83–100). These partnerships are the embodiment of reconciliation, offering an example of hope to all those with whom they come in contact. Furthermore, such cooperation towards the realization of a mutual goal creates what I would term a 'virtuous circle of reconciliation': having come to know and agree to work with the other despite previous conflicts, the resulting 'practical co-operation creates mutual esteem among all believers in God and stimulates the desire to learn from others and to work with them' (John Paul II, 1996).

Conclusion: the Church as a paradigmatic community of hope

In the Sermon on the Mount (which has provided the gospel basis for this theology), Jesus instructs his followers to provide an example to others of his teachings:

> Neither do people light a lamp and put it under a bowl. Instead they put it on its stand, and it gives light to everyone in the house. In the same way, let your light shine before others, that they may see your good deeds and glorify your Father in heaven. (Matt. 5.15–16, NIV)

There can be no denying that in Jesus' ministry and the early Christian communities, we are offered a future that, as imperfect as it may be on earth, amplifies the conditions that allow for human flourishing, creating a society in which justice and peace are the norm. Such an example offers religious institutions inspiration: first for creating a contextual understanding of the gospel for their milieu, and second, to practise the gospel in ways appropriate to the needs and wants of their constituency. Once the balance is perfected, the resulting tension between theology and praxis will result in paradigmatic communities of hope that live the alternative possible futures that will lie at the centre of the Church's moral vision.

That balance has never been struck in Northern Ireland – a place with plenty of praxis but little overt or public theologizing. People of all faiths and none engage in reconciliation and partnerships because it is the right and logical thing to do, given their unique set of circumstances. However, the theology is needed if such praxis is going to have longevity and scope for reaching out beyond a committed few believers into wider society, effecting the type of change that will result in justice and peace. The leadership and the clergy of the Catholic Church in Ireland have suffered massive reputational damage as a result, among other things, of the clerical abuse scandals that came to light in the 1990s. While this is incredibly painful and must be addressed, it offers the Church a chance to reconstitute itself as the Council Fathers would have wished and rid itself of the clericalism and sexism that taint, rightly or wrongly, any of its dealings with society. This can be achieved through the active engagement of the laity, once they have heard and understood the message of the gospel, combining spirituality and activism to manifest powerfully and tangibly the alternative possible future offered by faith. In this, they must be supported by theologians who partake in a hermeneutical circle of reading and interpreting the Gospels and magisterium, researching and understanding the society that they wish to serve, and disseminating the public theology that results as accessibly as possible.

This dialogue between theologians (both clergy and lay) and the laity putting their faith into practice in their everyday lives, which both inspires and results from a public theology for Northern Ireland, must be treated as a living organism, the entire *raison d'être* of which is to ensure that justice and peace are the norm rather than an eschatological hope offered to people as a reward for the injustice, violence and degradation that they suffer during their worldly lives.

Notes

1 Catholic Social Teaching is also known as Catholic Social Thought, or sometimes as Catholic Social Thought and Practice. I use the term Catholic Social Teaching as it represents to me a more iterative process that allows for an interactive process of dialogue and praxis to develop, thus creating a unified whole rather than two separate elements, as the former terms suggest.

2 The preferential option for the poor was a phrase first used by Fr Pedro Arrupe SJ, Superior General of the Society of Jesus from 1965 to 1983, in a 1968 letter to the Jesuits of Latin America. This term was then developed by the Dominican Fr Gustavo Gutiérrez in *The Theology of Liberation* (1974 [1971]). However, it has been implicit in papal teachings since Leo XIII's (1891) *Rerum Novarum* (§23, 29), with these ideas further developed in *Mater et Magistra* (1961, §157), *Gaudium et Spes* (1965, §63), and *Populorum Progressio* (1967, §23, 53, 75). It was first explicitly articulated in 1987 by John Paul II in *Solicitudo Rei Socialis* (§§39, 42), and further emphasized in *Centesimus Annus* (1991) when he stated that 'love for others, and especially for the poor, is made concrete by promoting justice' (§58). It was embraced as a true Catholic obligation during Benedict XVI's papacy (2005–13) in *The Compendium of the Social Doctrine of the Church* (2005, §182). More recently, Francis (2013–) re-emphasized its importance to the mission of the Church in his 2013 apostolic letter, *Evangelii Gaudium* (§§186–212).

3 Community, although an 'aerosol' word, is defined here as those living within council wards on the Springfield Road.

References

Atherton, J. R., 2000, *Public Theology for Changing Times*, London: SPCK.
Atherton, J. R., 2003, *Marginalization*, London: SCM Press.
Atherton, J. R., 2004, 'Marginalisation, Manchester and the Scope of Public Theology', in E. Graham and E. Reed (eds), *The Future of Christian Social Ethics: Essays on the Work of Ronald Preston, Studies in Christian Ethics*, 17(2), London: T&T Clark.
BBC News, 1998, 'Trimble and Hume Centre Stage for Referendum', http://news.bbc.co.uk/1/hi/events/northern_ireland/latest_news/97031.stm (accessed 21 September 2017).
BBC News, 2009, 'Reaction to the Eames/Bradley Report', http://news.bbc.co.uk/1/hi/northern_ireland/7856590.stm (accessed 22 September 2017).
BBC News, 2015, 'Northern Ireland Welfare Reform Bill Fails to Pass', www.bbc.co.uk/news/uk-northern-ireland-32894371 (accessed 22 September 2017).
Blair, A., 2010, *A Journey*, London: Arrow.
Boff, L., 2011, *Virtues for Another Possible World*, Eugene, OR: Wipf & Stock.

Brown, M. (ed.), 2014, *Anglican Social Theology: Renewing the Vision*, London: Church House Publishing.
Buchanan, S., 2011, 'Examining the Peacebuilding Policy Framework of the British and Irish Governments', in M. Power (ed.), *Building Peace in Northern Ireland*, Liverpool: Liverpool University Press, pp. 172–90.
Buchanan, S., 2014, *Transforming Conflict through Social and Economic Development: Practice and Policy Lessons from Northern Ireland and the Border Counties*, Manchester: Manchester University Press.
Charity Commission Northern Ireland, 2014, 'Farset Youth and Community Development Ltd', www.charitycommissionni.org.uk/charity-details/?regid=100248&subid=0 (accessed 24 September 2017).
Consultative Group on the Past, 2009, *Report*, http://cain.ulst.ac.uk/victims/docs/consultative_group/cgp_230109_report.pdf (accessed 22 September 2017).
Dorr, D., 2016, *Option for the Poor and for the Earth: From Leo XIII to Pope Francis*, Maryknoll, NY: Orbis Books.
Elliott, M., 2009, *When God Took Sides: Religion and Identity in Ireland – Unfinished History*, Oxford: Oxford University Press.
Farset International, 'About Us', www.farsetinternational.co.uk/page4.html (accessed 24 September 2017).
Forrester, D. B., 2001, 'Social Justice and Welfare', in R. Gill (ed.), *The Cambridge Companion to Christian Ethics*, Cambridge: Cambridge University Press, pp. 195–208.
Francis, 2013, *Evangelii Gaudium*, http://w2.vatican.va/content/francesco/en/apost_exhortations/documents/papa-francesco_esortazione-ap_20131124_evangelii-gaudium.html (accessed 24 September 2017).
Galtung, J., 1964, 'An Editorial', *Journal of Peace Research* 1:1, pp. 1–4.
Girard, R., 1989, *The Scapegoat*, trans. Y. Freccero, Baltimore, MD: Johns Hopkins University Press.
Gutiérrez, G., 1974, *The Theology of Liberation: History, Politics, Salvation*, trans. C. Inda and J. Eagleson, London: SCM Press.
Heaney, S., 1975, *North*, London: Faber & Faber.
Hrynkow, C. and Power, M., 2017, 'Best Kept Secret', *Catholic Worker*, New York edn (August–September), p. 7.
Hrynkow, C. and Power, M., forthcoming, 'Transforming the Centre: Popes on Inter-Religious Dialogues as a Path to Multi-Track Peacebuilding', *International Journal of Peace Studies*.
Jenkins, R., 2004, *Social Identity*, 2nd edn, London: Routledge.
John XXIII, 1961, *Mater et Magistra*, http://w2.vatican.va/content/john-xxiii/en/encyclicals/documents/hf_j-xxiii_enc_15051961_mater.html (accessed 24 September 2017).
John Paul II, 1996, 'Address to the Episcopal Conference of Indonesia on their Ad Limina Visit', http://w2.vatican.va/content/john-paul-ii/en/speeches/1996/june/documents/hf_jp-ii_spe_19960603_bishops-indonesia.html (accessed 21 July 2017).
John Paul II, 1986a, 'Address to the Diplomatic Corps in Wellington', 23 November 1986, https://w2.vatican.va/content/john-paul-ii/en/speeches/1986/november/documents/hf_jp-ii_spe_19861123_corpo-diplomatico-wellington-nuova-zelanda.html (accessed 21 July 2017).

John Paul II, 1991, *Centesimus Annus*, http://w2.vatican.va/content/john-paul-ii/en/encyclicals/documents/hf_jp-ii_enc_01051991_centesimus-annus.html#-10 (accessed 24 September 2017).

John Paul II, *Laborem Exercens*, 1981, http://w2.vatican.va/content/john-paul-ii/en/encyclicals/documents/hf_jp-ii_enc_14091981_laborem-exercens.html (accessed 10 May 2017).

John Paul II, 1987, *Solicitudo Rei Socialis*, http://w2.vatican.va/content/john-paul-ii/en/encyclicals/documents/hf_jp-ii_enc_30121987_sollicitudo-rei-socialis.html (accessed 24 September 2017).

Knox, C., 2016, 'Northern Ireland: Where is the Peace Dividend?', *Policy and Politics*, 44:3, pp. 485–503.

Irish Stationery Office, 2015, *Bunreacht Na hÉireann – Constitution of Ireland*, www.taoiseach.gov.ie/eng/Historical_Information/The_Constitution/Bunreacht_na_hÉireann_October_2015_Edition.pdf (accessed 21 September 2017).

Leo XII, 1891, *Rerum Novarum*, http://w2.vatican.va/content/leo-xiii/en/encyclicals/documents/hf_l-xiii_enc_15051891_rerum-novarum.html (accessed 24 September 2017).

McGuinness, F., Brown, J. and O'Neill, M., 2017, *Unemployment by Constituency*, House of Commons Library Briefing Paper, no. 7868, http://researchbriefings.parliament.uk/ResearchBriefing/Summary/CBP-7868#fullreport (accessed 22 September 2017).

Morrow, D., 2016, 'From Enemies to Partners? Reconciliation in Northern Ireland', *Accord*, Insight 3, pp. 39–44, www.c-r.org/news-and-views/news/new-accord-publication-reconciliation-and-peace-processes (accessed 26 September 2017).

Northern Ireland Office, 1998, *The Belfast Agreement*, www.gov.uk/government/publications/the-belfast-agreement (accessed 21 September 2017).

Northern Ireland Statistics and Research Agency (NISRA), 2017, *Labour Force Survey*, www.nisra.gov.uk/statistics/labour-market-and-social-welfare/labour-force-survey (accessed 22 September 2017).

O'Connor, R. C. and O'Neill, S. M., 2015, 'Mental Health and Suicide Rise in Northern Ireland: A Legacy of the Troubles?' *The Lancet Psychiatry* 2:7, pp. 582–4.

O'Hara, M., 2012, 'Communities Worried that the Worst is Yet to Come in Northern Ireland', *Austerity in the UK*, www.jrf.org.uk/austerity-uk-communities-worried-worst-still-come-northern-ireland (accessed 22 September 2017).

Paul VI, 1971, 'If you Want Peace, Work for Justice', World Day for Peace Message for 1972, https://w2.vatican.va/content/paul-vi/en/messages/peace/documents/hf_p-vi_mes_19711208_v-world-day-for-peace.html (accessed 25 September 2017).

Paul VI, 1967, *Populorum Progressio: On the Development of Peoples*, http://w2.vatican.va/content/paul-vi/en/encyclicals/documents/hf_p-vi_enc_26031967_populorum.html (accessed 28 February 2017).

Pius XI, *Quadragesimo Anno*, 1931, http://w2.vatican.va/content/pius-xi/en/encyclicals/documents/hf_p-xi_enc_19310515_quadragesimo-anno.html (accessed 5 May 2017).

Pontifical Council for Interreligious Dialogue (PCID), 1984, 'The Attitude of the Church Towards Followers of Other Religions: Reflections and Orientations on Dialogue and Mission', www.pcinterreligious.org/uploads/pdfs/Dialogue_and_Mission_ENG.pdf (accessed 21 July 2017).

Pontifical Council for Justice and Peace, 2005, *Compendium of the Social Doctrine of the Church*, London: Burns & Oates.
Power, M., 2003, 'Developing a Theology of Reconciliation for Northern Ireland? The Irish Inter-Church Meeting', *Search* 26:1, pp. 21–9.
Power, M., 2007, *From Ecumenism to Community Relations: Inter-Church Relationships in Northern Ireland 1980–2005*, Dublin: Irish Academic Press.
Power, M., 2011, 'Building Peace in Northern Ireland', in M. Power (ed.), *Building Peace in Northern Ireland*, Liverpool: Liverpool University Press, pp. 1–17.
Power, M., 2013, 'Cardinal Cahal Daly', *Oxford Dictionary of National Biography*, Oxford: Oxford University Press.
Power, M., 2008, 'Of some Symbolic Importance But Not Much Else: The Irish Inter-Church Meeting and Ecumenical Dialogue in Northern Ireland since 1980', *Journal of Ecumenical Studies* 43:1, pp. 111–23.
Second Vatican Council, 1965, *Gaudium et Spes*, www.vatican.va/archive/hist_councils/ii_vatican_council/documents/vat-ii_const_19651207_gaudium-et-spes_en.html (accessed 12 May 2017).
Second Vatican Council, 1964, *Lumen Gentium*, www.vatican.va/archive/hist_councils/ii_vatican_council/documents/vat-ii_const_19641121_lumen-gentium_en.html (accessed 12 May 2017).
Tonge, J., 2006, *Northern Ireland*, Cambridge: Polity Press.
Verstvaeten, J., 2011, 'Towards Interpreting the Signs of the Times, Conversation with the World, and Inclusion of the Poor: Three Challenges for Catholic Social Teaching', *International Journal of Public Theology* 5, pp. 314–30.
Williamson, C., 2017, 'Record High 30,000 Domestic Abuse Incidents Reported to Police in Northern Ireland – Sexual Assaults Also Reach Peak Level', *Belfast Telegraph*, www.belfasttelegraph.co.uk/news/northern-ireland/record-high-30000-domestic-abuse-incidents-reported-to-police-in-northern-ireland-sexual-assaults-also-reach-peak-level-35725590.html (accessed 21 September 2017).
Young, D., 2017, 'Irish Language Act War of Words Continues as Sinn Fein [sic] Hits Out at "Insulting" Comments by Foster', *Belfast Telegraph*, www.belfasttelegraph.co.uk/news/northern-ireland/irish-language-act-war-of-words-intensifies-as-sinn-fein-hits-out-at-insulting-comments-by-foster-36145919.html (accessed 21 September 2017).
Young, I. M., 1990, *Justice and the Politics of Difference*, Princeton, NJ: Princeton University Press.

12

Afterword: Genealogy and Generativity

CHRISTOPHER BAKER AND ELAINE GRAHAM

Writing about wellbeing in later life, the gerontologist William Randall stresses the benefits of living within what he terms 'a good strong story'. This is essential for nurturing the quality of resilience – a key feature of positive wellbeing – not least in so far as it enables us to take the long view, to see ourselves relationally, incorporated into a reality larger and more expansive than ourselves, and to view the span of our own lives in the wider perspective of an unfolding human story that stretches through past, present and future:

> A good strong story extends beyond us as well, beyond our family and community. Through *genealogy*, for instance, it reaches back in time to previous generations and, through *generativity*, it stretches out to future ones as well ... A good strong story reaches out in humility and awe – to something grander than ourselves, to a vaster narrative than that of our own little self. (Randall, 2013, p. 14)

In our Introduction, we began with the debt John owed to the multiple narratives of the Industrial Revolution, his own life-story and his intellectual forebears – whether we wish to call that a Manchester 'School' or 'Story'. These all represented significant genealogies in which John located and interpreted his concerns, and enabled us to trace some of the most important dimensions of his life's work. In this brief Afterword, we move now to evaluate the generative dimensions of John's contribution to Christian social ethics, as we look ahead to the future. What have we learned from this appreciation of his legacy; what challenges and priorities await; and what untapped potential in his work calls to us for further development?

CHRISTOPHER BAKER AND ELAINE GRAHAM

The Challenges and opportunities of the Fourth Great Awakening

As part of his magisterial synopsis at the end of *Challenging Religious Studies*, John validates his thesis regarding the development of measuring systems that gauged the huge contributions religion makes to the health, equality and wellbeing of nations. In charting the intimate relationship between religious, political and economic change in the USA, for example, John is indebted to the economist Robert Fogel's influential typology of epochs of religious awakening and socially progressive change, as well as the work of McLoughlin, Hunter and Putnam. Fogel's book, *The Fourth Great Awakening and the Future of Egalitarianism* (2000), suggests that every significant period of economic, national and technological upheaval since the eighteenth century has created a religious revival that in turn has generated a movement for progressive social change. These revivals start roughly in 1730, 1830 and 1920: the first era materializes the link between questioning religious authority and new forms of political thought that leads to post-colonial revolution. The second sees religious revival channelled into nation-building and national reform, leading to first-nation reforms and the abolition of slavery. The third sees the influence of the social gospel on welfare reform, culminating in the New Deal and huge advances in education, poverty reduction and healthcare. Fogel's thesis is that a fourth revival is taking place, beginning in the 1960s and 70s as the stability of the post-war era gives way to a new period of rapid social, economic and techno-physical change that we now associate with neo-liberalism, globalization and digital innovation.

However, unlike previous religious revivals, the 'Fourth Awakening' does not appear to have generated progressive change at a deep structural level. This is despite a huge global revival in religious awareness and practice associated with the Moral Majority in the United States, and global Islamic and Pentecostal revivals that show no signs of abating. Indeed, by 2060, largely due to demographic changes, it is projected that only 12.5 per cent of the world's population is likely to be religiously unaffiliated. There are perhaps two reasons for this lack of change. The first, echoing Putnam and Campbell's findings in *American Grace*, is that the conservative nature of much of the religious revival is privatizing volunteering with a focus on individual philanthropy rather than civic activism.

> The failure of American religion (and especially Evangelicals) today to mount a more vigorous campaign against class disparities could thus be seen as a sin of omission, especially compared to the struggles for social justice that people of faith mounted in comparable periods of American history. (Putnam and Campbell, 2010, p. 232)

A second obstacle to a leveraging of renewed spiritual energy on to progressive change is the full-spectrum way the forces, practices and imaginaries of neo-liberal ideology are constantly cutting the rug from under our feet. Naomi Klein, examining the rise of the Trump and Brexit phenomena, labels this deliberate sense of public and civic disorientation the 'shock doctrine', which relies on the extreme polarization of views and the false presentation of facts in the media (Klein, 2017). Every war, natural disaster or terrorist attack is used as a brutal excuse to implement neo-liberal economic policies such as privatization, deregulation and cuts to social services. Thus, the policy of austerity in the UK, the socially and individually destructive effects of which still lie deep within the fabric of national life, was one such response to the near breakdown of the global financial system in 2008 due to the collapse of the sub-prime or bad-debt market.

John's legacy therefore needs to be read against this deepening and ongoing crisis of public, economic and political life that continues to unfold as the hallmark of the twenty-first century. The first part of the narrative is the collapse of what might be called alternative meta-narratives or imaginaries that shape and guide the fundamental telos of our society. As Calhoun has described, social imaginaries are important ways of providing

> an established way of imagining that reproduces ways of thinking and acting with a high degree of regularity and thus gives them material force. The reproduction of this imaginary comes through text and language, narratives and rituals and constantly repeated practical experience. Much of what gives the world shape is held among us in forms of understanding. (Calhoun, 2016, p. 9)

Many political commentators and social theorists (Habermas, 2005; Beck, 2010; Taylor, 2007) have described the fracturing of these narratives into multiple and often disconnected fragments, although there is some evidence of creative ways in which these fragments are being linked together to create new and shared sets of deeper values and principles by which the public square can be reinvigorated and democracy revived: for example, the Black Lives Matter and #MeToo campaigns, which have also been recently augmented by #Neveragain movement. The deep-seated and institutionalized issues of racism, sexism and the power of the gun lobby, confronted by these mainly grass-roots and rapidly mobilizing campaigns, are led predominantly by young millennials. They deploy digital and social media technology to mobilize mass crowds. They are no longer prepared to tolerate the increasingly draconian ways in which white, male and conservative Christian hegemony is being perpetuated by the Trump administration. Theirs is a more radical vision of equality and economic and cultural inclusion, based on tolerance and respect, alongside the critical calling out of institutional corporate and state violence.

Marginalization versus revival

However, the a priori issue that John constantly addresses in his work, and is even more relevant in the current era, is how the extant tradition of Anglican social thought speaks into the present political vacuum, characterized by the erosion of trust and the rise in isolation and despair that is driving new expressions of nationalist and reactionary populism.

This, then, is the main problematic that needs to be addressed: the marginalization of a critical and credible Christian voice in the public square. Against this deficit, there are nevertheless key countervailing tendencies that are opening up new frontiers and spaces of post-secular rapprochement and engagement. The first is the renewed search for authenticity and re-enchantment that characterizes, in particular, the political and cultural aspirations of the millennial cohorts and those increasing numbers of citizens who define themselves as 'no religion'. We have elaborated in detail elsewhere on these emerging connections (Baker, 2017), but essentially the search for a more values-driven and ethical public life is a response to a post-2008 disenchantment with neo-liberal tactics focused on materialism, consumerism and individual autonomy that have left people anxious, disenfranchised and adrift from traditional communities of friendship and support. Meanwhile, many religiously affiliated citizens, motivated by the postmodern search for individual fulfilment, are forsaking the structures of the Church, which they perceive to be too materialistic and divorced from the problems of the world, and instead seeking a deeper, more rigorous and authentic sense of discipleship in the culture of the world via the establishment of various kinds of intentional communities (Bielo 2011; Martí and Ganiel, 2014; Moody, 2015).

Thus, a disenchanted religious cohort increasingly enchanted by the world is meeting a newly enchanted 'no-religion'/secular subjectivity in what we might call a 'messy middle' of potentially progressive political and spiritual resurgence. What unites the people in this still hazy but increasingly powerful hinterland is generally a willingness to move beyond (but without forsaking) ideological and dogmatic rules and formulae in order to bring about change on the ground – 'to do something about something'. This foregrounds ethics over morality; innovation and communication over rules-bound tactics of engagement. The opportunities are ripe for the Church, and indeed other institutions struggling to engage in a more fluid and fast-moving world, to act as curators of these new spaces of intentional ethical and civic performance in which both religious and secular identities and practices are to some extent deformalized: foodbanks, addiction and homeless services, transition towns and cities of sanctuary, community food projects and pop-up cafes, social enterprises and broad-based community networks, to name but a few.

These established but also emerging spaces reflect geographies of post-secular rapprochement, which Cloke and Beaumont define as

> a coming together of citizens who might previously have been divided by differences in theological, political or moral principles ... a willingness to work together to address crucial social issues in the city, and in doing so put aside other frameworks of difference involving faith and secularism. (2013, p. 28)

They are also spaces and places where people are prepared to invest their spiritual capital for the sake of creating an excess of meaning, value and problem-solving power. Spiritual capital is the motivating power of our beliefs, values and world views – it is the 'why' that drives the 'what'. For members of faith groups this spiritual capital is made up of a complex interaction between formal beliefs, social interactions and rituals (Baker and Skinner, 2006), which have been identified by sociologists such as Putnam and Campbell as ideal 'echo chambers' whereby deep morals and principles are 'freighted' (2010) into the public sphere.

We are now understanding better how 'no-religion' beliefs, values and world views are also potential catalysts for progressive as well as regressive forms of volunteering and civic and political engagement (Beaman, 2017). Concepts like these should help the churches and other faith groups better understand the new opportunities presenting themselves for vital public contributions in what is clearly both a post-Christendom but also a post-secular sphere, and thus counter a sense of impotence and irrelevance being experienced by many mainstream Christian denominations in the UK. These contributions are in John's own words a 'gift' to wider society, which perceives itself as secular but is simultaneously 'fascinated' and 'troubled' by religion (Graham, 2017). These interventions into the public sphere help create new and unexpected realignments between religious and secular spheres, as well as innovative insights and practices of belief. Far from representing the occlusion of the Church, this external and worldly interest in re-enchantment actually contains elements of its renewal, here understood not as great reformations of doctrine and practice from within the universal Church, as in the Great Reformation 500 years ago, but one brought about by the creative and disrupting actions of the Spirit of God, or *missio Dei*, at work in the wider world outside the

Church. It is an etic, not an emic, revolution to which the Church is being called to respond and by which it will be rejuvenated.

A call to arms

We have already alluded to John's anxiety that the Church would choose the path of self-inflicted obscurity rather than renewal. For him, the seeds to that renewal lay in the Church being a competent and empowered advocate for the wellbeing of individuals and of nations, expressed in what he defined in *Public Theology for Changing Times* as the paradigm of partnership and reconciliation. This era, beginning in the 1980s through to the present, has the following hallmarks:

> changes in context and religious life, evolving (reformulated) models of Christian and other faiths' involvements in such change in partnerships with government and other sectors, the fruitfulness of the relationship between religion and capital, the growth of religious involvement in interdisciplinary studies of wellbeing, and finally openings in relationships between Christianity and economics. (Atherton, 2014, p. 187)

We take the liberty below of developing these ideas, this legacy of thought that John has left us, into a mini-manifesto for an empowered and strategic theology and performative apologetics. This could potentially help the Church of England, and other faith groups, become curators of new politics of hope and renewal, rather than fearful arrangers of deckchairs on sinking ships. Five modalities of an ongoing search for an Anglican social theology now follow; strongly prominent in John's work, they serve as continuing generative sources for the future. Above all, they are characterized by a search for a rigorous and traditioned authenticity infused with the hallmarks of confidence, authenticity and partnership. The genius of John's work is that he recognizes that the secret of a robust and transformational Anglican social theology lies not in treating these elements in a piecemeal or episodic fashion but in incorporating all five into a critical and strategic whole.

1 *'Tradition' as organic, evolving and enabling*

Writing in a volume on the future of Anglican social theology, Alan Suggate comments on the nature of 'tradition' as one of its wellsprings (along with Scripture and reason). While all three generative sources are multifaceted, Suggate makes the point that 'tradition' is particularly complex, embodying a living thread of ideas and practices that is handed down through the generations, and evolves in response to new circumstances:

AFTERWORD: GENEALOGY AND GENERATIVITY

> One could not come to faith except through the tradition embodied in the church. Yet there is no safety in simply handing it down. Tradition is also the experience of Christians living adventurously in response to those central revelatory events. And since they inhabit societies and cultures that grow and change, they must take account of new knowledge. (Suggate, 2014, p. 29)

It is essentially dialogue between the wisdom of the past and the demands of the present that constitutes the generative source of creative and authentic Christian theology. Yet this requires a critical openness towards the tradition itself, acknowledging that it possesses a degree of provisionality and partiality. There are always new insights to be gleaned, new challenges to be faced. This receptivity to changing contexts must not be mistaken for capitulation to secular insights, however, since tradition proceeds dialogically, through respectful awareness of the integrity of inherited wisdom interpreted in the light of the immediate and concrete imperatives of daily living.

In terms of the likely possible future shape of Anglican social theology, this means it is neither fixed nor finished, as Malcolm Brown has suggested elsewhere (Brown, 2014). Inevitably, perhaps, it will always be something of a hybrid, standing at the confluences of other influences, notably Evangelical and Roman Catholic traditions. This offers some welcome ecumenical dimensions and may serve as a source of energy and renewal in so far as the public theologies of both these traditions (even as they are manifested within the Church of England) may represent alternative strategic repertoires beyond the predominance of traditional Establishment. This may, in turn, release the insurgent energies away from what John termed the 'social action curia' and the issuing of church reports to increasing emphasis on local activism, citizens' groups and broad-based alliances as alternative sources of 'soft power'.

2 *Attention to the empirical and contextual as the place of divine encounter*

The enduring missional and theological challenge of 'connecting God to the contemporary world' (Atherton, 2000, p. 1), therefore, both requires immersion in the traditions and practices of the Church and – as John always stressed – a rigorous and attentive listening to the ways of the world. As Will Storrar points out elsewhere in this volume, this was driven by a particularly high doctrine of creation and incarnation on John's part. By his own admission, John often felt like 'a fish out of water' (Atherton, 2000, p. 2) in more mono-disciplinary academic and ecclesial settings; but this was driven by a conviction that the world was a primary *locus theologicus*. 'Christian faith in itself demands participation' in the world, since 'God's word, communicated in and through the Scriptures, recounts public history powerfully as the very warp and woof of revelatory acts' (Atherton, 2000, p. 2).

3 Theology as practical divinity

One of the key priorities of Anglican social theology has been the task of mediating the wisdom of tradition into a pluralist public square – a tradition honourably upheld by such principles as middle axioms, for example. As contexts change, however, so too will the strategies adopted to communicate and embody its essential teachings:

> The test of Anglican social theology is whether it will in the end make the claims of Christ, the vision of Scripture and the rich Christian understanding of being human within community audible to the world at large. (Brown, 2014, p. 188)

As we argued earlier in this Afterword, the contemporary West is unaccustomed to mixing religion and politics, and yet a combination of the retrenchment of the state in many aspects of public policy, together with signs of the enduring afterlife of religion, combine to offer faith-based activism and citizenship a renewed visibility and political potential. Studies of post-secular rapprochement (Beaumont and Cloke, 2012) and post-secular apologetics (Graham, 2017) have argued strongly that it is in their dynamic demonstration of the virtues of presence and partnership that the churches will find the strongest warrant of their credibility and relevance to wider society.

Powerfully in John's work, reflecting trends in the discipline of practical theology, we see a model of theology as primarily a performative discipline, or what he termed 'practical divinity' (Atherton, 2000). This reflected a broader 'turn to practice' within practical theology, in which theology is framed as a form of 'practical wisdom' in which the aims and ends of theologizing are profoundly practical – instantiated and embodied in the practices of worship, care, public service, social transformation (Graham, Walton and Ward, 2005; Bass et al., 2016). It is echoed in John's sentiments in the essay included in this volume: 'By their fruits ye shall know them' (Matthew 7.16, 20, KJV). Yet this is more than a pragmatic decision to soft-pedal 'hard' theology in favour of meaningful relevance; nor is it some kind of applied theology; rather, theology is 'practical all the way down' (Korsgaard, 2003, p. 112):

It is not simply that theology is in some way proven by the actions of Christians; it is more that the actions of justice, right relation and reconciliation are the very expressions of the triune God. (Atherton, 2000, p. 5)

4 Christian realism

The discernment of signs of the times and embarking on practices of partnership and transformation was, therefore, for John, all about the 'tangible practical consequences' of theological tradition (2000, p. 3). Along with John's attention and attentiveness to the practical implementation of theological vision, however, goes a commitment to what he termed 'visionary pragmatism, realistic radicalism, and feasible alternatives' (1998, p. 101). Once more, this reflects a concern that theology should be capable of generating practical, credible and relevant contributions to public debate. This is in part about overcoming the 'fear of getting down to fundamentals, a reluctance ... to be really practical' (1988, p. 101) while taking due account of the complicating factors of timescale and political complexities – as the art of the possible and the ambivalence of human sin and finitude. 'There will be no Kingdom of God established by them on earth, and the moral judgements in the social arena are invariably profoundly relative' (Atherton, 1992, p. 159). Essentially, then, this points to the enduring value of the sensibilities of Christian realism, or a theology of both sides of the cross.

To offer a credible vision of the future inspired by Christian hope remains one of its most important gifts to public life. The Church lives in anticipation, 'living in the interim' (Atherton, 2000, p. 23), aware of the ways in which it falls short of ultimate perfection; yet it lives in the hope of ultimate transformation, through God's grace, that the Church can be 'a place of hope through what has been achieved and experienced and through what is yet to come' (Atherton, 2000, p. 24). This combination of the limitations and the possibilities of political change upholds the virtues of resilience and anticipation in the face of complexity. Yet amid the fragmented, tense and disillusioned climate of contemporary Western politics, perhaps these critical and tough virtues of pragmatism and Christian realism are infinitely preferable to the grandiosity of grand political narratives and the populism they attempt to whip up.

5 The 'capacious God'

John's legacy challenges us to acknowledge the significance, first, of tradition, second, of conversation with the non-theological and, third, the practical nature of social ethics. Yet above all, we note the supremely *theological* nature of his work. His vision of the 'capacious God' (2000, pp. 4ff.) runs throughout his work, and his convictions never departed from the sense that all was informed by the very nature and activity of God.

As Malcolm Brown's chapter in this volume indicates, the dichotomy of incarnation and atonement was already being breached in the shape of new initiatives within industrial mission and emergent theologies that stressed the unity of social justice and evangelism. This can be elaborated further by the notion of mission as *missio Dei* – as an expression or outworking of the nature of the triune God. God as creator, incarnate redeemer and Spirit outpoured in the faithful community serves as a model for the life of the Church in the world. It roots the life of the Church in the missionary activity of God as it takes place in the servant witness of Christ and in the outpourings of the Holy Spirit. But just as the life of the Spirit gives life to the Church, so it is also moving to effect reconciliation and transformation in the world beyond the Church. This must relieve the Church of any pretensions to exclusivity:

> [The church] has no need to maintain its special power and its special charges with absolute and self-destructive claims. It then has no need to look sideways in suspicion or jealousy at the saving efficacies of the Spirit outside the church; instead it can recognize them thankfully as signs that the Spirit is greater than the church and that God's purpose of salvation reaches beyond the church. (Moltmann, 1977, p. 65)

This new understanding affirms the universality of mission as God's redemptive work in creation in which humanity – including, but also increasingly beyond, the Church – is invited to participate. It comes to fruition in the advent of justice and peace and in the flourishing of social structures and communities, as well as through the conversion of individual souls. Once again, too, it is seen as a process in which the Spirit of God is evident in the often startling gravitation of secular structures and events towards the values of the Kingdom (Matthey, 2001, pp. 429–30). The winds of the Spirit blow in the life of the world to inspire all people to desire human dignity and promote the common good.

Yet this is not to diminish the role and significance of the Church as essential for the evangelization of the world – indeed, this kind of thinking contributes to a renewal of understandings of the Church as profoundly 'missional' in its very nature. This places renewed emphasis on local expressions of what it means to be church, the better to relate to its own immediate context – and returns us, significantly, to focus on the performative praxis of the Body of Christ as the sign and sacrament of divine activity in the world.

AFTERWORD: GENEALOGY AND GENERATIVITY

As Will Storrar observes in this collection, the task of overcoming public anger and disillusionment in an age of populism is not to withdraw but to engage with the theological resources – material, moral and imaginative – that are capable of setting out non-coercively a credible vision of the future. John's insistence on a public theology mindful of both sides of the cross – the ultimate victory of Christ over the sufferings of the world and a hope in the world's ultimate redemption by God's grace – clearly affirms a theological vision that is capable of transcending the immediate and the achievable to inspire forms of practical divinity that reach beyond the fragmentation and compromise of temporal affairs.

References

Atherton, J. R., 1992, *Christianity and the Market: Christian Social Thought for Our Times*, London: SPCK.

Atherton, J. R., 2000, *Public Theology for Changing Times*, London: SPCK

Atherton, J. R., 2014, *Challenging Religious Studies: The Wealth, Wellbeing and Inequalities of Nations*, London: SCM Press.

Baker, C. B., 2017, 'Mission and Authenticity', *Anvil* 33:3, online at https://churchmissionsociety.org/resources/mission-and-authenticity-chris-baker-anvil-vol-33-issue-3 (retrieved 30 March 2018).

Baker, C. R. and Skinner, H., 2006, *Faith in Action: The Dynamic Connection between Religious and Spiritual Capital*, Manchester: William Temple Foundation.

Bass, D. C., Cahalan, K. A., Miller-McLemore, B. J., Nieman, J. R. and Scharen, C. B. (eds), 2016, *Christian Practical Wisdom: What It Is, Why It Matters*, Grand Rapids, MI: Eerdmans.

Beaman, L., 2017, *Deep Equality in an Era of Religious Diversity*, Oxford: Oxford University Press.

Beaumont, J. and Cloke, P., 2012, 'Introduction to the Study of Faith-Based Organizations and Exclusion in European Cities', in P. Cloke and J. Beaumont (eds), *Faith-Based Organizations and Exclusion in European Cities*, London: Policy Press, pp. 1–36.

Beck, U., 2010, *A God of One's Own: Religion's Capacity for Peace and Potential for Violence*, Cambridge: Polity Press.

Bielo, J., 2011, *Emerging Evangelicals: Faith, Modernity and the Desire for Authenticity*, New York: New York University Press.

Brown, M. (ed.), 2014, *Anglican Social Theology: Renewing the Vision Today*, London: Church House Publishing.

Calhoun, C., 2016, *Religion, Government and the Common Good*, Temple Tract 2:2, William Temple Foundation, online at http://williamtemplefoundation.org.uk/wp-content/uploads/2017/02/Religion-Government-and-the-Public-Good_Craig-Calhoun_Temple-Tract.pdf (retrieved 30 March 2018).

Cloke, P. and Beaumont, J., 2013, 'Geographies of Postsecular Rapprochement in the City', *Progress in Human Geography* 37:1, pp. 27–51.

Fogel, R., 2000, *The Fourth Great Awakening and the Future of Egalitarianism*, Chicago, IL: University of Chicago Press.

Graham, E. L., 2017, *Apologetics without Apology: Speaking of God in a World Troubled by Religion*, Eugene, OR: Cascade.

Graham, E., Walton, H. and Ward, F., 2005, *Theological Reflection: Methods*, London: SCM Press.

Habermas, J., 2005, 'Equal Treatment of Cultures and the Limits of Postmodern Liberalism', *Journal of Political Philosophy* 13:1, pp. 1–28.

Klein, N., 2017, *No Is Not Enough: Defeating the New Shock Politics*, Toronto: Allen Lane.

Korsgaard, C. M., 2003, 'Realism and Constructivism in Twentieth-century Moral Philosophy', *Journal of Philosophical Research* 28 (Supplement), pp. 99–122.

Martí, G. and Ganiel, G., 2014, *The Deconstructed Church: Understanding Emerging Christianity*, Oxford: Oxford University Press.

Matthey, J., 2001, 'Missiology in the World Council of Churches', *International Review of Mission* 90:359, pp. 427–43.

Moltmann, J., 1977, *The Church in the Power of the Spirit: A Contribution to Messianic Ecclesiology*, Minneapolis, MN: Fortress Press.

Moody, K. S., 2015, *Radical Theology and Emerging Christianity: Deconstruction, Materialism and Religious Practices*, London: Ashgate.

Putnam, R. and Campbell, D., 2010, *American Grace: How Religion Unites and Divides Us*, New York: Simon & Schuster.

Randall, W. L., 2013, 'The Importance of Being Ironic: Narrative Openness and Personal Resilience in Later Life', *The Gerontologist* 53, pp. 9–16.

Suggate, A., 2014, 'The Temple Tradition', in M. Brown (ed.), *Anglican Social Theology: Renewing the Vision Today*, London: Church House Publishing, pp. 28–73.

Taylor, C., 2007, *A Secular Age*, Cambridge, MA: Harvard University Press.

Index of Names and Subjects

9/11 1

Aberdeen 38, 81
advertising 104–108
Age of
  Atonement 9, 18, 19, 30, 83–93, 184
  Incarnation 5, 9, 18–19, 21, 51, 81–93, 143, 146–147, 159, 181, 184
  partnership 4, 9, 18, 86–93, 144–145, 153–154, 164, 169–170, 180, 182–183
  reconciliation 9, 18, 86–93, 144–145, 164, 180, 183–184
  the State 9, 83, 92
  Voluntarism 9, 83
algorithms 18, 113, 118
Alinsky, Saul 132, 141n
altruism 11, 30
anger 18, 59, 85, 124–142, 185
Anglicanism 8, 47, 56, 60, 86, 156
  Anglican social theology 3, 19, 84, 90–93, 124, 178, 180–182, 186n
  see also Church of England
Archbishop's Commission on Urban Priority Areas (Faith in the City) 39, 41, 42, 49n, 53, 82, 85–86, 88, 92, 94n
Aristotle 127
Artificial Intelligence 110, 113
Atherton, John 20–36
  early life, family and marriage ix–x, 8, 15–16, 38
  Lancashire roots 5, 16–17, 50, 57, 62
  and Manchester Cathedral 3, 37, 38, 50–53, 57–58, 60, 62, 94n3
  and University of Manchester 38, 50–3, 57, 62, 111, 125

  and William Temple Foundation vii, 37–39, 50, 53–55, 62, 85–87, 124
  theological method 6–8, 15, 37, 39, 40, 159
Atherton, Lesley vii, ix–x, xi
autoethnography 3,15

Baker, Christopher R. vii, ix, 1–19, 32–33, 34, 35n , 44, 49n, 51, 53–54, 55, 57, 63n, 175–186
Beveridge, William 30
Bible 7, 14, 20, 21, 26, 29, 28, 55, 128, 182
Big Data 113, 118
'Black Lives Matter' 177
Blackstone Edge 5
Blair, Tony 9, 161, 162
blockchain 113, 114–117, 119, 120, 123n
'blurred encounters' 110–112, 123n, 144
Brown, Malcolm vii, 10, 18, 53–56, 63n, 81–95, 158, 172n, 181, 182, 184, 185n, 186n
Board for Social Responsibility viii, 38, 39, 52, 86, 94n4
Body of Christ 4, 11, 184
Boff, Leonardo 161, 171n
Brexit 18, 163, 177
Buddhism 8, 127

capital
  human 29, 31
  religious and spiritual 10, 34, 53, 152, 179
  social 10, 13, 44, 56, 62
capitalism 5, 10, 13, 14, 57, 65–79, 93, 94, 96, 98, 104, 140, 180
Catholic Social Teaching 19, 61, 74, 158–174

187

See also Church, Roman Catholic
Center for Theological Inquiry,
    Princeton viii, 4, 43
charity 97, 98, 101
character, see virtue ethics
Charry, Ellen 6 45, 49n
Chetham, Humphrey 29
Chetham's Library 31
China 135
Christendom 11, 13, 100, 179
Christian social ethics 3, 8–10, 11–14,
    17, 28, 45, 51, 53, 55, 65–80, 93,
    96, 124, 125, 135, 158, 175, 183
Christianity 13, 20
  and well-being 20–36
  and economics 20–21, 23
Christian social ethics 11, 14, 17, 28,
    34, 45, 53, 65–80, 96, 175
Christian Socialism 13, 67
Christian Realism 68, 72, 110,
    121–123, 183
Church Action on Poverty viii, 37, 39,
    47
Church, Roman Catholic 121, 160,
    163, 170
  and public theology
  Second Vatican Council 159, 160,
    164
  see also Catholic Social Teaching
Church of England 39, 52, 53, 61, 82,
    84–88, 90–93, 113, 180–181
  Industrial and Economic Affairs 52,
    94n4
  see also Anglicanism
churchgoing 29, 30, 44, 82, 151
Citizens UK 145
civil society 120, 134, 137, 139, 159
climate 5, 135
coal mining 42, 51
Cold War 2
common good 4, 6, 11, 12, 30–31, 48,
    58, 71, 133, 135, 140, 158, 166, 184
community organizing 62, 145
  faith-based 133–135, 141, 145
Conservative Party (UK) 40, 52, 58,
    67, 85, 93, 162
  See also economics, neo-liberal and
    Thatcherism
consumption 23, 44, 105, 107, 108,
    116, 144

consumerism 23, 25, 40, 96, 104–108,
    178
creation, doctrine of 74, 75, 84, 146,
    152, 181, 184
Cross, the 47, 84, 89, 183, 185
Christology 74, 75, 77, 79

Deaton, Angus 6, 22–24, 27, 31, 43,
    124, 130–131, 133, 135
democracy 10, 18, 29, 40, 67–68, 84,
    102, 115, 126, 132, 136, 177
development 7, 11, 16, 22, 33, 116,
    117, 122, 126, 158, 163, 165
Depression, Great 16
Durham
  Bishop of 53
  diocese of 15

Easterlin, Richard 21, 24, 27, 31
economic
  growth 10, 17, 21–24, 27, 31, 37, 46,
    54, 65, 70, 113,
  theory 61, 71, 75–79, 94n4, 96–109
  transformation 2, 22, 72, 183
economics
  and theology 10–12, 14, 52–53, 61,
    66–67, 68, 70, 72, 111, 124–125
  and well-being 31
  behavioural 6
  classical 12, 23, 58, 71, 75–78
  'faithful' 13–14, 71–73, 79
  Islamic 6, 13
  neo-liberal 52
  welfare 76, 96, 102, 104–106, 108
'economy of grace' 14, 57, 71–73, 79
ecumenism 3, 8–10, 48, 52, 53, 54–55,
    71, 82, 84, 92, 125, 140, 181
Eden Network 18, 143, 146–153,
    156n1
Edinburgh, University of 125, 128
education 16, 21, 22, 29, 31, 36, 97,
    103, 104, 176
empirical evidence 3, 7–8, 13, 17, 24,
    27, 28, 32, 40, 44, 54, 133, 137–
    138, 159–160, 181
  see also research, qualitative and
    quantitative
Engels, Friedrich 5, 6
entangled fidelities 110, 112, 120,
    123n

INDEX OF NAMES AND SUBJECTS

ethics 3, 11, 21, 27, 30, 32, 59, 93, 104, 112, 122, 139, 178
  see also Christian social ethics
emotion 16, 18, 24–25, 29, 30, 44, 57, 59–61, 62, 127–128, 129, 131–133, 141, 149, 151
environment 2, 5, 6, 8, 9, 12, 33, 48 68, 71, 103, 125, 126
Europe 24, 31, 53, 58, 67
evangelicalism 84, 92, 143, 147–148, 154, 156n3, 181
evolution 6, 15, 28

Faith in the City see Archbishop's Commission on Urban Priority Areas
family 30, 97, 103, 134, 159, 175
feminist
  economics 6
  ethics 77
finance 70, 110–123
  financial crises 92, 94, 129, 131, 177
free trade 56
Free Trade Hall, Manchester 5
friendship 30, 32, 58, 87, 117, 124, 125, 150, 168, 178
Fogel, Robert 6, 20, 23–24, 176, 185n

global economy 12, 18, 57, 62, 65–80, 87, 125, 129, 133, 140, 177
global ethics 71
globalization 2, 3, 5–6, 9, 11, 13, 16, 17, 42, 54, 56, 58, 8, 90, 113, 125–126, 133–136, 144–145, 153, 176
Graham, Carol 24–25, 27
Graham, Elaine vii, 1–19, 32, 51, 54, 57, 175–186,
'Great Awakenings' 176–178
'Great Transition' 10, 16
Grenholm, Carl-Henric vii, 17, 32, 65–80
Gore, Charles 3, 56, 86
Good Friday Agreement 161–162

happiness 6–8, 11, 13, 16–25, 34, 43, 49n, 59, 61, 77, 149
  see also wellbeing
health 10, 16, 18, 20–36, 38, 43, 97, 103, 104, 125, 128, 129–130, 141, 149, 176

mental 8, 130, 149, 163
history 2, 4, 6, 15, 17, 18, 21, 22, 25, 27, 56, 59, 82, 84, 88, 135, 176, 182
  cliometrics 148
  economic history 20, 28, 45, 96
hymns 30

Incarnation, see Age of
income 21–30, 33–34, 43, 96–97, 101, 103–104, 120, 131, 150
Indices
  Belonging, Becoming and Participation 33, 34, 152
  Human Development 7, 33
  Religion and Happiness 34
  Religiosity 34
  Social Development 33
  Sustainable Economic Welfare 33
India 99, 135
Industrial Mission 18, 52, 56–7, 81–82, 87, 89, 91, 94n, 95n, 184
Industrial Mission Association Theology Development Group 87, 94n
Industrial Revolution 5, 16, 17, 20–23 25–26, 29, 31, 37, 82, 110, 112, 113, 175
industrialization 2, 3, 5, 10, 37, 56, 125, 132, 135,
inequality 1, 8, 11, 22, 33, 34, 39, 43, 96, 102–104, 124, 125, 130, 131, 144, 161
interdisciplinarity 5, 6, 8–9, 12, 21, 43, 45, 54, 65, 94n6, 111–112, 144, 147, 155, 180
inter-faith 52
intermediate organizations 56, 86, 134, 139–140
Ireland 19, 158–174
Islam 17, 176

Jantzen, Grace 149, 152
Jubilee 2000 13
justice 4, 6, 12, 18, 29, 30, 40, 46, 47, 51, 58, 60, 61, 65, 67, 69, 74, 76–79, 87, 88, 91, 107, 125–128, 132–133, 134, 139, 158, 160, 162, 165, 168, 170, 171, 176, 183, 184

Kant, Immanuel 101, 107, 136–141

Keynes, John Maynard 6, 23, 40, 51, 52, 54, 70, 94n7
Kingdom of God 11, 30, 83, 90, 151, 152, 161, 164, 165, 166, 183, 184
Klein, Naomi 177

labour, see work
Labour Party (UK) 9, 40, 58, 93, 161
laity 53, 67, 159, 160, 164, 169, 170
Lancashire 2, 4, 5, 16–17, 50, 57, 62
Latour, Bruno 112, 120
Layard, Richard 24, 29, 30, 43, 77, 149
Leech, Kenneth 58
liberalism
  economic 42, 68, 71, 93, 176, 177, 178
  political 75, 90, 177
  theological 42, 68, 71, 73, 74,
life expectancy 20, 33, 43, 130, 149
Liverpool 46
  Bishop of 47
London School of Economics 50

Macintyre, Alasdair 55–56, 91
Malthus, Thomas 6, 12, 22, 23, 25
Manchester 2, 4, 5, 10, 15, 1, 29, 37, 38 81, 82, 94n2, 143–157
  Cathedral 3, 38, 50–53, 58–60, 94n3
  Diocesan Board for Social Responsibility 39, 111
  University of 3–4, 38, 39, 111, 125, 135
'Manchester School' of Christian social ethics 2 3–4, 17, 50–64, 113, 124
marginalization 2, 7, 9, 11, 13, 43, 54, 60, 67, 69–70, 78, 143–146, 155, 160, 165, 178
market 2–3, 9, 10–13, 17–18, 26, 40–42, 58–59, 62, 65–72, 70–71, 76, 78–79, 81, 86, 93, 96, 99, 102, 104, 113–114, 129, 131, 144–145, 177
Marshall, Alfred 6, 97, 99, 101
Marxism 67, 69, 86, 89
Maurice, F.D. 3, 41, 86
#MeToo 177
middle axioms 51, 53, 54, 86, 125, 135, 140, 141, 182
missio Dei 151, 152, 179, 184

mission 82–83, 85, 88, 90, 92, 143–157, 171n2, 181, 184
missional pastoral care 19, 147–153, 155–156
money 21, 23–25, 26, 56, 97, 99, 104, 114, 149
monovision 45
moral freighting 32, 34, 44
mortality 7, 10, 20, 21, 23, 26, 130
  see also life expectancy
Muslims, see Islam

neo-liberalism 71, 176–178
New Economics Foundation 30, 31
nutrition 23, 43, 103

paraenesis 57, 60
Pareto Efficiency 76, 102–103
participation 10, 29, 30, 34, 48, 59, 60, 65, 68, 71, 108, 144, 151, 152–153
pastoral care 4, 47, 129, 132
  see also missional pastoral care
Pendle Hill 16–17
pharmakon 116, 119, 122
political economy 3, 6, 10, 12, 17, 48, 54, 65–80
politics 2, 11, 13, 32, 40, 41, 65, 68, 70, 81, 86, 93, 117, 129–132, 136, 138–139, 159, 162, 180, 182–183
Pope Francis 165, 171n2
Pope John Paul II 165–166, 169, 171n2
Pope Paul VI 158, 168
population 5, 9, 22–23, 84, 92, 130, 134, 135, 143 162, 176
populism 1, 18, 124, 131–132, 135, 178, 183, 185
Positive Emotions, Engagement, Relationships, Meaning and Achievement (PERMA) 16
postmodernism 48, 56, 178
post-materialism 23–24
post-secular 53, 178–179, 182
poverty 5, 7, 8, 10, 11, 15–16, 17, 20, 22–23, 34, 38–41, 43, 47, 50–51, 59, 68, 69, 76–77, 79, 85 92, 130, 143–146, 148, 150, 153–155, 163, 176
Power, Maria vii, 19, 158–174

preferential option for the poor 46, 145, 160, 161, 164, 165, 171n2,
Preston, R.H. 3, 6, 38, 42, 50–55, 58, 60, 62, 66, 68, 72, 85, 94n6, 113, 124, 125, 135, 140
practical divinity 4, 8, 182–183, 185
Princeton, University of 4, 43, 124, 130
psychology 6, 7, 16, 27, 29, 43, 144
  positive 34
Puritanism 29, 31
Putnam, Robert 6, 29, 30, 31, 32, 34, 44, 176, 179

Quakers 17, 32

research
  qualitative 33, 44, 144, 148, 153
  quantitative 15, 33, 144, 148
Reader, John viii, 18, 110–123
religious studies 6, 8, 13, 27, 37, 44–45, 48, 112, 125, 135, 144, 148, 156
Ruddick, Anna viii, 18–19, 143–157
Russell, Hilary viii, 17, 37–49

sacrament 4, 5, 51, 84, 184
Salford 2, 3, 4, 5, 10, 15, 39, 143
salvation 86, 153, 184
Schwab, Klaus 110–111
secular 1, 2, 4, 6, 7, 8, 23, 27–34, 39, 42, 43, 45, 53, 71, 73, 83, 89, 129, 133–134, 135, 151, 159–160, 164–165, 166, 178–179, 181, 184
secularization 70, 89
Sedgwick, Peter viii, 3–4, 17, 50–64
Sen, Amartya 6, 12, 28, 34, 69–70, 76–78, 101
Sermon on the Mount 164, 167, 170
Sheffield
  Diocesan Bishops 82–83
  Industrial Mission 81–83, 86–87, 89
Slavery 20, 176
social media 116, 120–121, 177
socialism 10, 11, 40, 58, 65, 67, 69
sociology 6, 13, 27, 29, 43, 45, 61, 111, 144
South Africa 87–88, 126, 128, 132
spirituality 4, 8, 41, 149, 150, 170
state 9, 11, 51, 65, 67–68, 70, 83, 90, 92, 104, 136–140, 162, 178, 182
  see also welfare state

Steedman, Ian viii, 18, 96–109
Stiglitz, Joseph 6, 22, 28, 34
Storrar, William viii, 18, 124–142, 181, 185
Strängnäs diocese 30, 31
Sweden 12, 30
sustainable development 12, 126, 140

Tanner, Kathryn 6, 14, 57, 71
Tawney, R.H. 3, 6, 38, 50–51, 54–62, 66, 85, 86, 113
taxation 14, 103, 104, 167
technology/ies 12, 22, 31, 42, 88, 115–116, 119–123, 135, 176
  biotechnology 110
  digital, see information technology/ies
  information 18, 110, 112–114, 118, 119–123, 177
Temple, William 3, 6, 37, 50–56, 86, 94n7, 113, 124, 134, 139, 140
Thatcherism 1, 52–53, 67, 81, 86, 88–89
theological anthropology 71, 151, 164
theology 6–7, 8, 41–42, 76, 81–82, 86, 88, 90–93, 110, 122, 143, 151–152, 155, 166, 170, 179, 183, 184
  incarnational 4, 51, 84, 159, 182
  'ordinary' 39, 44–45, 147, 153, 155–156
  practical 4, 15, 27, 44, 62, 67–70, 129, 147, 182–183
  see also practical divinity
  public 1–3, 4–6, 15–17, 27, 37–49, 50, 52, 54, 62, 89, 110, 112, 124–142, 180–181, 184
  urban 144–146
  see also Archbishop's Commission on Urban Priority Areas
  see also Atherton, theological method
Thomas Aquinas 127–128
trade 26, 29, 65, 70
Trade Unions 29, 46, 47, 57, 134, 139
transmission processes 27, 28, 32–34, 153
trauma 1, 129–132, 141
Trump, Donald 18, 130, 177–178
trust 13, 29, 30, 32, 34, 61, 62, 77, 90–91, 112, 114–117, 120–122, 140, 141, 149–150, 163, 168–169, 178

Uppsala, University of vii, 4, 17, 43, 76
urban mission 143–157
urban regeneration 38, 52
unemployment 39, 41, 52–53, 60, 87, 163
United States of America 44, 126, 129–134, 176

voluntary sector 44, 97, 154
volunteering 29, 30, 34, 46, 149–150, 176, 179
virtue 4, 32, 44, 97, 168, 182, 183
virtue ethics 9, 55, 60–61, 100–101
violence 60, 78, 129, 135, 162–163, 168, 171, 178

welfare 14, 22, 27, 72, 89, 92, 163, 176
 economics 18, 33, 76, 96, 102–108
 state 38, 51, 68, 154
wellbeing 3, 6–8, 10–11, 13, 14, 16, 17, 20–36, 43, 45, 60, 62, 116, 124–125, 143, 155
 and health 18
 and income 143–144
 and religion 16, 44, 53, 59, 62, 124, 143, 146, 147–153, 155, 180
 measurement systems 27, 30, 31, 33–34
 subjective 6, 19, 21, 23, 24, 27–29, 33–34, 43, 149–150
 techno-physical 6
Wells, Sam 145–146
Wesley, John 83, 97, 99
Westcott, B.F. 3
William Temple Foundation vii, viii, 37–39, 50–64, 85–87, 124
worship 4, 5, 9, 11, 29, 30, 31, 34, 38, 39, 46, 151, 182
work 2, 23, 25, 39, 41, 51–52, 53, 82, 84, 92–93, 97–98, 99–100, 103, 130, 163
World Economic Forum 110, 114

www.ingramcontent.com/pod-product-compliance
Lightning Source LLC
Chambersburg PA
CBHW021948290426
44108CB00012B/991